For Ryan
a stalwart student
of the Bible

From Grandpa Brett
December 2018

JUDGES &
RUTH

Brazos Theological Commentary on the Bible

JUDGES & RUTH

LAURA A. SMIT
AND STEPHEN E. FOWL

BrazosPress
a division of Baker Publishing Group
Grand Rapids, Michigan

© 2018 by Laura A. Smit and Stephen E. Fowl

Published by Brazos Press
a division of Baker Publishing Group
PO Box 6287, Grand Rapids, MI 49516-6287
www.brazospress.com

Printed in the United States of America

ISBN: 978-1-58743-330-6

Library of Congress Cataloging in Publication Control Number: 2018011657

18 19 20 21 22 23 24   7 6 5 4 3 2 1

Judges
In memory of John H. Stek (1925–2009)
and Kenneth E. Bailey (1930–2016)

Ruth
To Sarah and Don Stevens-Rayburn

CONTENTS

SERIES PREFACE

Near the beginning of his treatise against gnostic interpretations of the Bible, *Against Heresies*, Irenaeus observes that scripture is like a great mosaic depicting a handsome king. It is as if we were owners of a villa in Gaul who had ordered a mosaic from Rome. It arrives, and the beautifully colored tiles need to be taken out of their packaging and put into proper order according to the plan of the artist. The difficulty, of course, is that scripture provides us with the individual pieces, but the order and sequence of various elements are not obvious. The Bible does not come with instructions that would allow interpreters to simply place verses, episodes, images, and parables in order as a worker might follow a schematic drawing in assembling the pieces to depict the handsome king. The mosaic must be puzzled out. This is precisely the work of scriptural interpretation.

Origen has his own image to express the difficulty of working out the proper approach to reading the Bible. When preparing to offer a commentary on the Psalms he tells of a tradition handed down to him by his Hebrew teacher:

> The Hebrew said that the whole divinely inspired scripture may be likened, because of its obscurity, to many locked rooms in our house. By each room is placed a key, but not the one that corresponds to it, so that the keys are scattered about beside the rooms, none of them matching the room by which it is placed. It is a difficult task to find the keys and match them to the rooms that they can open. We therefore know the scriptures that are obscure only by taking the points of departure

for understanding them from another place because they have their interpretive principle scattered among them.[1]

As is the case for Irenaeus, scriptural interpretation is not purely local. The key in Genesis may best fit the door of Isaiah, which in turn opens up the meaning of Matthew. The mosaic must be put together with an eye toward the overall plan.

Irenaeus, Origen, and the great cloud of premodern biblical interpreters assumed that puzzling out the mosaic of scripture must be a communal project. The Bible is vast, heterogeneous, full of confusing passages and obscure words, and difficult to understand. Only a fool would imagine that he or she could work out solutions alone. The way forward must rely upon a tradition of reading that Irenaeus reports has been passed on as the rule or canon of truth that functions as a confession of faith. "Anyone," he says, "who keeps unchangeable in himself the rule of truth received through baptism will recognize the names and sayings and parables of the scriptures."[2] Modern scholars debate the content of the rule on which Irenaeus relies and commends, not the least because the terms and formulations Irenaeus himself uses shift and slide. Nonetheless, Irenaeus assumes that there is a body of apostolic doctrine sustained by a tradition of teaching in the church. This doctrine provides the clarifying principles that guide exegetical judgment toward a coherent overall reading of scripture as a unified witness. Doctrine, then, is the schematic drawing that will allow the reader to organize the vast heterogeneity of the words, images, and stories of the Bible into a readable, coherent whole. It is the rule that guides us toward the proper matching of keys to doors.

If self-consciousness about the role of history in shaping human consciousness makes modern historical-critical study critical, then what makes modern study of the Bible modern is the consensus that classical Christian doctrine distorts interpretive understanding. Benjamin Jowett, the influential nineteenth-century English classical scholar, is representative. In his programmatic essay "On the Interpretation of Scripture," he exhorts the biblical reader to disengage from doctrine and break its hold over the interpretive imagination. "The simple words of that book," writes Jowett of the modern reader, "he tries to preserve absolutely pure from the refinements or distinctions of later times." The modern interpreter wishes to "clear away the remains of dogmas, systems, controversies, which are encrusted

---

1. Fragment from the preface to *Commentary on Psalms 1–25*, preserved in the *Philokalia*, trans. Joseph W. Trigg (London: Routledge, 1998), 70–71.
2. *Against Heresies* 9.4.

upon" the words of scripture. The disciplines of close philological analysis "would enable us to separate the elements of doctrine and tradition with which the meaning of scripture is encumbered in our own day."[3] The lens of understanding must be wiped clear of the hazy and distorting film of doctrine.

Postmodernity, in turn, has encouraged us to criticize the critics. Jowett imagined that when he wiped away doctrine he would encounter the biblical text in its purity and uncover what he called "the original spirit and intention of the authors."[4] We are not now so sanguine, and the postmodern mind thinks interpretive frameworks inevitable. Nonetheless, we tend to remain modern in at least one sense. We read Athanasius and think of him stage-managing the diversity of scripture to support his positions against the Arians. We read Bernard of Clairvaux and assume that his monastic ideals structure his reading of the Song of Songs. In the wake of the Reformation, we can see how the doctrinal divisions of the time shaped biblical interpretation. Luther famously described the Epistle of James as a "strawy letter," for, as he said, "it has nothing of the nature of the Gospel about it."[5] In these and many other instances, often written in the heat of ecclesiastical controversy or out of the passion of ascetic commitment, we tend to think Jowett correct: doctrine is a distorting film on the lens of understanding.

However, is what we commonly think actually the case? Are readers naturally perceptive? Do we have an unblemished, reliable aptitude for the divine? Have we no need for disciplines of vision? Do our attention and judgment need to be trained, especially as we seek to read scripture as the living word of God? According to Augustine, we all struggle to journey toward God, who is our rest and peace. Yet our vision is darkened and the fetters of worldly habit corrupt our judgment. We need training and instruction in order to cleanse our minds so that we might find our way toward God.[6] To this end, "the whole temporal dispensation was made by divine Providence for our salvation."[7] The covenant with Israel, the coming of Christ, the gathering of the nations into the church—all these things are gathered up into the rule of faith, and they guide the vision and form of the soul toward the end of fellowship with God. In Augustine's view, the reading of scripture both contributes to and benefits from this divine pedagogy. With countless variations in both exegetical conclusions and theological frameworks, the same pedagogy

---

3. Benjamin Jowett, "On the Interpretation of Scripture," in *Essays and Reviews* (London: Parker, 1860), 338–39.
4. Jowett, "On the Interpretation of Scripture," 340.
5. *Luther's Works*, vol. 35, ed. E. Theodore Bachmann (Philadelphia: Fortress, 1959), 362.
6. *On Christian Doctrine* 1.10.
7. *On Christian Doctrine* 1.35.

of a doctrinally ruled reading of scripture characterizes the broad sweep of the Christian tradition from Gregory the Great through Bernard and Bonaventure, continuing across Reformation differences in both John Calvin and Cornelius Lapide, Patrick Henry and Bishop Bossuet, and on to more recent figures such as Karl Barth and Hans Urs von Balthasar.

Is doctrine, then, not a moldering scrim of antique prejudice obscuring the Bible, but instead a clarifying agent, an enduring tradition of theological judgments that amplifies the living voice of scripture? And what of the scholarly dispassion advocated by Jowett? Is a noncommitted reading—an interpretation unprejudiced—the way toward objectivity, or does it simply invite the languid intellectual apathy that stands aside to make room for the false truism and easy answers of the age?

This series of biblical commentaries was born out of the conviction that dogma clarifies rather than obscures. The Brazos Theological Commentary on the Bible advances upon the assumption that the Nicene tradition, in all its diversity and controversy, provides the proper basis for the interpretation of the Bible as Christian scripture. God the Father Almighty, who sends his only begotten Son to die for us and for our salvation and who raises the crucified Son in the power of the Holy Spirit so that the baptized may be joined in one body—faith in *this* God with *this* vocation of love for the world is the lens through which to view the heterogeneity and particularity of the biblical texts. Doctrine, then, is not a moldering scrim of antique prejudice obscuring the meaning of the Bible. It is a crucial aspect of the divine pedagogy, a clarifying agent for our minds fogged by self-deceptions, a challenge to our languid intellectual apathy that will too often rest in false truisms and the easy spiritual nostrums of the present age rather than search more deeply and widely for the dispersed keys to the many doors of scripture.

For this reason, the commentators in this series have not been chosen because of their historical or philological expertise. In the main, they are not biblical scholars in the conventional, modern sense of the term. Instead, the commentators were chosen because of their knowledge of and expertise in using the Christian doctrinal tradition. They are qualified by virtue of the doctrinal formation of their mental habits, for it is the conceit of this series of biblical commentaries that theological training in the Nicene tradition prepares one for biblical interpretation, and thus it is to theologians and not biblical scholars that we have turned. "War is too important," it has been said, "to leave to the generals."

We do hope, however, that readers do not draw the wrong impression. The Nicene tradition does not provide a set formula for the solution of exegetical problems.

The great tradition of Christian doctrine was not transcribed, bound in folio, and issued in an official, critical edition. We have the Niceno-Constantinopolitan Creed, used for centuries in many traditions of Christian worship. We have ancient baptismal affirmations of faith. The Chalcedonian definition and the creeds and canons of other church councils have their places in official church documents. Yet the rule of faith cannot be limited to a specific set of words, sentences, and creeds. It is instead a pervasive habit of thought, the animating culture of the church in its intellectual aspect. As Augustine observed, commenting on Jer. 31:33, "The creed is learned by listening; it is written, not on stone tablets nor on any material, but on the heart."[8] This is why Irenaeus is able to appeal to the rule of faith more than a century before the first ecumenical council, and this is why we need not itemize the contents of the Nicene tradition in order to appeal to its potency and role in the work of interpretation.

Because doctrine is intrinsically fluid on the margins and most powerful as a habit of mind rather than a list of propositions, this commentary series cannot settle difficult questions of method and content at the outset. The editors of the series impose no particular method of doctrinal interpretation. We cannot say in advance how doctrine helps the Christian reader assemble the mosaic of scripture. We have no clear answer to the question of whether exegesis guided by doctrine is antithetical to or compatible with the now-old modern methods of historical-critical inquiry. Truth—historical, mathematical, or doctrinal—knows no contradiction. But method is a discipline of vision and judgment, and we cannot know in advance what aspects of historical-critical inquiry are functions of modernism that shape the soul to be at odds with Christian discipline. Still further, the editors do not hold the commentators to any particular hermeneutical theory that specifies how to define the plain sense of scripture—or the role this plain sense should play in interpretation. Here the commentary series is tentative and exploratory.

Can we proceed in any other way? European and North American intellectual culture has been de-Christianized. The effect has not been a cessation of Christian activity. Theological work continues. Sermons are preached. Biblical scholars produce monographs. Church leaders have meetings. But each dimension of a formerly unified Christian practice now tends to function independently. It is as if a weakened army has been fragmented, and various corps have retreated to isolated fortresses in order to survive. Theology has lost its competence in exegesis.

8. *Sermon* 212.2.

Scripture scholars function with minimal theological training. Each decade finds new theories of preaching to cover the nakedness of seminary training that provides theology without exegesis and exegesis without theology.

Not the least of the causes of the fragmentation of Christian intellectual practice has been the divisions of the church. Since the Reformation, the role of the rule of faith in interpretation has been obscured by polemics and counterpolemics about *sola scriptura* and the necessity of a magisterial teaching authority. The Brazos Theological Commentary on the Bible series is deliberately ecumenical in scope because the editors are convinced that early church fathers were correct: church doctrine does not compete with scripture in a limited economy of epistemic authority. We wish to encourage unashamedly dogmatic interpretation of scripture, confident that the concrete consequences of such a reading will cast far more light on the great divisive questions of the Reformation than either reengaging in old theological polemics or chasing the fantasy of a pure exegesis that will somehow adjudicate between competing theological positions. You shall know the truth of doctrine by its interpretive fruits, and therefore in hopes of contributing to the unity of the church, we have deliberately chosen a wide range of theologians whose commitment to doctrine will allow readers to see real interpretive consequences rather than the shadowboxing of theological concepts.

The Brazos Theological Commentary on the Bible endorses a textual ecumenism that parallels our diversity of ecclesial backgrounds. We do not impose the thankfully modest inclusive-language agenda of the New Revised Standard Version, nor do we insist upon the glories of the Authorized Version, nor do we require our commentators to create a new translation. In our communal worship, in our private devotions, and in our theological scholarship, we use a range of scriptural translations. Precisely as scripture—a living, functioning text in the present life of faith—the Bible is not semantically fixed. Only a modernist, literalist hermeneutic could imagine that this modest fluidity is a liability. Philological precision and stability is a consequence of, not a basis for, exegesis. Judgments about the meaning of a text fix its literal sense, not the other way around. As a result, readers should expect an eclectic use of biblical translations, both across the different volumes of the series and within individual commentaries.

We cannot speak for contemporary biblical scholars, but as theologians we know that we have long been trained to defend our fortresses of theological concepts and formulations. And we have forgotten the skills of interpretation. Like stroke victims, we must rehabilitate our exegetical imaginations, and there are likely to be different strategies of recovery. Readers should expect this reconstructive—not reactionary—series to provide them with experiments in postcritical doctrinal interpretation, not commentaries written according to the settled principles of a well-functioning tradition. Some commentators will follow classical typological and allegorical readings from the premodern tradition; others will draw on contemporary historical study. Some will comment verse by verse; others will highlight passages, even single words that trigger theological analysis of scripture. No reading strategies are proscribed, no interpretive methods foresworn. The central premise in this commentary series is that doctrine provides structure and cogency to scriptural interpretation. We trust in this premise with the hope that the Nicene tradition can guide us, however imperfectly, diversely, and haltingly, toward a reading of scripture in which the right keys open the right doors.

R. R. Reno

ABBREVIATIONS

General

CCSL   Corpus Christianorum: Series Latina. Turnhout: Brepols, 1953–
JSOT   *Journal for the Study of the Old Testament*
JSOTSup   Journal for the Study of the Old Testament Supplement Series
LXX   Septuagint
MT   Masoretic Text
NRSV   New Revised Standard Version
PL   Patrologia Latina [= *Patrologiae Cursus Completus*: Series Latina]. Edited by Jacques-Paul Migne. 217 vols. Paris, 1844–1864
VT   *Vetus Testamentum*

Biblical

Old Testament

Gen.	Genesis	1–2 Chron.	1–2 Chronicles
Exod.	Exodus	Ezra	Ezra
Lev.	Leviticus	Neh.	Nehemiah
Num.	Numbers	Esther	Esther
Deut.	Deuteronomy	Job	Job
Josh.	Joshua	Ps. (Pss.)	Psalm (Psalms)
Judg.	Judges	Prov.	Proverbs
Ruth	Ruth	Eccles.	Ecclesiastes
1–2 Sam.	1–2 Samuel	Song	Song of Songs
1–2 Kgs.	1–2 Kings	Isa.	Isaiah

Jer.	Jeremiah	Jon.	Jonah
Lam.	Lamentations	Mic.	Micah
Ezek.	Ezekiel	Nah.	Nahum
Dan.	Daniel	Hab.	Habakkuk
Hosea	Hosea	Zeph.	Zephaniah
Joel	Joel	Hag.	Haggai
Amos	Amos	Zech.	Zechariah
Obad.	Obadiah	Mal.	Malachi

Deuterocanonical/Apocryphal

Sir.   Sirach

New Testament

Matt.	Matthew	1–2 Thess.	1–2 Thessalonians
Mark	Mark	1–2 Tim.	1–2 Timothy
Luke	Luke	Titus	Titus
John	John	Philem.	Philemon
Acts	Acts	Heb.	Hebrews
Rom.	Romans	Jas.	James
1–2 Cor.	1–2 Corinthians	1–2 Pet.	1–2 Peter
Gal.	Galatians	1–3 John	1–3 John
Eph.	Ephesians	Jude	Jude
Phil.	Philippians	Rev.	Revelation
Col.	Colossians		

✠ JUDGES ✠

by Laura A. Smit

ACKNOWLEDGMENTS

Over the years that I have spent writing this commentary, many people have helped me to understand the book of Judges more clearly. Rusty Reno initially pushed me to be much bolder than I wanted to be in moving from exegesis to theology, which was painful but helpful. At the last, he gave me nothing but encouragement. Dave Nelson and the rest of the team at Baker have consistently demonstrated kindness and patience. I am especially indebted to Dwight Baker, who has frequently sat through my preaching on the book of Judges without ever once succumbing to the temptation to ask me when I was going to finish writing already.

The following groups gave me opportunities to test what I was thinking: the congregations of Forest Hills Presbyterian Church and Calvin Christian Reformed Church, both in Grand Rapids, who have heard many sermons on Judges, some at early stages when I was not yet clear in my own mind what I thought about the book; the members of the class on Judges that I taught in the spring of 2010 as part of the Calvin College Academy of Lifelong Learning, who patiently let me teach them and in turn taught me; and the participants in my six-day class on the book of Judges at the New Wilmington Mission Conference in the summer of 2014, whose enthusiastic response led me to hope that I was close to finished.

I have had more conversations about Judges with gracious individuals than I can possibly remember, but the following people have been especially helpful to me, though some of them may have no idea that I found our conversations significant: Jerry Andrews, Jill Carattini, Phil Cary, David Crump, Christiana de Groot, Elizabeth Holmlund, Brandon Hurlbert, John Jarik, Donna La Rue, Arie Leder, Won Lee, Peter Leithart, Darian Lockett, Margaret Manning, Jodi Mac-Lean, Richard Muller, John Natelborg, Ken Pomykala, Carolyn Poteet, Rebecca

Sitsapesan, John Thompson, Raymond Van Leeuwen, Richard Whitekettle, and Bryce Wiebe. My family have also been very supportive of my Judges obsession.

Finally, I have dedicated this commentary to the memory of two great teachers of the Bible. John Stek was my Old Testament professor at Calvin Theological Seminary, and he was the first person to show me how important structure is when reading Hebrew narrative. He is cited in the chapter on Deborah, but his influence is in every chiasm. Ken Bailey sat in on my New Wilmington Mission Conference class on Judges at a point where I needed reassurance, which he was gracious enough to give me. He told me that a good commentary needs to "marinate," which is why it is wise to take upwards of ten years to write one.

1

THE BIG PICTURE

Method

My first job out of seminary was directing a youth program. I soon discovered that the junior-high and high-school students for whom I was responsible had a strong knowledge of Bible stories. If presented with a collection of Sunday school flannelgraph pictures, any one of them could have stood in front of the group and retold the story of the crossing of the Red Sea, or the story of Jesus confronting Zacchaeus, or the story of Jesus dying on the cross and coming back to life three days later. And yet these students had absolutely no understanding of Christianity. They could not tell me what any of these stories had to do with their own lives, not even the story of the death and resurrection of Jesus. They had some vague sense that Jesus had "saved" them, but no ability to talk about what that meant or why the event recounted in this old story should make a difference in their lives today. Prior to that experience as a youth director, I had been inclined to trust the stories of the Bible to "speak for themselves" and was rather enamored of narrative preaching. After that experience, I decided that my preaching needed to include theology and doctrine as well as narrative.

The book of Judges is full of stories that make for thrilling Sunday school lessons, but few of the Christian people with whom I have spoken about those stories over the years that I have been working on this project have any idea of what they might mean. For most Christians I have encountered, the stories in the book of Judges are interesting curiosities that may be entertaining, exciting, or horrifying. But they are not meaningful. They are not relevant. They have no message for how we should live our faith today.

Some scholars of the book of Judges are content to be entertained. David Gunn observes, "It is my belief that much of the Old Testament narrative belongs naturally to the life-sphere of art and entertainment."[1] Similarly, in her introduction to the book of Judges, Ailish Ferguson Eves comments that "in its pathos and humor as well as its horror this kind of storytelling is the generic ancestor of modern action or adventure films. The most pressing question is what led the Hebrew people to preserve among their holy books these accounts of their ancestors' immorality, oppression and violence."[2] Because Eves understands the stories only as stories, she is at a loss to understand what meaning they might have that would explain their preservation, given that many of the stories reflect poorly on the people of Israel.

While it is tempting to package the message as a great adventure story, especially when trying to engage the attention of children and young adults, we should resist this temptation to read Judges from the voyeuristic, dramatic perspective appropriate to contemporary popular literature, thereby missing the prophetic nature of the book. The book of Judges was not written to entertain, nor is its primary meaning the preservation of the history of Israel. This is a book of prophetic proclamation, intended to communicate truth that is essential for faith and life. In other words, these stories are deeply meaningful. As a book of *prophetic* proclamation, the meaning that it contains is authoritative, for it is a message from God Himself.[3] The unflattering portrait of the people of Israel painted by the book of Judges makes sense when we remember that these stories were not written only by the people of Israel. God is the primary author, as well as being the chief actor in the book.

1. David Gunn, *The Fate of King Saul: An Interpretation of a Biblical Story*, JSOTSup 14 (Sheffield: JSOT Press, 1980), 11, quoted in Marty Alan Michelson, *Reconciling Violence and Kingship: A Study of Judges and 1 Samuel* (Eugene, OR: Pickwick, 2011), 25n30.

2. Ailish Ferguson Eves, "Judges," in *The IVP Women's Bible Commentary*, ed. Catherine Clark Kroeger and Mary J. Evans (Downers Grove, IL: InterVarsity, 2002), 128.

3. I mean no offense by using masculine language for God. I am well aware that God is not male; I capitalize pronouns referring to God in order to underscore the analogical nature of this language. I have tried other approaches to speaking and writing about God but have found that my current approach is the least bad in terms of its effects on how I think about God. I understand that language affects different people differently and that others may make other choices that are responsible and God-honoring. For an in-depth explanation of my choices, please see the section on language in "Who Is God?," in *Conversations with the Confessions: Dialogue in the Reformed Tradition*, ed. Joseph D. Small (Louisville: Geneva, 2005), 95–98.

To find the meaning in Judges, it is necessary to place this book in the context of God's entire message to us, connecting it to the unified revelation of the Christian Bible. I am aware that different parts of the Bible were written at different times, by different human authors, and in different contexts. In the field of biblical studies, particularly for those scholars whose interest is primarily historical or literary, it may make sense to focus on books of the Bible as independent units, without immediately (or ever) connecting the whole collection of books into one grand narrative. However, the *theology* of the book of Judges can only be understood by putting this book in the context of the whole of scripture. Judges can be a depressing book, documenting as it does a spiral into deeper and deeper sin, rebellion, and degradation. If it is considered apart from the entire sweep of salvation history, I see no way to interpret it as good news. But set within the grand narrative of scripture, Judges fills an essential role. If scripture is a long, coherent argument or presentation, then Judges is one necessary proposition in that argument, but not the conclusion. If scripture is a long drama with a happy ending, Judges is that moment in the first act when it seems that all is lost.

This unified approach to reading the Bible is not as natural for us as it was for people of earlier eras, in part because we do not know the Bible nearly as well. The thirteenth-century theologian Bonaventure once said that the difficulty with interpreting scripture accurately is needing to have so much of it memorized before one can even begin. "No one will find this an easy task unless, by constant reading, he has fixed in his memory the text of the Bible to the very letter; not otherwise shall he ever have the ability to interpret Scripture."[4] Bonaventure assumed that the Bible can only be understood in light of itself, and that such understanding requires having a great deal of scripture in one's memory so that, as one reads along, word associations and connections will leap to mind. Our easy access to the printed word, so easy that now many of us have searchable copies of the Bible with us at all times on our phones and tablets, is a great gift, but such access discourages memory, meaning that we often miss the interconnectedness of the text. When we read that an event in the biblical narrative took place at Shechem, most of us do not immediately remember all the other events that occurred at Shechem in the course of biblical history. The first writers, readers, and hearers of the texts would have thought of those connections.

Those first writers, readers, and hearers were immersed in a great system of symbols that enriched their communication and their understanding of the world.

---

4. Bonaventure, *Breviloquium*, trans. José de Vinck (Paterson, NJ: St. Anthony Guild Press, 1963), 18.

Most of us are deaf to that system of symbols as we read the Bible, and we therefore miss large portions of the meaning. When we read a story about Gideon putting out a fleece and inspecting the dew that had fallen or had not fallen on it, we need to be aware of the meaning of a fleece and the meaning of the dew if we are to hear all that was there for the first hearers. I make no claim to having mastered this system of symbols, but I have caught enough hints of it to believe that it cannot be learned apart from approaching the Bible as a unified whole.

To find the meaning in Judges, it is also necessary to determine the book's genre. Judges is a historical book, as evidenced by the effort to locate events at specific times and places and by the frequent references to current commemorative markers or place names. So, for instance, we are told that Judah attacked the Canaanites living in the town now known as Hebron, then known as Kiriath-arba (1:10). However, the primary genre of the book of Judges is not history; it is prophecy. The book of Judges is rightly categorized as one of the former prophets. That is to say that the narrator of Judges is not so much concerned to give an accurate historical account of a particular era as to present that story in a prophetic way, a way that conveys meaning and a message. The book of Judges has an undisguised perspective, which is part of this prophetic nature. As Daniel Block observes:

> The author's intent is not to produce a cold, rational, and objective record of events; this is literary rhetoric, the language of persuasion, designed to challenge prevailing notions and effect a spiritual and moral transformation in readers of the composition. The book represents an extended sermon, or a series of sermons, that draws its "texts" from the real historical experiences of the Israelites in the premonarchic period. But like a modern preacher, the biblical author selects, organizes, arranges, shapes, and crafts his material for maximum effect. Recognizing this guards the readers against *the fallacy of misplaced literalism*, by which we force the text to carry freight it was not intended to carry. (Block 1999: 52–53)

This does not mean that the text is an invention or fiction; it is history, but prophetic history. The telling of the historic events has been shaped by a particular message, and so the literary structure and rhetorical effect of the account should be understood as deliberately serving the prophetic message. Part of the book's prophetic nature is seen precisely in its incisive application to and interpretation of real historical events, but those events may be told out of chronological order, emphasize the actions of a person who would have seemed unimportant to many bystanders, or connect the historical events to other events that would happen hundreds of years later. Events that happened during the same time period but that do not contribute to the book's message—such as the stories of Ruth and Samuel—are omitted from Judges and find their home elsewhere in the canon. Furthermore, the narrator has access to God's judgments, feelings, plans, and reactions—which marks the book as prophetic. Bruce Waltke observes, "The implied author's omniscience and omnipresence, apart from modern demands of documentation, are due to his heavenly inspiration, not his fictitious inventiveness" (2004: 36).

To see how this works, consider one of the secondary messages our prophet is communicating to us: that God has chosen Judah over Benjamin, which is to say David over Saul. In the service of this message, Judah is credited with taking the city of Jerusalem, and Benjamin is blamed for the failure to make that conquest permanent (or perhaps failure to conquer a different section of the city). This is not how the story is told in the book of Joshua, which has a different prophetic agenda. There we read that it was the tribe of Judah who failed to drive the Jebusites out of Jerusalem (15:63). The historical truth, as we would understand it in our post-Enlightenment terms, was probably some combination of these stories: since Jerusalem is on the border of the territory of Judah and Benjamin, it is likely that both tribes shared credit for its capture and blame for its loss. But since Judges is in part a prophecy against Benjamin, the failures of Benjamin are highlighted.

However, the choosing of Judah is not without qualification. Throughout the book, Judah's role degrades from being the leader of the occupation to being the betrayer of Samson to being the leader in civil war. More basically, the book of Judges offers a criticism of both David and Saul, since at the heart of Judges is a claim that only YHWH is King of Israel and that for Israel to have any other king is a failure in keeping covenant. The fact that Judges in its canonical form was almost certainly compiled during the time of the exile helps us understand this theme. From the perspective of the exile, the ultimate inadequacy of human kingship has become clear. The coming of Jesus as Messiah reveals that the only legitimate human king, the only king who can secure for us both freedom and a lasting homeland, is the Incarnate One, who is YHWH Himself.

Prophetic literature is uncomfortable literature, and the book of Judges certainly creates discomfort in many readers. Prophecy brings us into contact with the normative word of God, and when we are out of harmony with that word (as, thanks to our sin, we always are to a greater or lesser extent), the contact can be painful. This is not because God has it in for us or enjoys seeing our pain. Rather, the way the world is constructed is such that sin produces pain, because sin drives us away from God, who is the source of all goodness, fullness of joy, and everlasting pleasure (Ps. 16:11).

Even though the book contains few morally exemplary stories, several characters from Judges rate a mention in the "heroes of faith" list of Heb. 11. This has led many preachers to try to rehabilitate the characters in Judges. I have listened to many sermons that attempt to explain away the apparent failings of Gideon, Jephthah, and Samson. But the list in Hebrews is not describing heroes of the law, people whose virtue earns them a place on a list of moral exemplars. Rather, the list in Hebrews is describing heroes of *faith*, people whose lives made clear that the law cannot save and who were driven to a desperate hope in a God of grace. These are people who clung to God and His promises in the midst of dark times, especially the dark times brought about by their own sin, from which they could not free themselves. Their inclusion in Heb. 11 does not set them beyond moral criticism any more than contemporary Christians' assurance of membership in the covenant community of the church sets us beyond moral criticism.

Most of the moral lessons in the book of Judges concern examples of what *not* to do. In the children's book *The Bike Lesson*, by Stan and Jan Berenstain, a father bear attempts to teach his son how to ride a bike; however, the father's own bike riding leaves a good deal to be desired. He is constantly ending up in disastrous situations, after which he says to his son, "This is what you should not do."[5] Or consider the terrifying films often shown as part of driver's education courses in which the consequences of failing to wear one's seat belt are portrayed in bloody detail. The book of Judges may function in this way for us. It is a warning or counterexample. Eugene Merrill observes, "It is fair to say that the book is an account of how not to live out the creation mandate as it was placed in the custody of God's chosen nation Israel."[6] The anarchy of the end of the book is where we will end up if we fail to honor our covenant with God, fail to practice right worship, fail to live courageously, and fail to recognize God's authority over all of life. More than that, this anarchy is where we in fact are located apart from God's grace. We are not invited to read the book of Judges from a perspective of distance or superiority; we are invited to see it as our own frightening story.

The people of Israel spent forty years under Moses's leadership in the wilderness, learning how to be YHWH's covenant people. They had received the law

5. Stan Berenstain and Jan Berenstain, *The Bike Lesson* (New York: Random House, 1964).
6. Eugene H. Merrill, *Everlasting Dominion: A Theology of the Old Testament* (Nashville: B&H Academic, 2006), 421.

at Sinai, including detailed instructions for a system of worship that included feasting, sacrifice, prayer, and priesthood. YHWH governed them closely during that time, taking care of their daily needs by sending manna and quail, making sure that their clothing did not wear out, and giving Moses meticulous guidance about their oversight. Once the people crossed into the land of Canaan under Joshua's leadership, they began to step toward more independence. For instance, the manna and quail ceased, and they needed to think about how to cultivate food. And yet they still had a parental leader who spoke with YHWH directly and implemented His will for them in great detail. Or, to use a different metaphor, they moved from a tutorial about the law into an apprenticeship or internship, with Joshua as their mentor and supervisor. With the death of Joshua, the people of Israel are meant to enter a more adult stage of their covenantal life, living out the law that they have been taught under Moses and Joshua.

At the heart of the book of Judges are the twin claims that YHWH Himself is both King (8:23) and Judge (11:27) in Israel. With the occupation of the land, YHWH intends to rule His people directly, without a central mediator. Moses was a tutor, Joshua a mentor, but now, after forty years of wandering, they have come back into the promised land, where they are again given the commission to fill and subdue the land. Each person in Israel is now in a direct covenantal relationship with YHWH, which is to be lived out in the claiming of the land. This is the test of their adulthood, a test that they are about to fail.

The book of Judges is thus an extensive proof of the ineffectiveness of the law to save and of God's people's ongoing need for His gracious intervention generally and for the sending of a mediating deliverer specifically. As Paul tells us, "But law came in, with the result that the trespass multiplied" (Rom. 5:20). In Judges we will be watching as sin increases all the more, underscoring that the people of Israel cannot save themselves. More significantly, they cannot keep the law on their own power. Like all of us, they are prone to wander. Their slavery is not to foreign powers but to idolatry.

Unlike the first readers or hearers of Judges, we come to these scenes already knowing the next act of the play. It is futile for a Christian to read the Old Testament as if unaware of the gift of Jesus Christ. Given that Jesus, the Son of God, is also the Logos, the Word that is spoken, the fullness of God's law revealed in a human life, we should expect the written word of God to testify to Him. As a Christian reader of the Old Testament, I also assume that when the scriptures speak of God, or YHWH, or the Lord, without specifying one of the three persons of the Trinity, then it is the triune God who is meant, for there is no other God who could be intended. So I do not believe that the God of Israel is solely the Father of Jesus Christ; rather, the God of Israel is the one God, who is Father, Son, and Holy Spirit. For this reason I also take references to the Spirit in the Old Testament and specifically in the book of Judges to be references to the Third Person of the Trinity, the Holy Spirit, even though I am aware that the first readers of this text could have had no such idea.

In Judges in particular, Jesus is also present in two additional ways. First, in common with much Christian tradition, I take it that the Angel or Messenger of the LORD who appears at Bochim, then later to Gideon, and finally to Manoah's wife and to Manoah, simply *is* the Second Person of the Trinity. We will consider this in more detail as we come to those episodes.

Second, there is a long tradition of seeing all or most of the judges as types of Christ, pointing forward to His saving work. Insofar as the judges act as saviors or deliverers of their nation, that may perhaps be appropriate. I believe that most basically the judges are to be understood as Israel in microcosm—the whole people being reflected in their leader. They should only be understood as types of Christ at moments when Israel as a whole can be understood as a type of Christ. I am not convinced that such instances occur often in the book of Judges, if at all, since this book generally presents the people of Israel as YHWH's unfaithful bride. Some judges may do particular things that can be seen as prefiguring Christ, but other parts of their stories do not fit well into such typology. There are, however, several characters whose interactions with Israel or with the judges who represent Israel appear to me to point to Christ: Achsah, Jael, Jephthah's daughter, and the unnamed concubine, to name the most probable. Even though all these characters are women, my own reading of this book is neither especially feminine nor feminist. I am simply open to the idea that both men and women are made in God's image and can reflect Christ's glory, and therefore to the possibility that types of Christ may as easily be female as male. Being closed to that possibility has led to some very odd interpretation in the past, particularly of this book. Again, we will consider ways in which these characters foreshadow Christ as we come to them in the text.

The Book as a Whole

In the chapters that follow, we will consider each episode of the book of Judges, but first it makes sense to consider the book in its entirety, both in terms of themes that are present throughout and in terms of the book's overall structure.

Occupying the Land

Throughout the scriptures, the promise of rest in the promised land has multiple layers of meaning. There is a strictly literal promise of a place in which the people of Israel will be able to live in social and political security. But the promise of the new land is also a promise of a new way of living, a way of living in union with God as His set-apart and holy people.

Eden was a holy land made for holy people. It was not only a land externally, where humans were meant to move about physically; it was also a holy land in which they were to live spiritually, in a relationship with God that Jesus will characterize as "abiding" in the Gospel of John (15:4–10). This relationship of abiding is transformative, making God's people into *holy* people. Not only do they abide in the holy land, which is God's own presence, but God abides in them, making them into His image and likeness (John 14:20–23). This was the Edenic design, restored and completed in Christ. The Bible thus presents holiness in two ways. From the side of its cause, holiness comes from God's interior presence in the person within the relationship of true worship of God (holy land). From the side of its effect, holiness is the justice or righteousness manifested by the person and community (holy people). The fall signals the loss of holiness, the loss of both holy land and holy people; it is no wonder that at the east "gate" of the garden of Eden there are now found "cherubim, and a sword flaming and turning to guard the way to the tree of life" (Gen. 3:24).[7]

The covenant with Abraham is a promise of a new land, a promise that Abraham's descendants will be a holy people living in a holy land. This is more than a geographical and political promise. It is a promise to restore the abiding relationship with God in which God's people live in a constant state of intimacy with Him that then transforms them into holiness. The covenant at Sinai offers Abraham's descendants the tools they need for this promise to come true: the law and the tabernacle. The law allows them to become a holy people, and the tabernacle is an in-breaking of the holy land, the place where YHWH meets with his people. The structures of worship that are given at Sinai are structures that allow for the expansion of this land, so that all of life becomes a place of holy encounter with the holy God. The promise of the land of Canaan is that it will be a great tabernacle where YHWH will dwell among His people, a foretaste of the new creation. "The Law and the tabernacle/ark make clear that it is not

7. Michael Dauphinais and Matthew Levering, *Holy People, Holy Land: A Theological Introduction to the Bible* (Grand Rapids: Brazos, 2005), 58. Also Arie Leder, "Holy God, Holy People, Holy Worship," *Calvin Theological Journal* 43, no. 2 (November 2008): 213–33.

land and descendants per se that God intends to provide; rather, it is 'holy land,' symbolized by God's presence with the people in the ark of the covenant that dwells in the tabernacle, and 'holy people,' informed and governed by divine Law."[8] It is because the land is holy that everything and everyone not holy, not dedicated to YHWH, will be removed.

This promise is brought to pass through YHWH's work, by means of His word, and not by the work of the people of Israel. Deuteronomy thus foresees a time when the people will live in "a land with fine, large cities that you did not build, houses filled with all sorts of goods that you did not fill, hewn cisterns that you did not hew, vineyards and olive groves that you did not plant" (Deut. 6:10–11). Meditating on this text, Walter Brueggemann says:

> The rhetoric at the boundary [i.e., at the Jordan, before entering Canaan] is that of pure gift, radical grace. There is no hint of achievement or merit or even planning. It is all given by the giver of good gifts and the speaker of faithful words. At the boundary Israel affirms that being landed is *sola gratia*: You did not build . . . ; you did not fill . . . ; you did not hew . . . ; you did not plant. The new land is in a peculiar way like the wilderness. It wells up with life-giving power, unplanned by Israel, in inscrutable ways. Deuteronomy reflects early: Israel cannot and does not and need not secure its existence for itself. It is all done for it by the same One who gave manna, quail, and water. Only now the gifts are enduring and not so precarious.[9]

Brueggemann goes on to observe that because the land is gift, under the care not of Israel but of YHWH Himself, it is also inscribed with the words of covenant. "The gifted land is covenanted land. It is not only nourishing space. It is also covenanted place."[10]

For New Testament people, the land of Canaan thus becomes a type of the new life of union with Christ into which we are invited through the in-breaking of God in the new tabernacle that is the incarnation. The book of Hebrews makes this explicit:

> For if Joshua had given them rest, God would not speak later about another day. So then, a Sabbath rest still remains for the people of God; for those who enter God's rest also cease from their labors as God did from his. Let us therefore make every effort to enter that rest, so that no one may fall through such disobedience as theirs.

8. Dauphinais and Levering, *Holy People, Holy Land*, 59.
9. Walter Brueggemann, *The Land* (Philadelphia: Fortress, 1977), 4
10. Brueggemann, *The Land*, 52.

Indeed, the word of God is living and active, sharper than any two-edged sword, piercing until it divides soul from spirit, joints from marrow; it is able to judge the thoughts and intentions of the heart. And before him no creature is hidden, but all are naked and laid bare to the eyes of the one to whom we must render an account.

Since, then, we have a great high priest who has passed through the heavens, Jesus, the Son of God, let us hold fast to our confession. (Heb. 4:8–14)

There is no change of subject when the author of Hebrews moves from the discussion of rest to the discussion of God's word and then to a discussion of our High Priest in heaven, for it is God's word that guarantees and makes possible our rest in the true promised land, which is union with Christ in heaven. He has made a safe path for us into the presence of the Father, a path that we can only travel by being united with Him, which can only happen through the work of the Holy Spirit. So, then, when the Spirit unites us with Christ and we, in union with Him, travel the path through the heavens into the presence of the Father, we find ourselves embraced and surrounded by the overflowing love of the three persons, resting in the very nature of God. When, in the Gospel of John, Jesus promises to "prepare a place" for us in His Father's house (14:2), this is the place that He is promising. Earlier in the Gospel, John tells us that when Jesus spoke of His "Father's house," He was speaking of His own body (2:21). The place that Jesus prepares for us in His Father's house is a place of union with and as His body.

For Christians, as for the people of Israel, this process of being brought into the promised land of union with God is something we pursue by means of right, God-ordained worship. Thus the almost complete absence of right worship in the book of Judges is ominously significant. The people have come into the land in a literal way, but they are not coming into the holy land of union with YHWH by means of the worship structures He established on Sinai. The tabernacle is *never* mentioned in the book of Judges, and the ark is mentioned only at the very end of the book. Wrong worship—worship of Baal, but also twisted versions of YHWH worship—is characteristic of the people of Israel in every episode throughout the book and is even characteristic of Israel's leaders in the stories contained in the second half, from Gideon onward. Without right worship at the heart of their communal life, the people of Israel will not find rest in Canaan, because without right worship—no matter how effectively they may conquer territory—they will not be living as holy people in a holy land.

Reversing the Fall

Judges thus recounts a failed venture. Behind the failure to inhabit the land of Canaan as a holy land lies the ongoing reality of the fall. The book of Judges shows the people of Israel attempting to undo the double effects of sin articulated by God in the double curse on Adam and Eve. Adam's sin had brought down a curse regarding his relationship to the land, and in the book of Judges we see the people of Israel beginning but ultimately failing to restore an appropriate dominion over the land. Eve's sin had brought down a curse regarding her relationship to Adam, and in the book of Judges we see the people of Israel beginning but ultimately failing to restore a life-giving relationship between women and men. These two themes—the broken relationship of Israel to the land and the broken relationship of women to men—each wind through the entire book from beginning to end. They are related to the two great sins of Israel in the book of Judges: idolatry and intermarriage with the Canaanites.

In the beginning, Adam was made to be a priest to the creation, a steward of God's blessings who names the animals brought before him. As George Herbert taught in his poem "Praise,"

> Of all the creatures both in sea and land
> Only to man Thou has made known Thy ways,
> And put the pen alone into his hand,
> And made him secretary of Thy praise.
>
> Man is the world's high priest: he doth present
> The sacrifice for all; while they below
> Unto the service mutter an asset,
> Such as springs use that fall, and winds that blow.[11]

Both creation accounts give testimony to this priestly role. In the first creation account, Adam and Eve are told to have dominion over the earth, but it is a dominion that is to result in the fruitful flourishing of the creatures that they rule. They are named as God's image, or representative (Gen. 1:26–28). In the second account, Adam is described as being made from the dust of the earth and from the breath of God, as one who stands between the creation and the Creator. He is placed in the garden in order to tend it and "serve" the soil. He is given the task of naming the animals, reflecting analogically God's own act of speaking in

---

11. *Lyra Sacra: A Book of Religious Verse*, ed. Henry Charles Beeching (London: Methuen, 1895), 82, lines 5–12.

the creation (Gen. 2:7–8, 15–20). In all these ways, Adam is seen as a mediator between God and the nonhuman creation.

On the seventh day God rests, which is to say that He takes His seat to rule over this new world. Adam and Eve are at rest because they are in harmony with that rule. This is what it is for them to be at rest in the land. Being a Presbyterian, I think of this rest in terms of the first question and answer of the Westminster Shorter Catechism. Adam and Eve are at rest when they are living toward their "chief end," the purpose for which they have been made, and this end is "to glorify God and enjoy Him forever." Resting in the land is possible for Adam and Eve because in a state of holiness they are achieving their end by living in a right relationship of abiding with God.

After the fall into sin, the curse on Adam reflects the disruption of this relationship and also the disruption of his priestly vocation. When Adam and Eve hear God approaching "as the Spirit of the day" (which is to say, the day of judgment), they hide from Him (Gen. 3:8).[12] They have a new fear of God, a fear rooted in disobedience and shame. They are alienated from God, and therefore they are also alienated from their own nature. They are no longer living as "spiritual bodies" (1 Cor. 15:44) in which their physical existence is intimately maintained by their abiding within God's life-giving grace. Instead, they have become perishable bodies, drawing their life from the creation rather than from their Creator. They have become people "of dust" (1 Cor. 15:49), and death is now their future.

Sin has alienated Adam from God, but it has also alienated him from the land. The very dust from which he himself was taken will now rebel against him as he tries to make it into a garden, a place of fruitfulness. His work of serving and tending will now be met by thorns. He will be in harmony with the land only in his death, when he returns to it (Gen. 3:17–23).

There is, however, a promise that one of Eve's descendants will crush the serpent's head and break the curse (Gen. 3:15). Could it be that Joshua, whose very name is salvation, is that one? Could it be that the move into the promised land is the restoration long hoped for? The book of Judges explores this possibility and demonstrates with no room for doubt that the promise is not fulfilled. By the end of the book, it is obvious that (despite several heads having been crushed) the curse has not been rolled back, the effects of sin are not diminished, and the people of Israel are not yet at rest in the land. If education and self-discipline could have led

12. Meredith G. Kline, "Primal Parousia," *Westminster Theological Journal* 40, no. 2 (Spring 1978): 245. See chap. 4 on Othniel for a further discussion of this understanding of the Spirit's presence in the Old Testament.

to salvation from sin and the restoration of the order of creation, this should have been the moment. Instead, the book of Judges is a lived-out proof of the doctrine of original sin, of the fact that human beings cannot save ourselves because we are dead in our sin. We need a Savior who offers more than education and law, more even than a divinely given education and a divinely given law. We need a Savior who offers a new creation.

For a brief while at the beginning of the book, things look hopeful. The first judge, Othniel, conquers the Canaanites and receives from Caleb good land, with springs of water, along with a faithful wife with whom he can be fruitful and multiply. Later, when Deborah and Barak go to battle against Sisera, the creation joins in fighting at their side. The river and the stars fight for them (5:20–21). The head of their adversary is literally crushed (4:21). Perhaps the creational harmony of human beings with the natural world is being restored.

But by the time of Gideon things are already growing more dire. The Midianites attack the crops of Israel and are likened to swarms of locusts destroying the land (6:3–5). Gideon is first seen in the midst of an awkward harvest, separating wheat from chaff while hiding in a winepress (6:11). Gideon wins a great victory over the Midianites but then turns his wrath on his fellow Israelites, whom he attacks using thorns and briars (8:16), the emblems of an untamed land in God's curse on Adam (Gen. 3:18). By the end of Gideon's story, he—like fallen Adam—is so alienated from God that he sets up his own form of worship, which leads his people into idolatry. Gideon's son Abimelech is likened to a thornbush (9:15), and in Abimelech's attempts to make himself king the people of Israel continue to experience the punishing effects of Gideon's wrath and disobedience. By the time we arrive at Samson, things have grown yet worse. Samson's relationship with the creation is consistently disordered and marked by death: he eats honey taken from a lion's corpse (14:8–9), he destroys crops by setting foxes on fire (15:4–5), and he kills his enemies with the jawbone of a donkey (15:15–17). The last two stories in the book are about people who cannot keep still, who are traveling and relocating, who are anything but at rest. All of which culminates in a civil war, in which it becomes clear that the land must be cleansed of the people of Israel as much as the people of Canaan. The first curse, the curse on Adam and the land, remains in effect.

In the beginning, Eve was made to be a priest to Adam. In the second creation account, Adam is made before Eve, and his state of aloneness is the first thing in this sinless creation that God identifies as "not good" (Gen. 2:18). Our familiarity with the story may make it difficult to see how odd this is. Adam is in a state of sinless communion with God Himself. Shouldn't a relationship with God be enough for us? How is it that Adam is described as alone in a not-good way? Furthermore, God is our Help, the original Help from whom all other help derives. This is a common theme throughout the Bible.[13] How is it that Adam needs another helper? Eve's creation suggests that our need to encounter God's helping presence in human form, that is, our need for the incarnation, is not simply a response to sin. Even apart from sin, Adam needs to encounter God in one who is bone of his bone, flesh of his flesh (Gen. 2:23).[14]

In the first creation account, Eve shares Adam's commission to be God's image in the world He has made. In the second creation account, the particular way in which Eve is to do this is made explicit, even as the particular way that Adam is to do it is made explicit. Adam is made from the earth; Eve is made from Adam. Adam is the mediator to the land from which he is made; Eve is the mediator to Adam from whom she is made. Adam is priest for the creation; Eve is priest for Adam. She is the one who is named the *ezer* or helper, a word used over and over in the Old Testament to describe God. She is created as a type of Christ, a forerunner of the incarnation. Her calling is to embody God's word to Adam.[15]

The fall into sin is initiated because Eve fails in this calling and fails spectacularly. Instead of bringing God's word to Adam, she brings the word of the serpent. Because she is his bone and flesh, Adam receives that lie in the place of God's truth and acts on it. The curse on Eve is twofold, changing her relationship with her children and with her husband. God tells her, "I will greatly increase your pangs in childbearing; in pain you shall bring forth children, yet your desire shall be for your husband, and he shall rule over you" (Gen. 3:16). Up until this point in the story, if there is a hierarchy between Adam and Eve, Eve is at the top of that hierarchy. It may be that other passages of scripture, such as Gal. 3:28, give us reason to assume that there was no hierarchy in the sinless creation and that Adam was meant to be a priestly helpmeet back to Eve in a mutual showing forth of God's presence, but Gen. 2 alone makes no such suggestion. After the fall, however, a hierarchy is definitely established by the new experience of sin. From now on, husbands will rule over their wives, and women's needy desires will make them complicit in their own subordination. And from now on through the whole of

13. For a start, see Pss. 54:4; 121:2; Heb. 13:6.

14. I take this as evidence that the incarnation would have been fitting anyway, even if there had been no sin, though of course that is not the same as saying that it would have been necessary.

15. Also see Laura A. Smit, *Loves Me, Loves Me Not: The Ethics of Unrequited Love* (Grand Rapids: Baker Academic, 2005), chap. 2.

the Old Testament, though women may occasionally function as prophets and as rulers, no women will serve as priests in Israel's worship.

But again, Gen. 3:15 promises that the disordered state of alienation reflected in the curse on Eve will not endure forever, any more than the alienation from the land reflected in the curse on Adam will. Could it be that the new life in Canaan will be a life in which this curse is rolled back?

Again, things begin positively. At the very beginning of the book, we have the figure of Achsah, who fulfills the role with her husband Othniel that Eve failed to fill with Adam. Othniel is the faithful, victorious one (Rev. 2:26–29) to whom Caleb, the father, gives his child as a spouse. Achsah then intercedes with her father on behalf of the man she has married, so that Caleb gives Othniel good land with springs of water. Here we have a woman fulfilling the role of the priestly helpmeet, serving as a type of the High Priest who is also the Bridegroom, who intercedes with His Father for His bride and who comes to the marriage with the gift of living water. We also see Othniel fulfilling the role toward Achsah that Adam failed to fulfill with Eve. Othniel uses his power to dominate the powers of evil rather than living into the post-fall paradigm of dominating his wife.

There are many women in the book of Judges, and Achsah is the benchmark against whom they are to be measured. Deborah and Jael seem to come close. At the beginning of Deborah's story, she is recognized as a prophet and a judge. Barak, the Levite, is reluctant to perform his priestly duty of leading the army into battle unless Deborah joins him in this role as well, and so she does. The battle is waged against Sisera, who can be understood as an embodiment of the curse on Eve. His own mother testifies (with approval) to his use of rape as a routine weapon in war. He is oblivious to the very existence of Deborah and to the threat of Jael. Dominating and ruling over women is central to how he is portrayed in the story. Ultimately, Jael, the seed of the woman, crushes his head with a tent peg (5:26–27). Barak and Deborah join together to sing a song of triumph summing up this victory, in which Deborah is described as "a mother in Israel" who has cared for the people of Israel so that they have enough to eat (5:7). There is much here that appears to be an undoing of the curse on Eve, and yet it is all done in an atmosphere of threatening violence that is far removed from the Edenic ideal. Although Deborah and Jael measure up to the benchmark of Achsah, their circumstances do not. This is also true of the next story featuring a woman: the false king Abimelech is killed by a woman dropping a millstone on him, crushing his skull (9:52–54), again an echo of the promise in Genesis that the serpent's head will be crushed.

Beginning with chapter 11, however, women prefigure Christ not by being priestly helpmeets but by being sacrifices. Jephthah's daughter is sacrificed by her father, in sharp contrast to the loving treatment that Achsah receives from her father Caleb. Samson's wife is burned to death by the Philistines, and her father is burned with her (15:6). The Levite sacrifices his concubine to protect himself (19:25), and after she has been raped to death, he cuts her body into pieces and distributes them to all the tribes of Israel (19:29).

The final story in Judges shows two groups of young women taken by force to be the wives of the Benjaminites, with whom the army of Israel has been at war. First, four hundred young virgins from Jabesh-gilead are taken, after the inhabitants of the city are slaughtered by the men of Israel (21:8–14). Then two hundred of the daughters of Shiloh are abducted by the remnant of the tribe of Benjamin with the collusion of the other tribes (21:15–23). The pairing of violence and marriage takes place on a grand scale. It is clear that the curse on Eve has not been undone any more than has the curse on Adam. These stories of horror in the last part of the book demonstrate the ongoing reality of men dominating women in ways that lead to death. Most of the women in the last part of the book are unnamed and do not speak, clearly not fulfilling the role of priestly helpmeets.

But the male priests also fail to fulfill this helpmeet role. Barak is a timid Levite who needs to be cajoled into doing his job. The Levite who serves as Micah's priest in chapters 17 and 18 is leading worship of an idol, and the Levite who sacrifices and then cuts up his concubine in chapter 19 leads the tribes of Israel into war while denying his own cowardice. In the last half of the book, there is no faithful priestly presence in Israel, no one—male or female—who speaks the word of God and embodies His helping presence, other than an indirect reference to Phinehas, grandson of Aaron, who is still serving before the ark at Bethel (20:28).

The coming of Jesus addresses both the curse on Adam and the curse on Eve. Jesus is the second Adam who leads us into rest (Heb. 4). In the new heaven and the new earth, our right relationship with the creation will be restored, and already now the power of Christ allows us to anticipate that restoration. Jesus is also the second Eve, our great High Priest who is bone of our bone, flesh of our flesh. The reconfiguring of marriage in the New Testament as a relationship of mutual submission is a step toward the rolling back of the curse, as is the new creation promise that in Christ there is neither male nor female, for all Christians are united into one body, a promise that begins to work itself out in the new creation reality of the church, where men and women work together as brothers and sisters, as equals. While a direct reflection of the curse on Eve is seen in that there are no women priests in the Old Testament, in the New Testament our only priest is Christ, but men and women alike receive His Spirit, are transformed into His likeness, and share in His offices. Jesus also transforms the role of the sacrifice into a role of power, for in His person He combines the role of the priest with the role of the one who is offered up.

The book of Judges serves to demonstrate with stark clarity how deep is our need for a Savior who will rescue us from the effects of our sin, specifically sin manifested according to these two patterns. In so doing, this book prepares us for the good news of the New Testament. The Heidelberg Catechism teaches that, in order to know the comfort of belonging to Jesus Christ, I must first know "the greatness of my sin and wretchedness."[16] When Paul unpacks the mystery of salvation in the book of Romans, he begins by spending significant time driving home the depth and breadth of sin in a straightforward and dogmatic way. Judges makes the same point, but more viscerally. Our sin and misery are very great. The consequences of sin articulated in the curse on Eve and the curse on Adam continue to spin out in vast patterns of destruction throughout human history, and our own power is not sufficient to stop the spinning.

Structure

The artistry of the book of Judges contributes to its searing impact. A didactic warning about idolatry would not have the power of this carefully structured telling of horrific events in which we are invited to participate imaginatively. The intentional patterning of the book overall and of each episode invites us into this imaginative participation, shaping our reaction to the stories, whether or not we are aware of that pattern consciously. When we enter imaginatively into the world of Judges, the horizon of our worldview fuses with the horizon of ancient Israel, so that this story becomes our story. This is exactly the right reaction to the book, for this story of sin, idolatry, and rebellion against God really *is* our story, and the primary prophetic goal of the book is to bring us to that realization.

Every chapter in this commentary thus begins with a section on literary structure. Such structural analysis is immensely fruitful, especially in preaching. First, structure reveals meaning. The typical structural approach of Hebrew narrative is the chiasm, in which the passage's key idea is placed *centrally*, framed by parallel

16. "The Heidelberg Catechism," *Book of Confessions: Study Edition* (Louisville: Geneva, 1999), Q/A 2, p. 59.

structures before and after. English literature does not typically follow this pattern, so it takes practice for people whose reading experience is mostly in English to see it. Once we develop that ability, we can see much more clearly what the passage is supposed to be about. For instance, it is significant that Gideon is the figure in the middle of the book of Judges; the Gideon story with its focus on YHWH's kingship is central to the meaning of the book.

Second, in my experience as a preacher, analyzing the structure of a passage often makes obvious what is the best way to structure a sermon on that passage. It becomes easier to see where the units are within the story, and these units typically translate into the main points of the sermon. It becomes easier to see parallels and contrasts, which typically reveal a lot about whether an action is one we should imitate or one we should condemn. It becomes easier to understand what the point of the story was intended to be.

Third, most thoughtful adults can learn to think about a text in terms of its structure, and that makes this approach especially useful for homiletics. When the sermon depends on knowledge of languages or history not available to people in the pew, it is easy to send a message that understanding the Bible is a special form of secret knowledge only available to educated clergy. I have had people in the church tell me that they have stopped trying to read the Bible for themselves precisely because they so admire their pastor's depth of knowledge and know that they cannot replicate it. This is not the message any good preacher wants to send. If instead we can communicate that the keys to understanding the Bible as a guide to faith and life are paying attention to the structure of the text (which is generally perfectly discernible even in translation) and knowing the Bible well enough to notice cross-references, then we are inviting members of the congregation into an accessible sort of study. This is not secret knowledge. This is knowledge available to anyone who reads persistently and with loving attention.

D. W. Gooding has identified a chiastic structure to the entire book of Judges, an identification that is now widely, though not universally, accepted.

Introduction: Part I (1:1–2:5)
Introduction: Part II (2:6–3:6)
Othniel (3:7–11)
Ehud + Shamgar (3:12–21)
Deborah (4:1–5:31)

Gideon (6:1–8:32)
Abimelech + Tola + Jair (8:33–10:5)
Jephthah + Ibzan, Elon, Abdon (10:6–12:15)
Samson (13:1–16:31)
Epilogue: Part I (17:1–18:31)
Epilogue: Part II (19:1–21:25)[17]

Marc Zvi Brettler, among others, has complained that this structure is unrealistic because the parallel sections are not of equal length, so that the judgeship of Othniel, which is four verses long, is set in parallel with the judgeship of Samson, which is four chapters long. As we move through the book, we will need to consider just why that is so, but the parallels are so theologically and exegetically fruitful that I cannot dismiss Gooding's theory. When the book is examined in light of this structure, the truly beautiful nature of its literary composition becomes obvious, and new levels of meaning are exposed.

In addition to this primary and basic chiastic structure, there are two other overlapping structures: first, a through structure, which moves from beginning to end, demonstrating a trajectory of decline into apostasy (which we have already begun to consider in the previous section); second, a parallel structure, in which the first half of the book is recapitulated and developed in the second half of the book. There are also smaller patterns that cut across these structures, such as several sets of three that run throughout the book: three appearances by the messenger of YHWH, three times when women attack men's heads, three prophetic speeches, and three encounters with the tribe of Ephraim at the Jordan.

Some contemporary readers find it difficult to imagine that all these structural pieces are really there, really intended by the author or editor of the book. I believe they are intentional, meaningful, and elegant. I am not a great stylist, but even I am capable of writing a sentence that has meaning on more than one level. Even I am capable of constructing parallels and patterns in my writing that convey meaning. The author or editor of the book of Judges is a very great stylist. But more than that, the ultimate Author of this book, as of all of scripture, is the Holy Spirit, who is more than able to embed many levels of meaning into

---

17. D. W. Gooding, "The Composition of the Book of Judges," *Eretz Israel* 16 (1982): 70–79, cited approvingly by Daniel Block (1999: 49), Bruce Waltke (2004: 190), and many others. An alternate organization that some find persuasive is suggested by Jay G. Williams in his article "The Structure of Judges 2:6–16:31," *JSOT* 49 (1991): 77–86. Williams identifies a more complex structure of interrelation between all twelve of the judges according to the four seasons.

the text, including meanings that may not have been clear or comprehensible to the first readers or even to the human authors themselves. The book of Judges is a sophisticated piece of writing, constructed with a careful view toward maximizing meaning through structure, and paying attention to structure will therefore be central to our examination.

2

THE FIRST PROLOGUE

1:1–2:5

Structure

Judges opens with two parallel prologues, the first of which recounts the history of the invasion of Canaan and the relationship that the people of Israel have with the people of the land, and the second of which speaks of the temptation to idolatry and the relationship that the people of Israel have with YHWH. The book ends with two parallel epilogues, the first of which speaks of the relationship that the people of Israel have with YHWH, and the second of which recounts the history of a disastrous civil war. The two prologues and two epilogues thus form a great chiasm around the book, framing the narratives of the judges with the themes of the establishing of the people in the land and the insistence on right worship of YHWH as opposed to idolatry. These two themes are connected to each other in that the Israelites can only be formed into a holy people who are able to inhabit the land under the kingship of YHWH when their worship lives are rightly ordered. The structure of the book makes clear that Israel's failure to conquer and inhabit the land as they were commanded to do is a direct result of their turn toward idolatry and of the collapse of the right worship of YHWH that they had learned under Moses.

In the opening scenes of this first prologue, the action moves from south to north, taking in the entire land. The tribes mentioned in the first chapter correspond with the tribal affiliations of the six major judges, and the order in which those tribes are treated here corresponds to the order in which they are treated in the body of the book. The structure of Judges underscores the totality of Israel's apostasy in that there are twelve judges, six major and six minor, one for each of the twelve tribes. Just as the prologue moves from the most obedient to the least, so the book as a whole moves from Othniel, the most faithful, to Samson, the least faithful. Although the stories of Judges may have originally been more localized tales, they have been knit together in an elegant and intentional way to tell a story of all God's people.

K. Lawson Younger notes that the first prologue is framed by the question "Who will go up?" (1:1–2a) and by the ultimate answer that it is the messenger of YHWH who will go up to proclaim judgment against Israel (2:1–5). The body of the passage is divided into two: the account of Judah going up (1:2b–21) and the account of Joseph going up (1:22–36).[1] The question of who should go up returns in the final epilogue, signaling the connections between that story and this one.

Both Judah and Joseph start with success, then move to failure. These failures are evaluated and judged in the final going up of the messenger of YHWH. Setting the two sections next to each other reveals that the taking of the lord of Bezek by Judah is parallel to the taking of the Canaanite informer at Bethel by Joseph. This highlights Joseph's inferiority to Judah, since Judah does at least capture the lord of Bezek whereas Joseph shows more faithfulness to the Canaanite informer than to the command of YHWH.

Election

Judges begins with an echo of the book of Joshua. That book begins by saying that "after the death of Moses" God raised up Joshua. Now, with a parallel introduction ("After the death of Joshua"), we expect to read of a new leader. But there is no new leader, at least no one individual. The tribe of Judah is given corporate leadership over the other tribes, as Jacob had already prophesied would happen (Gen. 49:8). Caleb, who is not biologically a descendent of Abraham but is a member of the covenant community affiliated with Judah, does have leadership

1. K. Lawson Younger Jr., "The Configuring of Judicial Preliminaries: Judges 1:1–2:5 and Its Dependence on the Book of Joshua," *JSOT* 68 (1995): 77.

within Judah as the last member of Joshua's generation, but whereas the book of Joshua highlights his individual accomplishments, the book of Judges highlights the accomplishments of the tribes. For instance, Joshua attributes the taking of Hebron to Caleb, whereas Judges attributes the taking of Hebron to Judah. The claims are not contradictory, but different values are being expressed.

The first act of YHWH in the book of Judges is an act of election. Judah is chosen. Judah does not merit this choice, as will become obvious (15:9–13), and yet YHWH will remain faithful to His choice not only throughout Judges but throughout the sweep of scripture. Why are some chosen and others not? Prior to the question of the election of Judah is the assumption that the tribes of Israel are all elect over against the reprobate Canaanites. It is tempting to justify this act of election on YHWH's part by pointing to the heinous nature of much Canaanite religious practice, which included cultic prostitution and child sacrifice. However, by the end of the book of Judges this argument has been effectively undermined, since the people of Israel have themselves done every heinous thing imaginable, such that they certainly have no grounds to claim any moral superiority to the Canaanites. Election is not about merit.

The election of Israel as a people occurred at Sinai, when they entered into a suzerain covenant with YHWH. Jon Levenson explains that a suzerain covenant is not the same as a simple recognition of divine sovereignty, which would allow for the existence of lesser monarchs along with YHWH's claims to kingship. Rather, a suzerain covenant is marked by exclusivity. There is only one suzerain, and there is no tolerance for competition, no willingness to share authority. Levenson observes, "This proscription is the ultimate source of the prohibitions upon the worship of other deities in Israel, and . . . it underlies the depiction of them as unworthy, even, finally, unreal."[2] It also underscores a central idea in Judges, that YHWH Himself is King over Israel, which is why they do not and should not have any other king (8:23).

The suzerain has vassals, each of whom shares indirectly in his royalty and owes him absolute allegiance. In the case of Israel, YHWH names all the people of Israel as His vassals, calling them "a priestly kingdom and a holy nation" (Exod. 19:6). The election of Israel is thus rooted in a covenantal, two-sided relationship in which YHWH endows the people of Israel with royalty and holiness and they are given the right to claim Him as their Emperor, the one great King to whom they owe loyalty. This covenant includes the recognition that to worship any other god would be treasonous, a violation of the covenant promises.

2. Jon Levenson, *Sinai and Zion: An Entry into the Jewish Bible* (San Francisco: HarperSanFrancisco, 1985), 71.

Throughout the Old Testament, human marriage is understood as pointing toward and being enfolded within the larger covenant of Israel with YHWH. When Paul describes marriage as an illustration of the relationship between Christ and His bride, the church (Eph. 5:21–33), this is not a new idea. The commandment against marriage with the Canaanites is explained in terms of infidelity against YHWH because the people of Israel are to understand themselves as joined to YHWH in an exclusive covenant analogous to marriage. The analogy is used frequently in prophecies against Israel. For example: "As a faithless wife leaves her husband, so you have been faithless to me, O house of Israel, says the LORD" (Jer. 3:20). Within the symbol system of the Bible, the proscription against marrying Canaanites is naturally connected to the sovereign claims of YHWH; marrying outside the covenant community is considered infidelity to the covenant head.

The primacy of Judah in this covenant points us forward both to David and to Jesus. Judah is appointed to lead within the twelve tribes, even though Judah was not the oldest of the twelve sons of Jacob. We will see disintegration within Judah's role over the course of the book. Judges has an inclusio uniting the first prologue and the last epilogue by asking the same question of who should go up, and in each case Judah is selected. However, by book's end the going up will be against Benjamin in civil war rather than against the people of the land in obedience to YHWH. Judah fails to fulfill the terms of the covenant, fails to live up to YHWH's electing choice. However, here as elsewhere in the Bible, when God's people fail to meet their covenant obligations, YHWH Himself fulfills their obligations and bears the consequences of their disobedience.

The Angel of the LORD

As the structure shows us, even in this prologue Judah's election is fulfilled by the Angel of the LORD rather than by the tribe of Judah. It is the Angel (or, in some translations, the "messenger") who "goes up" at the end of the prologue, after Judah has "gone up" only imperfectly.

The Angel of the LORD appears many times throughout the Old Testament and is often addressed as God Himself. In Judges, the Angel of the LORD appears to Gideon and to Manoah and his wife. Both Gideon and Manoah initially take the Angel to be a human being, but by the end of each story each man is worried that he is about die because he has seen the face of God. Many Christian interpreters throughout history have thus concluded that these visits from the Angel of the LORD are theophanies. At Bochim, the people of Israel are indeed encountering

God, even as Jacob encountered God at the Jabbok and Moses encountered God at the burning bush. More specifically, these manifestations may be understood as Christophanies, preincarnate appearances of the Second Person of the Trinity. Within the triune Godhead, who is known in the Old Testament as YHWH, it is the Father who is the Source and Sender; it is the Son who is the Word that is spoken, the "exact imprint" of the Father's nature (Heb. 1:3); it is the Spirit who is the binding Love between the Father and the Son. Therefore, when we encounter a divine figure who is sometimes addressed as God and whose primary task is revelatory, it is reasonable to identify Him with the Son, the one who is sent.[3]

The Son is also the person of the Trinity who, in His human nature, is a member of the tribe of Judah. Although Judah is chosen to lead the people of Israel in the taking of the land, it is Jesus Christ, the Son of God and the Lion of Judah, who completes and fulfills the terms of Judah's election, in a preliminary way at Bochim and in a final way in His incarnation, or more specifically in his being lifted up on the cross, raised up from the dead on the third day, and raised to the right hand of the Father in His ascension. In this passage He fulfills the terms of Judah's election by insisting on purity in the land, an insistence that condemns the people of Israel as well as the Canaanites. Here in the first prologue, the Messenger of the LORD goes up to Bochim to announce that rest is not coming yet because the terms of the covenant are being broken. When He comes again, He will fulfill the terms of Judah's election by going before His people into the rest prepared for them in the heavenly kingdom (Heb. 4:1–11).

The Destruction of the Canaanites

Perhaps no episode in the Bible is more troubling than the command to eradicate the people of the land in the taking of Canaan. What are we to make of the "Canaanite genocide," as it is now often called?[4] For some people, this command to exterminate the native peoples of the land effectively renders this portion of scripture (and perhaps by extension the entire Old Testament) illegitimate. In his book on the Former Prophets, Robert Alter observes that the details of the

3. David Gunn (2005: 18) notes that the Rabbinic tradition identified this angel/messenger as Phinehas, reasoning that since he went up to Bochim from Gilgal rather than going down to Bochim from heaven, he must be a human messenger rather than an angelic messenger, and that the high priest was the most likely human messenger.

4. See, e.g., Stanley N. Gundry, ed., *Show Them No Mercy: Four Views on God and Canaanite Genocide* (Grand Rapids: Zondervan, 2003).

conquest as we find them in Joshua and Judges are not supported by archaeological evidence. He concludes:

> The fact that this narrative does not correspond to what we can reconstruct of the actual history of Canaan offers one great consolation: the blood-curdling report of the massacre of the entire population of Canaanite towns—men, women, children, and in some cases livestock as well—never happened. . . . The *ḥerem*, the practice of total destruction that scholars call "the ban" . . . , was not unique to ancient Israel, and there is some evidence that it was occasionally carried out in warfare by other peoples of the region. The question is why the Hebrew writers, largely under the ideological influence of Deuteronomy, felt impelled to invent a narrative of the conquest of the land in which a genocidal onslaught on its indigenous population is repeatedly stressed. (Alter 2014: 4)

I do not share Alter's assumption that archaeology is more trustworthy and accurate than scripture, but it is certainly the case that Israel is roundly condemned throughout Judges for *not* exterminating the Canaanites as commanded. Even if it were the case that the violence was less than as reported in Joshua and Judges, if this is the result of the disobedience of God's people, should we be comforted by it?

I suggest that the story of the destruction of the Canaanites has some structural similarities to the story of the sacrifice of Isaac. In Gen. 22 Abraham is commanded by God to sacrifice his son Isaac, a command that he prepares to obey. However, at the last minute he is told that his willingness to perform the sacrifice was the key and that the sacrifice of Isaac is not required. Earlier Abraham had told his son, "God himself will provide the lamb for a burnt offering" (Gen. 22:8), and this proves to be true. This terrifying story communicates truths that stand in tension with each other. On the one hand, God claims the right to require Abraham to sacrifice his son. Life belongs to God, and He has a right to demand it when He chooses. On the other hand, through this enacting of the sacrifice, God is also teaching Abraham something about one way in which He is not like the gods of the nations. He cannot be bought off, and His desire is not ultimately for sacrifice—even though He has a right to sacrifices. His desire is *not* that people sacrifice their children, and after the terrifying events of the Akedah (i.e., the binding of Isaac) it becomes clear in Israel that whereas pagans send their children through the fire, the people of Israel do not. God still claims all firstborn sons, but the Israelites are supposed to *redeem* their eldest sons. In the Passover, all the Israelite firstborn sons were redeemed with the blood of the Passover lamb. This obligation to redeem the firstborn son continues after the exodus, communicating both the truth that God is the Lord of life and also the truth that God provides a lamb to take the place of the deaths that are owed to Him.

In Deut. 18 Moses teaches, "When you come into the land that the LORD your God is giving you, you must not learn to imitate the abhorrent practices of those nations. No one shall be found among you who makes a son or daughter pass through fire. . . . For whoever does these things is abhorrent to the LORD; it is because of such abhorrent practices that the LORD your God is driving them out before you" (18:9–10, 12). Later, after the kingship was established in Jerusalem, the prophet Micah could ask:

> "With what shall I come before the LORD,
>   and bow myself before God on high? . . .
> Shall I give my firstborn for my transgression,
>   the fruit of my body for the sin of my soul?"
> He has told you, O mortal, what is good;
>   and what does the LORD require of you
> but to do justice, and to love kindness,
>   and to walk humbly with your God? (Mic. 6:6–8)

The possibility of child sacrifice is now self-evidently rejected with a rhetorical question.

When YHWH first commanded Abraham to sacrifice his son, it was not a trick. It was a serious commandment, and Abraham was right to say yes to it, because YHWH truly does have the right of life and death over all those we love. And yet YHWH used that command to teach Abraham and all His people a different, deeper lesson about His nature. He does not insist on His rights. He chooses to be the one who pays what is due to Him, rather than having us pay, both because we can never pay enough and, more explicitly, because our children are precious to Him, which makes child sacrifice abhorrent to Him. The refusal of child sacrifice becomes a moral distinctive that sets Israel apart from the peoples around them.

Similarly, God has every right to require the destruction of the Canaanites—a claim we will explore in more detail in a moment. However, in the event, the attempt to destroy the Canaanites fails, and through that failure the Israelites learn the other side of the equation—that YHWH's favor cannot be earned by zealous acts of war, that they themselves are too sinful to offer the *herem* sacrifice with any efficacy, and that there will be another lamb to take the place of the Canaanites.

Let us first consider the claim that God has every right to require the destruction of the Canaanites, that this requirement is not in itself immoral or illegitimate.

Many people in contemporary Western culture find this claim difficult to swallow. In a Doonesbury cartoon, a young woman questions her pastor, saying, "Reverend Sloan, I've been noticing something about the readings in church." "What's that, Sam?" he asks. Her answer encapsulates a popular reading of scripture: "Whenever you read from the Old Testament, God is always crabby and snarky to everyone, but the New Testament isn't about anger at all—it's about love. God's only Son is this total pacifist—he wouldn't harm a flea. He's just this humble dude who's mellow to everyone—even the Romans! He only really snaps once, right?" She is thinking of Jesus with the moneylenders as the one time he really "snapped," which leads her mother to ask, "Oh right. What *is* it about moneylenders?" to which Reverend Sloan replies, "They do seem to set people off, don't they?"[5] Apparently, Garry Trudeau is confident that Jesus would never punish people for alternative religious practices, but even Jesus would punish bankers. Already in the early church, Marcion used similar reasoning to discredit the Old Testament as teaching a different ethic than that taught by Jesus. The idea of a discontinuity between the ways in which God operates in the Old Testament and the ways in which God operates in the New Testament continues to surface throughout the history of the church.

One way to resolve the conflict is to say that the deity portrayed in the Old Testament is someone other than the triune God of the New Testament. The early church ruled out this approach in its response to Marcion. Another way to resolve the conflict is to say that the Old Testament reflects a radical misunderstanding of God's true nature, that it is not normative or inspired in the same way as the New and so may be set aside by Christians. This appears to be the approach taken by C. S. Cowles in his essay "The Case for Radical Discontinuity," in which he argues that the people of Israel were not capable of correctly understanding God's will and that they therefore misinterpreted God's command to inhabit the land of Canaan as a command to commit genocide. That this was not in fact God's intention, Cowles argues, is seen in that the New Testament teaches a very different ethic. "That a radical shift in the understanding of God's character and the sanctity of all human life occurred between the days of the first Joshua and the second Joshua (i.e., Jesus) is beyond dispute. It was nothing less than moving from the assumption that God hates enemies and wills their annihilation to the conviction that God 'so loved [enemies] that he gave his one and only Son'" (John 3:16).[6] Cowles asserts that a Christocentric hermeneutic will guide us in setting aside certain portions of the Old Testament as misguided.

5. Garry B. Trudeau, *Doonesbury*, May 31, 2009.
6. C. S. Cowles, "The Case for Radical Discontinuity," in Gundry, *Show Them No Mercy*, 41.

If ours is a Christlike God, then we can categorically affirm that God is not a destroyer. Death was not a part of God's original creation, neither will there be any more "death or mourning or crying or pain" in the new (Rev. 21:4). God does not engage in punitive, redemptive, or sacred violence. Violence and death are the intrinsic consequences of violating God's creative order; they are the work of Satan, for he was a "murderer from the beginning" (John 8:44). God does not proactively use death as an instrument of judgment in that death is an enemy, the "last enemy" to be destroyed by Christ (1 Cor. 15:20–28). And God does not deal with the enemy.[7]

Therefore, Cowles concludes, God did not actually intend the annihilation of the Canaanites, though He did not blame the Israelites for their failure to understand this. They did the best they could with their limited understanding. From our vantage point as followers of Christ, we can see that they misunderstood God's will when they set out to use violence as the means by which they would take the land.[8]

This may sound very much like the position I was articulating a few paragraphs ago, but it is not quite the same. Cowles thinks that the people of Israel misunderstood YHWH, that He never required them to cleanse the land. I think that the clear witness of the text is that He did lay that requirement on them, that it was a serious requirement, and that their disobedience in the face of that requirement was the source of many of their problems. To return to the parallel with Abraham, how different would that story have been if Abraham had never brought Isaac up the mountain and made the initial motions of offering a sacrifice? Would YHWH have taught His people not to sacrifice their children if He had not first seen the willingness to make such sacrifice? Cowles assumes that God is too nice ever to seek the death of a people, but such an assumption requires setting aside the scriptural witness at many points.

Many such assumptions are at play in Cowles's argument. Most obviously, his argument assumes that some parts of scripture are more authoritative than others, and that some parts of scripture reflect actual misunderstanding and inaccurate teaching that never came from God. It is no longer necessary to wrestle with difficult texts in the Old Testament, since anything that contradicts one's assumptions about how Christ works may be set aside as misguided. Cowles argues that any Christian who doesn't keep all the Old Testament sacrificial and dietary laws is already doing this, but most Christians who take a high view of the inspiration

7. Cowles, "Radical Discontinuity," 30.

8. Cowles's argument could easily be combined with Alter's claim that the genocide never happened and that this is a good thing by suggesting that in His providence God prevented the people of Israel from doing what they thought He commanded.

of all of scripture would argue that there is a difference between believing that God intended certain practices only for a time during the old covenant, since those practices were later fulfilled in the work of Christ, and believing that God never intended those practices in the first place. There is also a difference between believing that God's intentions for our practice have changed and believing that God's very nature has changed.

The problems in Cowles's argument stem from two primary sources. The first is a tendency common to contemporary Christians: underestimating human sinfulness. Even those, like myself, who come from the Calvinist tradition and who are prepared to sign on to the doctrine of total depravity with conviction find in practice some difficulty in believing that our sins are truly serious. When scripture speaks of God's judgment against the nations, or against the people of Israel, or against all humanity—in our heart of hearts most of us tend to think that He is overreacting. Rather than seeing our sin as making us genuinely worthy of damnation, we typically understand our sin as a small matter that we should be able to settle by the payment of a fine or by receiving a slap on the wrist. Therefore, the question of the slaughter of the Canaanites is often presented as the slaughter of innocents, or at least as the slaughter of those who do not deserve to die.

The scriptural assumption, of course, is that we all deserve to die. The book of Romans teaches us that we are all "without excuse" (Rom. 1:20), that there are no innocent people, since everyone has been given enough revelation about God to be justly held accountable for worshiping Him rightly. And yet none of us worship Him rightly, meaning that we are all guilty, all deserving of judgment, and that God is well within His rights to kill any one of us. Until we genuinely believe this, it will be difficult to make sense of the book of Judges.

A second source of difficulty in Cowles's argument is a common problem leading to many misunderstandings of God's nature: underestimating the analogical gap between God's nature and our own. Because it is wrong for us to engage in the extermination of an entire people, Cowles and those who share his reasoning assume that it would be wrong for God to engage in such extermination. Because it is wrong for us to engage in retributive violence, they assume it would be wrong for God to engage in retributive violence. Because it is impossible for us to resort to violence without also indulging in sinful rage, disdain, hatred, or vengefulness, they assume that God would also be contaminated by such sinful emotions were He to engage in such acts.

All these assertions are grounded in the assumption that we may make deductions about God's inner life and ethical behavior based on our own experience.

This is clearly false. Our lives and God's life are not univocal. God does not exist on the same scale of being as we do; God is the ground and source of all created beings. Where we are finite, temporal, dependent, vulnerable, and in constant flux, He is infinite, eternal, self-sufficient, impassible, and fully actual. His ways are not our ways, and His way of existing is always radically unlike our own. When we move easily between our experience of reality to deductions about God's experience, we are inviting error.

More specifically, on the matter of killing and violence, all life belongs to God. He is the source of all that is. He repeatedly claims authority over issues of life and death throughout the scriptures. As only one example, consider Deut. 32:39, where God says, "See now that I, even I, am he; there is no god besides me. I kill and I make alive; I wound and I heal; and no one can deliver from my hand." One reason, perhaps the main reason, that killing is sinful for human beings is that we are claiming an authority over life and death that belongs only to God. God had the right to declare judgment on the earth in the flood, God had the right to declare judgment on Sodom and Gomorrah in raining destruction down on them from heaven, God had the right to declare judgment on Israel by handing them over to a series of oppressors, and God had the right to declare judgment on Canaan by decreeing the extermination of the pagan people of the land.

God's claim to this right of judgment does not go away with the coming of the new covenant. Despite the *Doonesbury* view of Jesus as "this total pacifist," Jesus is at times presented as a warrior, fighting against the forces of darkness. Jesus Himself is not simply a victim of human violence but uses violence and sacrifice as tools in his battle against sin and death. He ascends to rule the world with authority, an authority that continues to manifest God's claim to decide between death and life. Indeed, that authority expands in the New Testament, for now we know surely that the death and life over which God claims absolute authority is eternal death and eternal life. It is God who predestines some for the one and some for the other,[9] and in doing so God is not overstepping His own authority but exercising His right as the sovereign Creator to control all matters of death and life. At some point in the future, Jesus will come again to be our judge, at which point it will not only be moneylenders who experience his justice and authority.

In both the Old and the New Testaments, this claim of authority and judgment is mitigated by grace and mercy. In the stories of the occupation of the land, we find instances of people who have left their membership in the group of the condemned

---

9. Though I believe that the predestination to eternal death is passive, whereas the predestination to eternal life is active. As noted previously, it is our own sin that makes us worthy of damnation.

in order to join with Israel. Rahab and Ruth are two such people, but also Caleb and Jael and Moses's father-in-law. Shamgar, one of the minor judges, may also have been a Gentile convert, given that he does not have a Hebrew name. This is evidence that God is not engaged in an act of ethnic cleansing, since the line of demarcation between those who are liable to judgment and those who are to serve as the instrument of judgment is not an ethnic line but a religious line. Those who acknowledge the lordship of YHWH are His instruments and representatives; those who rebel against His lordship receive His judgment.

But the claim that YHWH has the right to exterminate whole peoples if He wills is not the end of the story of the conquest of Canaan. In practice, here as with the sacrifice of Isaac, God over and over provides a lamb in the place of the people of Canaan. For throughout the book of Judges, YHWH's judgment is most often turned not against the people of the land but against Israel: "For the LORD reproves the one he loves, as a father the son in whom he delights" (Prov. 3:12). This, of course, is the judgment not of destruction but of purification, yet in the midst of the experience of judgment that distinction may not be detectable. During the course of Judges, we read that YHWH did the following to Israel: He "sold them into the hand of King Cushan-rishathaim of Aram-naharaim" for eight years (3:8); "strengthened King Eglon of Moab against Israel" for eighteen years (3:12–14); "sold them into the hand of King Jabin of Canaan," who oppressed them for twenty years (4:2–3); "gave them into the hand of Midian seven years" (6:1); "sold them into the hand of the Philistines and into the hand of the Ammonites," who oppressed them for eighteen years (10:7–8); and "gave them into the hand of the Philistines for forty years" (13:1). YHWH had promised to give the land "into the hand" of Judah, but because of the faithlessness of the people, they were themselves given into the hands of their enemies. In both cases, the active agent was YHWH.

Cowles is certainly right that there is an eschatological discontinuity between the stories of the occupation of the land that we find in Joshua and Judges and the promise of the new creation. The promise of the book of Revelation is that "the leaves of the tree"—the tree with twelve kinds of fruit on either side of the river, standing for the twelve tribes and the twelve disciples, and so for the fullness of God's community—"are for the healing of the nations" (Rev. 22:2). This is the fulfillment of the original promise to Abraham that all the nations of the earth would be blessed through him. But throughout scripture we see that before one may receive God's blessing, one must die, that "the path of life" (Ps. 16:11) descends to hell and goes through it before rising to the throne room of God (Acts 2:30–33).

It is not for us to know the final destiny of the Canaanite peoples condemned by God in the conquest; however, since death is not the end of anyone's story but is rather a necessary prerequisite for the entrance into life, it is at least possible that God has a redemptive purpose in mind even for those who appear to be the most vile and rebellious.

Lex Talionis

In the first prologue, a conquered Canaanite king expresses no outrage at the Israelites' attempts to conquer his land. Instead, he sees his defeat at their hands as just, given his own aggression against other kings (1:7). Adoni-bezek articulates the Deuteronomistic theology that is the starting point (though not the ending point) of the book of Judges: that God's blessing and curse correspond to our behavior, that what goes around comes around, summarized as "life for life, eye for eye, tooth for tooth, hand for hand, foot for foot, burn for burn, wound for wound, stripe for stripe" (Exod. 21:23–25). The warning of Deuteronomy is that this retributive justice applies not only in a human court but also in our relationship with God. After spelling out with vivid clarity all the blessings and curses that await the people of Israel, depending on their choice to obey or disobey YHWH, Moses says:

> If you obey the commandments of the LORD your God that I am commanding you today, by loving the LORD your God, walking in his ways, and observing his commandments, decrees, and ordinances, then you shall live and become numerous, and the LORD your God will bless you in the land that you are entering to possess. But if your heart turns away and you do not hear, but are led astray to bow down to other gods and serve them, I declare to you today that you shall perish; you shall not live long in the land that you are crossing the Jordan to enter and possess. (Deut. 30:16–18)

This is the threat articulated in Judg. 2: if you break covenant with the Lord, he will break covenant with you.

The lord of Bezek is thus expressing the theology of Deuteronomy: "Know therefore that the LORD your God is God, the faithful God who maintains covenant loyalty with those who love him and keep his commandments, to a thousand generations, and who repays [*shalam*] in their own person those who reject him. He does not delay but repays [*shalam*] in their own person those who reject him"

(Deut. 7:9–10). The verb *shalam* can also be translated "to make good" or even "to make peace." See, for instance, Prov. 16:7: "When the ways of people please the LORD, he causes even their enemies to be at peace [*shalam*] with them." The connection between peace and retribution makes sense when retribution is seen as a rebalancing of YHWH's order, a reestablishing of the shalom that is a function of His law/logos. This is why the path to peace is the observance of His commandments. The Deuteronomy passage continues, "Therefore, observe diligently the commandment—the statues and the ordinances—that I am commanding you today" (Deut. 7:11).

Although the verb *shalam* does not appear again in Judges, the concept of a God-ordained natural law that rebalances the order of creation by giving people what they have given resurfaces repeatedly. Already at the end of this prologue, YHWH invokes the breaking of the Deuteronomic covenant to explain why He will break covenant in return and not drive the Canaanites out of the land (2:1–3). Eglon has brought uncleanness and shame into Israel, and so he is shamed and made unclean. Abimelech beheads his seventy brothers on a stone, and so he is slain by a stone dropped on his head. Samson is led astray by his eyes, and so his eyes are gouged out.

The punishment fits the crime, not because YHWH is creatively dreaming up interesting punishments á la Gilbert and Sullivan's Mikado, whose "object all sublime" is "to let the punishment fit the crime," so as to amuse Himself and other onlookers.[10] YHWH takes no such pleasure in the suffering of His creatures nor in the death of the wicked, and evil is not punished to indulge a sadistic streak in His nature. Rather, the punishment fits the crime because that is the orderly way in which YHWH has designed the world; the world is ordered so that those who do wrong will (eventually) experience their wrongdoing coming back to them, on their own heads. The retribution or setting right that follows when YHWH's people fail to keep the commandments is not a matter of YHWH becoming annoyed and punishing people with whom He is displeased. Rather, the power of the law is such that it compels a self-correction on the part of the world. When people do wrong, they suffer consonant consequences.

Tom Boogaart summarizes the Old Testament understanding of such retribution: "The acts directed by one party towards another, either good or evil, have a tangible, independent existence and an efficacy all their own. Once launched, these acts return to surround the agent and determine his fate. The impetus behind this

10. W. S. Gilbert, "My Object All Sublime," *The Mikado*, act 2.

movement of the act, its launching and returning if you will, is inherent in the act itself, yet God participates in this movement as well."[11] Boogaart goes on to point out that the most important feature of this understanding is the "exact correspondence of act and consequence."[12] The action really does have causal power to replicate itself, rebounding on the one who acted. This does not undermine God's sovereign power as the primary cause but rather acknowledges the genuine free agency of human beings as secondary causes whose actions really do have consequences.

However, throughout the book we see that God is more gracious than the pagan Adoni-bezek could understand, for God does not carry through on the abandonment of Israel to which He is entitled by virtue of Israel's abandonment of Him. Daniel Block observes:

> Adoni-Bezek's comment is loaded with irony. On the one hand, it reminds the reader that in the ancient world everyone, even pagans, perceived life theologically. On the other hand, the author hereby employs a Canaanite to announce that human beings will account to God/the gods for their action. Furthermore, by quoting the governor the author offers the first hint of the Canaanization of Israelite society in this period. The Judahite treatment of Adoni-Bezek is often perceived as an application of the law of *lex talionis*, "an eye for an eye and a tooth for a tooth," which represents an acceptable ethic in the Old Testament but was set aside by Christ (Matt. 5:38–39). However, not only does this interpretation fail to understand this law as an intentional effort to curb the escalation of violence (by proscribing a reaction greater than the action), but it fails to recognize here the irony of the present situation. The author hereby declares obliquely that the newly arrived Israelites (including the tribe of Judah) have quickly adopted a Canaanite ethic.... The Israelites use the Canaanites as models when deciding how to treat captives. (Block 1999: 90–91)

By book's end, the civilizing limits of *lex talionis* will be overcome, since throughout the book reactions are disproportionate to actions, culminating in the horrors of the second epilogue.

As Block notes, in the New Testament, Jesus explicitly sets aside the *lex talionis*.

> You have heard that it was said, "An eye for an eye and a tooth for a tooth." But I say to you, Do not resist an evildoer. But if anyone strikes you on the right cheek, turn the other also; and if anyone wants to sue you and take your coat, give your

---

11. Thomas A. Boogaart, "Stone for Stone: Retribution in the Story of Abimelech and Shechem," *JSOT* 32 (1985): 47–48.
12. Boogaart, "Stone for Stone," 48.

cloak as well; and if anyone forces you to go one mile, go also the second mile. Give
to everyone who begs from you, and do not refuse anyone who wants to borrow
from you.

You have heard that it was said, "You shall love your neighbor and hate your
enemy." But I say to you, Love your enemies and pray for those who persecute you,
so that you may be children of your Father in heaven; for he makes his sun rise on
the evil and on the good, and sends rain on the righteous and on the unrighteous.
(Matt. 5:38–45)

Despite the Deuteronomistic rhetoric of Judges, we see YHWH Himself turning
the other cheek again and again in this book and throughout the biblical narrative, remaining faithful despite the unfaithfulness of Israel.

Worship

The gathering at Bochim reminds the people of Israel of what God has said to them
in the past. This word of YHWH delivered here is especially linked to Exod. 23:20–
33 and 34:11–15. Specifically, Judg. 2:3 is harking back to Exod. 23:29, in which
YHWH warns Israel that the driving out of the occupants of the land will be
gradual, because if it were sudden "the land would become desolate and the wild
animals would multiply against you." This is not meant to give the people of Israel
permission to dawdle in implementing YHWH's commandment. Rather, it is a
gracious promise that YHWH will support them during the transition.

The repentant gathering at Bochim is one of the few mentions of appropriate
worship in the book of Judges. The absence of corporate worship throughout
the book is clearly significant, since worship was central to the way of life taught
to the people of Israel by Moses. When Joshua addressed the people before the
initial occupation of the land, he repeatedly commanded them in the name of
YHWH to "be strong and courageous" (Josh. 1:6, 7, 9), telling them that their
strength and courage would be made possible by YHWH's presence with them
(1:9). But they could only be aware of that presence by acting "in accordance
with all the law" given to Moses (1:7), which in turn required constant meditation on that law: "This book of the law shall not depart out of your mouth; you
shall meditate on it day and night, so that you may be careful to act in accordance
with all that is written in it" (1:8). So the causal chain works like this: constant
meditation on the law leads to acting in accordance with the law, which leads to
living in a state of awareness of YHWH's presence, which leads to the strength

and courage necessary for the taking of the land. Everything starts with meditating on the law day and night.

For the people of Israel, meditating on the law and acting in accordance with the law are both social acts, involving gathering for worship to hear the law recited and responding to the law with appropriate prayers and ceremonies, such as ritual washing and offering sacrifice. These are acts that require the presence of Levitical priests, who are meant to spread out throughout the land of Israel in order to enable the right worship of God's people. They are acts of corporate worship—to which the people here commit themselves, with many tears. This commitment ceremony sets us up to expect repeated moments of worship in what follows and makes clear that the absence of such moments is not an oversight but deeply significant. Some commentators read the book's silence regarding tabernacle worship to mean that of course such worship was continuing and did not need to be mentioned, but I am convinced that the silence here signifies what Meier Sternberg calls a "gap"—an intentional omission that is meant to be noticed and to convey meaning—and not a "blank" (1985: 236). We are supposed to notice the lack of worship practice.

The lack of right worship creates a vacuum that will be filled by wrong worship, such as Gideon's establishment of the ephod, Jephthah's sacrifice of his daughter, Micah's shrine, and the misbehavior of multiple Levites. It is also filled by the active adoption of Baal worship, seen especially in Gideon and Abimelech.

3

THE SECOND PROLOGUE

2:6–3:6

Structure

David Dorsey (1999: 107) demonstrates that the second prologue has an elegant structure, highlighting a theme otherwise easy to miss:

a **positive beginning**: during lifetime of Joshua and elders, Israelites set out to take their inheritances and they <u>serve</u> Yahweh (2:6–9)

  b **sin of next generation** (2:10–13)
- contrasted with their <u>fathers</u>
- <u>served</u> the Baals; <u>worshiped</u> other gods
- <u>went after other gods</u>
- occurred once; and they had an excuse ("they did not know")

    c **judgment**: military defeat from surrounding nations (2:14–15)
- begins: <u>Yahweh was angry with Israel</u>

      d **CENTER: Yahweh's gracious intervention** (2:16)

  b′ **worse sins of each successive generation** (2:17–19)
- contrasted with their <u>fathers</u>
- <u>served</u> the Baals; <u>worshiped</u> other gods
- <u>went after other gods</u>

- not just once, but repeatedly; and no excuse given
- c′ **worse judgment**: Yahweh will no longer enable Israel to take their own land (2:20–3:4)
  - begins: <u>Yahweh was angry with Israel</u>
- a′ **disheartening conclusion**: Israelites, having failed to take their land, settle among the Canaanites, intermarry, and <u>serve</u> their gods (3:5–6)

Dorsey suggests that YHWH's gracious intervention is placed in the center to highlight that it was ineffective, since even after He intervened, the pattern grew worse. It seems to me more likely that it is placed in the center to highlight that YHWH's grace is the stable core of the story around which everything else rotates. The subsequent stories of the judges demonstrate that point. YHWH's ongoing gracious intervention is seen in the raising up of judges, and so the heart of the book focuses on judges, people who are symbols of God's redemptive grace to Israel.

Israel's Unfaithfulness

Like the first prologue, the second prologue also begins with the death of Joshua (2:6), underscoring that the two prologues are meant to be parallel to one another. Although he was not a king in Israel, Joshua foreshadowed the later kings by performing many royal functions. He led the people of Israel in holy war, always depending completely on YHWH to be the real savior and claiming no credit for himself. He administered the land, especially by making sure that the conditions for holding the land that YHWH had established would be met. He studied the law himself and taught it to the people. Both formally and informally, he was the mediator and administrator of the covenant between the people of Israel and YHWH.[1]

So why does Joshua not have a successor? To some extent the judges will be his successors, though their work is clearly more local and a good deal less successful. But at the beginning of the book of Judges, there are as yet no such leaders appointed by YHWH. It seems that YHWH is insisting on at least trying the ideal form of government in which each citizen in Israel accepts the responsibility of being in a direct relationship of vassal to the High King YHWH. At times, this looks as if it is working. Throughout the books of Judges and Ruth,

---

1. Gerald Eddie Gerbrandt, *Kingship according to the Deuteronomistic History*, SBL Dissertation Series 87 (Atlanta: Scholars Press, 1986), 116–23.

we encounter the idea of elders who rule over a particular village or city. There seems to be a more or less egalitarian pattern of leadership and responsibility that is emerging, at least in some places. In many instances, the elders function as the judges of the city, adjudicating cases and distributing justice to those who come "to the gate" to ask for their help (Matthews 2004: 119–20). The people of Israel are to be "a kingdom of priests and a holy nation" (Exod. 19:6 NIV). Under the new covenant, mediated by the new Joshua, God's people are promised that they may be inheritors of the kingdom (Matt. 5:3; Mark 10:14; 1 Cor. 6:9), that the kingdom is among them (Luke 10:9), and that they possess the keys to the kingdom (Matt. 16:19). God's people are now "a royal priesthood" (1 Pet. 2:9). The dividing wall of hostility between Jews and Gentiles has been broken down in Christ (Eph. 2:11–22), and the things that once divided God's people do so no longer, for in Christ "there is no longer Jew or Greek, there is no longer slave or free, there is no longer male and female" (Gal. 3:28). One of the functions of the book of Judges in the context of the entire Christian canon is to demonstrate that God's people are not able to live out this calling as undivided kings and priests apart from the work of Christ.

In this second prologue, the narrator does not recount the history of conquest but rather looks forward to the history of Israel's infidelity, with the subsequent spiral into ever greater rebellion against God and ever more desperate abandonment by him. The people will be faithful only as long as there remain any who have *seen* the great works of YHWH. This is like the problem of the disciple Thomas, who also needs to see in order to believe. Jesus responds to Thomas by saying that those who believe without seeing are blessed (John 20:29). Similarly, the people of Israel are being asked now to walk by faith and not by sight (cf. 2 Cor. 5:7). There is still miraculous intervention throughout the book of Judges, but it is not as constant as in the days of Moses—the days of the manna and the quail, the pillar of fire and the pillar of cloud, the tabernacle overshadowed with the Shekinah—when there were daily supernatural evidences of God's intervention. In this way, the book of Judges more closely approximates our own age. What is striking is the almost immediate loss of memory among the people of Israel as soon as the supernatural signs become less frequent. There are other signs—the stones that Joshua had instructed the people to raise at the Jordan, for instance, and altars that Joshua had built at key moments in the recent past—but such memorials are apparently not sufficient.

The prophets Jeremiah and Ezekiel both promise what the New Testament tells us has come to pass: that the law will now be written not on tablets of stone but on the heart. That is, memory of YHWH's mighty deeds (at the exodus, but even more at the resurrection) will no longer be prompted by external helps but will be inscribed on the very person of the believer, so that the law/logos/image of the Son will now be a matter of internal conformity and participative union through the indwelling of the Holy Spirit rather than an externalized ethic. Judges shows us why this is necessary: the external will never be enough.

God's Wrath

God's anger burns hot against the people of Israel when they are unfaithful and disobedient. This does not mean that God is short-tempered or lacking in self-control. First, we must note that God's anger is redemptive. Since idolatry is self-destructive, it is grace for God to punish and discipline Israel, a means of bringing His people back into right relationship with Him. Second, we must note that God is not at the mercy of Israel's behavior for His peace of mind. Scriptural language about God is metaphorical and analogical; we must not make the mistake of interpreting that metaphor as if it were univocal. In our everyday usage, we regularly speak about the sun rising and setting, and there is no problem at all with such language. It is not deceptive, it is not inaccurate, and it is not untrue. However, when we start to do astronomy and talk about the nature of the sun, we need to use different language, language that recognizes that the sun is not moving around the earth (as the metaphor of rising and setting would suggest) but that the earth is orbiting the sun. Similarly, when we come to think *theologically* about God's nature, we may need to use some rather different language than the language we use when speaking in everyday discourse about our *experience* of God. Naturally, we experience God as being sometimes more gracious than at other times, sometimes angry, sometimes distant, sometimes loving and attentive. But none of these ways of speaking is an accurate way of describing God in Himself.

Scripture sometimes describes God as changing, sometimes as unchangeable; sometimes as moving along in time, sometimes as eternal and timeless; sometimes as emotionally responsive to us, sometimes as steadfastly loving. Therefore, all readers of scripture must ask: Which set of texts should be understood literally and which should be understood metaphorically? Since we have no human experience of unchangeability, eternality, timelessness, or steadfast love, such descriptions *cannot* be metaphorical. A metaphor attempts to describe something unknown in terms of the known. But these ways of describing God are not describing Him in terms of things we know. Therefore, it must be that the more anthropomorphic descriptions of God are the metaphorical ones.

As we think about the function of scripture, this makes perfect sense. God is translating Himself into terms that we can understand, culminating in the ultimate translation of Himself into human nature in the incarnation. Scripture itself reminds us that it is a translation by also speaking from time to time in language that is not metaphorical, such as in 1 Sam. 15:29: "The Glory of Israel will not recant or change his mind; for he is not a mortal, that he should change his mind." Abraham Heschel introduced the language of divine *pathos* into popular biblical studies, yet Heschel is clear and explicit in saying that scripture uses such changing and suffering language about God only analogically, arguing, "Pathos must be sharply contrasted with the theme of divine passion. . . . Pathos is a relative state, it always refers to humanity."[2] In other words, the language of wrath is not describing an internal state within God but rather is saying something about the relationship between God and those people described as the objects of His wrath. The New Testament tells us that God is love—not that God is loving, but that God is love itself. We are never told that God is wrath itself, suggesting that this attribute of God describes something other than God's essence. Confessional Christian orthodoxy affirms that God is impassible, that is, not vulnerable to externally caused emotions. This claim is linked to the claims that God is ontologically immutable and that He is eternal—that is, beyond temporality—such that He knows all human time simultaneously. Heschel argues, "As a mode of pathos, it may be accurate to characterize the anger of the Lord as suspended love, as mercy withheld."[3]

People exist not for their own sake but rather to give God glory, which is to say that the goal and end of human life is beyond human life, in God Himself. Apart from God we are incomplete; we are a mass of desire that has failed to reach its proper object. We are tormented by the fact that what we most want and need is not within our own capability to produce, that our own efforts at self-satisfaction are not only worthless but actively counterproductive. That experience of tortured and frustrated desire is the experience that we call "the wrath of God." It is not that God changes His emotional state toward us; it is not that some quality of anger exists in God—for if it did, then it would have to exist eternally and unchangingly, which is nonsensical. God has no lack, no need, no dependence on us. Rather, God is always and forever the abundant overflowing source of all love and blessing and

---

2. Abraham Heschel, *The Prophets* (New York: Perennial, 2001), 410–11.
3. Heschel, *Prophets*, 378.

goodness. As William Law once observed, "As certainly as he is the Creator, so certainly is he the Blesser of every created Thing, and can give *nothing* but Blessing, Goodness, and Happiness from himself because he has *in himself* nothing else to give. It is much more possible for the Sun to give forth Darkness, than for God to do, or be, or give forth anything but Blessing and Goodness."[4] When we say that we are experiencing the wrath of God, that means we are experiencing our own lack of that blessing and goodness because we have separated ourselves from God as the goal and end of our lives. More than that, we are further saying that in such a state of rebellion and disorder, the goodness of God is now experienced by us as searingly painful, as judgment, as wrath. It is not that God is feeling wrathful but rather that we—being improperly oriented toward the fire of His love—cannot experience His presence as blessing but are instead incinerated by it. "For indeed our God is a consuming fire" (Heb. 12:29; cf. Deut. 4:24).

Consider the story of Nadab and Abihu, who came into the presence of God carrying unfit fire, wanting to make an offering to Him on their own terms rather than via the safe path that God had revealed to Moses and Aaron. They were incinerated by God's holiness, not because God was angry with them—the text includes not one word about God's emotional response—but more as if they had stupidly wandered into an electrical fence (Lev. 10:1–3). There is a gate, a door, a way that gives safe access to the blessing and goodness for which we are made, but when we attempt to storm the walls, we find ourselves in pain. This is exactly what the people of Israel are doing throughout the book of Judges, and this is why over and over we encounter the wrath of God burning hot against them.

Again, as in the first prologue, the issue is idolatrous worship: the people choose to worship other gods rather than remaining faithful to the God of Abraham, Isaac, and Jacob. In place of right worship of YHWH, they turn to Baal, Astarte, and Asherah (2:11, 13; 3:7). These pagan religious systems suggest a pantheistic understanding of divine presence, undermining any sense of God's transcendent otherness or sovereignty. Astarte is the goddess of war, most often seen as Baal's consort. Asherah is the consort of El, the mother of all the gods, including Baal. Baal himself is the god of thunder and storm. These are fertility gods, part of a pantheistic pantheon of deities of a type that is common enough throughout the world's cultures. YHWH is absolutely intolerant of any worship of such deities.

This sort of pantheistic understanding of deity puts gods on the same scale of being as humanity and the rest of the natural world. The gods are like us, just bigger

---

4. William Law, *The Spirit of Love* (London: G. Robertson and J. Roberts, 1752), §§1–2.

and more powerful. Like us, they also eat and drink, marry and have children, are faithful or not, get angry and can be appeased, and so on. The pantheistic mind may allow for a division between spirit and body, but that division cuts through all of reality—both divine and nondivine. The claim that YHWH makes is that He is not like this. He is not one being among beings. His ways are not our ways. The great division is not between spirit and body but rather between the Creator God and everything that He has made, which is to say, everything else. We see the same cultural conflict that is here in Judges between Baal worshipers and YHWH worshipers resurfacing in the early church between worshipers of Greco-Roman gods and worshipers of YHWH. Early Christian theologians such as Augustine were constantly drawn to meditate on the stories of creation because the claim that God had created everything out of nothing, that God was not a being among beings but rather the ground of all existence, the one "in whom we live and move and have our being"—that claim required a radical shift in understanding reality. It is on the basis of that claim that we see the emerging awareness of God's nature as fundamentally unlike our own, such that there is no univocal access to God's nature but only analogical access, the greatest analogy being God's own translation of Himself into human nature through the incarnation. Even in the incarnation, however, God cannot be grasped or controlled or manipulated by us. The nature-focused religions of the Canaanites (paradigmatically the worship of Baal and Astarte, but also the worship of other Canaanite gods) are precisely aimed at grasping, controlling, and manipulating divine power. They are aimed at the erosion of any distance between humanity and deity, the denial that God is Other. This is what YHWH will not tolerate.

It is my conviction that this is the primary reason YHWH is never depicted as a female deity. There are instances of female metaphors applied to YHWH; indeed, as already noted, I am convinced that there are women in the book of Judges who are types of Christ. But YHWH is never depicted as a goddess. Every human person has at some time been inside his or her mother, and perhaps that is why religions that acknowledge a goddess instead of or in addition to a god tend more strongly to pantheism than those religions that do not. Of course, God is neither male nor female, and all of our gendered language for God is also metaphorical and analogical.[5] Women as well as men are made in God's image and are capable of reflecting his nature. But some metaphors are more dangerous than others.

5. My habit of capitalizing male pronouns referring to God is an effort to underscore the analogical nature of such language, that these pronouns are not being used in the same way that they would be used when referring to a male human being.

There is archaeological evidence that Israelites sometimes imported the idea of Asherah as Baal's consort into their own worship, suggesting that Asherah was YHWH's consort instead. In addition to all the problems with this idea that are spelled out above, it also undermines Israel's awareness of her own identity as the bride of YHWH.[6] YHWH has no consort or partner existing on the same plane as Himself, but has only the consort He has chosen and raised up into a relationship with Himself.

The paradigm established here in Judg. 2:11–19 is what Sternberg calls "foreshadowing by paradigm" (1985: 269). The paradigm set out here will be followed, with interesting and significant variations, throughout the book. First, the people do what is evil in the eyes of YHWH; that is, they are idolatrous. Then the anger of YHWH "burns hot" against them, so that He "sells" them to their enemies to be oppressed. After some time of this discipline, they cry out for help to YHWH, and in response He raises up a judge to save them. They're delivered, but after a time of rest they stop listening to their judge and go back to their idolatrous ways. This paradigm helps to structure the book and gives us as readers a tool for understanding what is happening. But it is not a straitjacket. According to the value system built into the paradigm itself, the moral choices that the people of Israel make will influence the fortune of their nation. When they are repentant, redemption is just as natural a consequence as subjugation is when they are idolatrous.

One might think that such a clear paradigm would remove all suspense from the story, but Sternberg insists that it does not: "The variations prove no less integral to structure and effect than the uniformities. Indeed, their enrichment motivates the book's repeated and otherwise disproportionate lingering over the terminal link in the chain. The three antecedents may enjoy moralistic superiority; but it is in the Deliverance that the stuff of drama lies, that the figure of each judge waits to be explored, that the plot brings God and Israel into concerted action, that the theme may freely move between the actors and the cycle between historical generality and specificity" (1985: 271). Sternberg points out that the paradigm means we always know how the story will end, but we do not know how we will get to that end, and the variations between the narratives within the book of Judges allow room for "opacity and suspense" (1985: 271). The paradigm further allows the narrator to surprise us, for we are led to expect uniformity, and when that collapses, we notice.

6. J. A. Emerton, "'Yahweh and His Asherah': The Goddess or Her Symbol?," *VT* 4 (1999): 33; John Day, *Yahweh and the Gods and Goddesses of Canaan*, JSOTSup 265 (Sheffield: Sheffield Academic, 2000), 47, both cited in Matthews (2004: 80).

Divine Agency

YHWH's response to Israel's idolatry is to assert His sovereignty with a vengeance. "The anger of the LORD was kindled against Israel, and he gave them over to plunderers who plundered them, and he sold them into the power of their enemies all around, so that they could no longer withstand their enemies" (2:14). Significantly, as we have already considered in connection with the first prologue, YHWH Himself takes responsibility for the Israelites' troubles. He does not merely withdraw passively; He actively turns them over to their enemies. Throughout the book, we will see this same claim of agency whenever the people of Israel are suffering.

Charles Scobie suggests that God's agency is seen through "divine intervention" (when God acts directly to save, as in the miracles of the exodus) and "divinely inspired leadership" (as in the judges), but also in the use of "nation-states as his agents" both of judgment against Israel and of deliverance of Israel. "Although God uses world powers, he does so without their being aware of it; in Isa 45:5 God says of Cyrus, 'I arm you, though you do not know me.' In Isa 10:5 God refers to Assyria as 'the rod of my anger.' God can call King Nebuchadrezzar of Babylon 'my servant' (Jer 25:9)."[7] Certainly, throughout the book of Judges, YHWH claims to be using Israel's oppressors in this way. The Midianites and the Philistines may think that they are serving their own ends in attacking Israel, and they may consider that their success in oppressing Israel is evidence that their gods are stronger than the God of Israel. YHWH is not concerned with their misapprehensions on this point, so long as the people of Israel understand that their suffering is a result of His judgment.

Contemporary Christian theology typically avoids attributing responsibility for our suffering to God, claiming instead that God is sharing our pain. That is certainly not the theology of the book of Judges. God is quite willing to inflict pain on His own loved people, both to discipline and to correct them. Notice, however, that the goal of turning them over to their enemies is redemptive. At the time that they are handed over to foreign oppression, they are apostate, in rebellion against the covenant, living out of alignment with the law/logos of God. When they are oppressed but crying out to YHWH for deliverance, they are already in a better state morally and eternally than when they were prosperous but worshiping the Baals.

7. Charles H. H. Scobie, *The Ways of Our God: An Approach to Biblical Theology* (Grand Rapids: Eerdmans, 2003), 199.

In addition to the discipline of oppression, YHWH also uses the discipline of warfare. Throughout the history of humanity, warfare has been understood as having an ambiguous character. On the one hand, it is a terrible disaster. On the other hand, it is an arena within which people—typically men, less often women—may cultivate virtues such as honor and courage. Many contemporary Christians are uncomfortable with the idea that war can be glorified in this way. I well remember memorizing a poem when I was a young girl, a poem that I thought was very stirring and exciting: "The Charge of the Light Brigade" by Alfred Lord Tennyson. When I recited it to some members of my family, one of my uncles lectured me about what a bad poem it was since it was glorifying a horrific military debacle. Although I now see my uncle's point, I also see that his attitude reflects a cynicism about war that is typical of post-Vietnam thinking among American Christians but not of most people throughout history. Even if we want to defend that cynicism, we must recognize that it is eccentric in the history of the world, which is to say, it is off-center. Most people throughout the world and throughout history have believed that being able to show courage in the face of a hopeless military situation is both honorable and glorious. Those of us who react cynically to such a claim must deal with the reality that YHWH sees warfare—not just spiritual warfare but real, gritty, violent warfare— as potentially valuable training for His people. One of the themes of the book of Judges is courage—both the need for courage in order to be YHWH's faithful people and the absence of courage that is being displayed by YHWH's people during this period. Warfare is a way of training in courage. In a book about the life of George Washington, Joseph Ellis observes that "standing calmly at attention while the man abreast of you is disemboweled by a cannon ball is an acquired skill and not a natural act."[8] YHWH wants His people to display more than just physical courage, but the physical courage taught by war is preparation for the moral courage required to resist the temptations of idolatry and disobedience.

8. Joseph J. Ellis, *His Excellency: George Washington* (New York: Vintage, 2005), 117.

4

OTHNIEL

1:12–16; 3:7–11

Structure

The central body of the book begins with the brief but important story of Othniel, the first and paradigmatic judge. This story completes the Othniel narrative begun in chapter 1, where we read of his conquest of the city of Kiriath-sepher (the "City of the Book") and his subsequent marriage to Caleb's daughter Achsah. The division of his story into two sections serves several purposes. One advantage of this decision is that the Achsah story can be placed in parallel with the second epilogue, which includes the story of the Levite's concubine. Another advantage is that the portion of the story found in chapter 3 can be pared down to the bare bones, making obvious just how clearly it follows the paradigm established in chapter 2. The steps of the paradigm are these:

- Israel does what is evil in the sight of YHWH.
- Therefore, the anger of YHWH is kindled.
- Therefore, He sells (or, later, gives) them into the hand of some oppressor.
- They suffer for a specified amount of time, in this case eight years.
- The suffering people cry out to YHWH for deliverance.
- YHWH hears their cry and raises up a deliverer.

In this story, the evil that the Israelites have done is specified: they have forgotten the Lord their God and have worshiped the Baals and Asherahs (3:7). In the various iterations of the paradigm through the book, the sin is not always specified. YHWH always claims responsibility for the subsequent suffering that comes to His people.

Othniel is from the tribe of Judah. So just as the first prologue opened with Judah's work in the taking of the land, now the sequence of Judges opens with a judge from the tribe of Judah. The major judges will follow the order of the prologue in that Othniel is from Judah, Ehud from Benjamin, Deborah from Ephraim, Gideon from Manasseh, Jephthah from Gilead, and Samson from Dan. Othniel's status as the paradigmatic judge thus serves as a foil against which Judah's subsequent decline will be measured. In Deut. 33:7, Moses gives a blessing to Judah as the kingly tribe, a blessing that is not contingent on Judah's faithfulness but on God's faithfulness. Therefore, despite Judah's failures in this premonarchic time, the Davidic line still comes from Judah, and—far more importantly—so does Jesus.

As noted in chapter 1, Judges can be understood in terms of three overlapping structures: a through structure, a parallel structure, and a chiastic structure. First, in terms of the through structure, Othniel is the pattern and standard against which the story of each subsequent judge must be understood. Just as chapter 1 began with Judah, so now this central section of the book in which individual judges are described begins with the paradigmatic Judahite judge, who, interestingly enough, is Judahite by adoption, not biology. A. G. Auld observes that this story "has formal connections with almost every other story in the book."[1] For the first half of this progression (Othniel, Ehud, Deborah, and the first part of Gideon's story), the judges themselves are not caught up in degeneration but are responding to it. They themselves are faithful representatives of what Israel should be, but the apostasy of the people and the consequent oppression grow in intensity. The suffering experienced by Israel is meant to be redemptive, driving the people to a place of brokenness from which they cry for help, but as we move through the book, it will require longer and longer periods of oppression to produce this reaction. Before Othniel, the people of Israel suffered for eight years; before Ehud, it will be for eighteen, and before Deborah, it will be for twenty.

Second, there are two series of three judges each that are set parallel to each other. In terms of this structure, Othniel is especially set in parallel with Gideon, who initiates the second series. Gideon is greeted as a "mighty warrior" at the

---

1. A. G. Auld, "Gideon: Hacking at the Heart of the Old Testament," *VT* 39, fasc. 3 (July 1989): 259.

beginning of his story, a puzzling designation since at the time Gideon is manifesting only cynical cowardice. In contrast, Othniel really is a mighty warrior, arguably the strongest military leader in the book. His military sorties in chapters 1 and 3 are decisively victorious, empowered by confidence in YHWH and by obedience to the command to take the land. Since the weaker judge is best understood in terms of the stronger, these parallels will be investigated more deeply when looking at the Gideon story.

Third, in terms of the chiastic structure, Othniel is especially set in contrast to Samson, the last and most disappointing judge in the book. Othniel is an outsider, a Kenite, who becomes part of the people of Israel because of his decision to recognize YHWH as the true God and his willingness to be obedient to YHWH's commandments. His obedience wins him a faithful and God-fearing wife. He earns her hand by obedience in taking the land. The result of their marriage is that they are established together in a well-watered portion of the land. His name means "lion of God." He exhibits physical courage and the prowess of a warrior, traits that he puts in service of the safety of Israel, the taking of the land, and the protection and flourishing of his wife. Although in Othniel's day the people of Israel were sinning against YHWH by marrying with the people of the land, Othniel is a strong moral leader, modeling a marriage within the covenant community that honors the commands of YHWH. When Othniel is raised up against Israel's oppressor Cushan-rishathaim, his victory brings rest to the land.

Samson is an insider, a Danite, who is constantly drawn to the world of the Philistines. He is chosen by YHWH from birth but treats that choosing with disdain until the very end of his life. He is a would-be husband of an unworthy wife. He does not earn her hand but instructs his parents to acquire her for him. Unlike Othniel, Samson never claims any portion of the land, nor does he ever live at rest with his wife. The end result of his marriage is that his wife and her family are burned to death and Samson himself is left parched. In all, he chooses three different women in the stories that we have of him, and each choice is a choice of disobedience. Each choice leads to conflict for him, and finally Delilah leads him to be captured by the Philistines. He begins his pursuit of a Philistine bride by killing a lion and eating honey that is made within its corpse. He exhibits physical courage and the prowess of a warrior but uses these capabilities for personal vengeance, not for the deliverance of Israel. Samson has no standing as a moral leader and does nothing to help the people of Israel resist their fall into sin. Samson brings no rest to the land. His judgeship gives way to the time when everyone in Israel does what is right in his or her own eyes because the kingship of YHWH is no longer recognized.

The foil of Samson shows us more clearly how admirable Othniel truly is. So why does this initial story of a good judge receive so much less attention than the story of Samson, a bad judge? Othniel's story is told in ten verses, whereas Samson receives four chapters. In contemporary fiction, it is often the case that evil characters are more interesting and even more compelling than virtuous characters, that virtue is difficult to portray in a winsome and attractive way. But I do not believe that this can be the explanation for the focus on Samson over Othniel. God is not simply indulging our voyeuristic preference for stories about wrongdoing. Rather, the story of Samson receives more attention because it is our own story; it is the story of rebellion and failure. That is who we are.

In addition, as mentioned above, the compression of Othniel's story makes it easier for him to function as a model. Tammi Schneider points out that if the narrator had included more personal details about Othniel, the structure of the model would be less clear. The description of his tenure in office reveals the bare essentials of the office. This is the perfect situation for a model. Too many particulars would confuse the essential elements. The downward spiral of Israel is reflected in her later judges, who erred in the elaboration and details of the model set by Othniel (Schneider 2000: 40).

There is an additional reason for the brief nature of Othniel's story. Othniel is the paradigmatic judge within this book, but within the Deuteronomistic History it is Joshua who is the paradigm. Joshua is never called a judge, but his name includes the root from which both the word "judge" and the word "deliverer" are formed, the two words most commonly used to describes the judges. Joshua is the one who leads the people of Israel into the promised land and initiates the campaign against the Canaanites. Joshua never seeks kingship, and yet he is a prophetic teacher to his people, a leader in times of battle, and a magistrate who rules on the proper implementation of the law given to Moses. The first statement in the book of Judges is that Joshua has died, and the entire book may be seen as a fruitless search for his successor. The story of the good judge Othniel does not need lengthy development; we already have a developed story of the paradigmatic judge in the book of Joshua. On the other side of the book of Judges, we have the story of the last judge of Israel, who is also a great and good judge: Samuel. Othniel is a placeholder for these extensive stories.

Although Othniel is the best of the judges within this book, his story already reflects a falling off from the level of leadership that had been offered by Joshua.

Although Othniel is described in only positive terms, there is no mention of his relationship to the law. As a personally virtuous man, he may well have understood himself as guided by the law of YHWH, but there is nothing to indicate that he was a public teacher of that law. When Joshua took the mantle of leadership from Moses and led the people into the promised land, he set up standing stones at Gilgal as witnesses to the Lord's care for them (Josh. 4:1–9), he led the men of Israel in a service of circumcision (Josh. 5:2–9), and he celebrated the Passover in the new land (Josh. 5:10–12). Once Israel had conquered Jericho and Ai, Joshua gathered the people for a covenant renewal in which they again pledged fidelity to YHWH and during which Joshua read them the law (Josh. 8:31–35). Near the end of his life he called all the people of Israel together for another time of covenant renewal at Shechem, during which he rehearsed the history of God's care for His people (Josh. 24). None of the judges, not even Othniel, make any similar gesture to indicate the centrality of the teaching of YHWH to their work. Othniel is not mentioned in connection with the covenant renewal at Bochim, where we might have expected him to be a leader. Silence on this topic could mean that such a ritual is assumed, but given the pattern of disintegration in Judges and the complete disregard for the law that is to follow, such an interpretation is not justified. Rather, the silence on this topic appears to be another genuine gap—a significant omission that is meant to be noticed.

Achsah and Othniel

Judges 1 includes the story of Caleb, who promised to give his daughter Achsah as wife to whichever soldier took the town of Kiriath-sepher. Othniel responded to the challenge by winning the town, and Achsah was given to him as his wife. Caleb gave Achsah some land as her dowry, but the land did not have sufficient water on it. So Achsah asked Caleb for water, and he granted her two additional pieces of land, each having springs of water. This seems an odd story to find in the midst of an account of battles, especially since the story was already told to us in the book of Joshua.

As the book unfolds, however, the treatment of women is central to several stories, and the proportion of the book given over to stories about women is higher than is typical in other biblical books, suggesting that this is something we are supposed to notice. In the introduction, we considered that there is a theme in Judges of undoing the double curse on Adam and Eve after the fall, such that the stories focus both on restoring right relationship with the land and on restoring right relationships between men and women. One of the clear patterns is that, as the book unfolds, women are treated less and less well, showing Israel's failure at reversing the curse on Eve. Putting the happy story of Achsah in the first prologue encourages the reader to compare the subsequent treatment of women to how she is treated. Her story becomes a benchmark for right behavior in a godly society. Since the fall of Adam and Eve, human beings are naturally prone to relationships of domination and manipulation, violence and subjugation, between men and women. When YHWH's people keep His law, these effects of the fall are controlled to some extent (though they will not be undone until Jesus forms His body in the New Testament). One sign that the law is being lived out is that fathers and husbands cooperate for the flourishing and safety of their daughters and wives. Achsah provides a striking foil for many of the other women in this book, especially Jephthah's daughter, whose father also made a vow about her, and the Levite's unnamed concubine, who also rode a donkey on a journey between her husband and her father. These are not accidental parallels. YHWH is telling His people that a symptom of holy communal living is that women flourish and a symptom of rebellious communal living is that women suffer. In his poem "Manifesto: The Mad Farmer Liberation Front," Wendell Berry gives this advice:

> So long as women do not go cheap
> for power, please women more than men.
> Ask yourself: Will this satisfy
> a woman satisfied to bear a child?
> Will this disturb the sleep
> of a woman near to giving birth?[2]

Judges suggests a similar test. When evaluating the ethics of a decision, ask yourself: Will this lead to the flourishing of women and their children?

Much has been made by some commentators of Achsah's fearlessness in approaching her father and asking him for water. But surely it should not be unusual that a daughter dare to approach her father with such a request? Water is necessary for life. She is not requesting something frivolous. Jesus tells us that even sinners know how to give good gifts to their children (Matt. 7:9–11), and one would think that in a normal world even sinners would keep their children safe and alive. So Achsah's story is not unusual, though what follows is unusual. Achsah's

2. Wendell Berry, *The Mad Farmer Poems* (New York: Counterpoint, 2008), 13.

relationship with Caleb and with Othniel reflects the order of creation. What follows with Jephthah, Samson, and the cowardly Levite is the order of the fall.

James Jordan suggests that in the story of Achsah, Othniel should be seen as a type of Christ in that the father sends the son to conquer the enemy in order to win the bride.[3] However, Caleb is not Othniel's father; he is Achsah's father. As already explicated in the introduction, if there is a typology, it would seem more obvious for it to go in the other direction. The judges function as representatives of Israel, not of YHWH, and their stories generally recapitulate the state of Israel at the time of their judgeship. Othniel is an image of Israel as YHWH intends Israel to be, obediently and courageously taking the land. When the people of Israel do this, the reward is a loving and faithful helpmeet who unites them to their Father in heaven and who brings blessing to the marriage—specifically, the blessing of water, which is tied to fertility. This is what the Israelites seek from the Canaanite gods but do not find. Jordan is certainly right that this imagery is easier from a christological and trinitarian perspective: the Father gives his only-begotten in marriage to the one who is faithful, or (as Jesus says in the book of Revelation) to the one who *overcomes*. Othniel is an overcomer, a warrior whose faith leads to victory. It is Achsah who is a type of Christ, set at the beginning of the book in contrast to the unnamed concubine, another type of Christ, who dies on behalf of the faithless spouse by book's end.

Daniel Block notes, "Ironically, none of the characters in this note is a native Israelite. They are Kenite proselytes, who have been so thoroughly integrated into the faith and culture of the nation that Caleb could represent the tribe of Judah in reconnaissance missions, and all model the life of Yahwistic faith in the face of the Canaanite enemy" (1999: 97). Block sees this as ironic because he also understands the interrelations of these three people to stand as a paradigm of what Israelite community should be and so to be a foil against which the later treatment of women is exposed as particularly disordered, a symptom of "the progressive Canaanization of Israelite society in the course of the book" (97). The end of 1:16 is ambiguous in that it says the Kenites settled with "the people," not specifying which people. In 4:11 we are told that "Heber the Kenite had separated from the other Kenites," which results in his living far away from the people of Israel, apparently close to the lands occupied by Jabin. This suggests that the Kenites other than Heber were still living as allies of Israel.

3. Jordan 1999: 8. Othniel is also described as a savior or deliverer who will save (*yasha*) Israel (3:9). This language is used for many of the judges, which is another reason why it has been so common for Christians to read these stories typologically.

Cushan-rishathaim

When Othniel is introduced as a judge, he is again an overcomer, conquering Cushan the Doubly Wicked (3:7–11; rishathaim means "doubly wicked"). Just as Othniel is paradigmatic in the effort to roll back the curse on Eve, so too he is paradigmatic in the effort to roll back the curse on Adam, restoring a right relationship with the land. The Doubly Wicked one has taken possession of the land set apart for YHWH's people because they have *forgotten* YHWH. This has happened before. In Deut. 32, Moses reflects on their time in the wilderness, saying, "You were unmindful of the Rock that bore you; you forgot the God who gave you birth" (32:18). The theme of forgetfulness will continue throughout Judges: the people of Israel fail to remember again after Gideon (8:34), Abimelech tells his family in Shechem to remember that he is their bone and flesh (9:2), and Samson asks God to remember him (16:28). To remember is to call to mind, which requires being consciously alert. This is a mark of love. We do not forget those we love. Indeed, they are always in our mind; as we go about our day, we think, "I will have to tell him that," or "Perhaps she would enjoy this." Real love is the appreciation of the other's independence, an enjoyment precisely of the fact that the other does not exist merely to meet my needs. We must especially learn to love God in this way, to hold Him before our minds in love, glorifying and enjoying Him. This is what it is to remember. But Israel forgets.

It may be startling that YHWH used Cushan the Doubly Wicked. Of course, God uses many people, including those who do not know Him. But this king is presented as the embodiment of evil. Shouldn't the holy God keep His hands clean by not using such tools? Augustine and Aquinas both claim that God's ability to use evil and turn it to good is a greater sign of His unchanging goodness than would be His aloofness from evil.[4] Though this is not always experientially or existentially convincing, texts like these tell us that it must be true. God did not make Cushan doubly wicked, but given Cushan's rebellion into wickedness, God makes use of that wickedness for His own purposes, including the disciplining of His beloved covenant people.

It is easier to understand how YHWH can make use of an evil person without being contaminated when we remember the long-standing Christian teaching that evil is not an independent force in the world generating new things that stand

4. Thomas Aquinas, *Summa Theologiae* Ia, Q. 2, Art. 3, ad. 1, in *Summa Theologica: Complete English Edition in Five Volumes*, trans. Fathers of the English Dominican Province (Notre Dame, IN: Ave Maria Press, 1981), 14, citing Augustine, *Enchiridion* 11.

in contrast with goodness. Evil has neither independence nor generative power. Evil can only destroy and take away, existing as a parasite on goodness. YHWH is fully actual; everything that He can be He is maximally at all times. There is no becoming within YHWH, and so there can be no lessening, no falling away, no lack. YHWH is not vulnerable to evil as we are. So whereas we need to be careful when interacting with evil powers and evil people, since there is a very real possibility that we will be influenced by them, YHWH has no such need for care. Just as He called the world into existence out of nothingness, so He can call good out of evil. This has nothing to do with evil progressing into good and everything to do with the fruitfulness of YHWH's own goodness, a fruitfulness that is supremely generative, filling in the holes that evil makes.

The Gift of the Spirit

Othniel is described as receiving the Spirit of God, a description that recurs in most of the other judges' stories (3:10; 6:34; 11:29; 13:25; 14:6, 19; 15:14). Since many of these instances precede behavior that is clearly and explicitly disobedient to YHWH, we may not interpret the descent of the Spirit as proof of full and complete sharing in YHWH's mission. The observation that the Spirit of YHWH has come on a person generally precedes an act of exceptional valor or physical strength, suggesting that God is the ultimate agent in such moments.

In his book *Images of the Spirit*, Meredith Kline links the presence of the Spirit in the book of Judges to the presence of God "as the Spirit of the day" in Gen. 3:8, a reference already alluded to in chapter 1. In a lengthy and carefully developed argument, Kline examines places in scripture in which God's presence makes a direct appearance, seeing Gen. 3:8 as the "primal parousia." The King James Version translates this verse as "They heard the voice of the LORD God walking in the garden in the cool of the day," as if the reference to the spirit/*ruah* here means evening breezes. Kline argues that this verse is not really about God's desire for a refreshing walk after a long day of work but instead describes "the advent of the Lord in his awesomely fearful judicial Glory" (1999: 97). He suggests that the appropriate translation is "They heard the sound of Yahweh God traversing the garden as the Spirit of the day," which is to say, the Spirit of the day of judgment (106).

In keeping with this identification of *ruah* as the Spirit in the judgment context of Gen. 3:8, we find that the divine Spirit is closely linked with the function of divine judgment elsewhere in scripture too. Of primary importance is the fact that "Spirit" appears as the designation of the Glory-chariot, the Presence of God in sovereign power, specifically the power of ruling and judging. Sometimes the human beings on whom the Spirit comes serve as the chariots or vehicles for this presence of judgment. In such cases, the Spirit empowers human beings to do the work of implementing God's judgment (Kline 1999: 104).

Kline then points to the instance of the Spirit coming on Othniel as an example of the same sort of presence, in which Othniel "became the agent of God's judicial action in behalf of Israel, going to war and delivering them from the oppression of Cushan-rishathaim" (1999: 104). It is quite possible for God to use a human being as an agent of His judgment without endorsing everything that person does. Indeed, it is quite possible for God to use a human agent who is outside the covenant community altogether. In Num. 24:2, the Spirit of YHWH comes upon Balaam, for example. In the book of Judges, YHWH Himself is King, and the judges do not function as governors or lesser kings but rather as agents directly under his royal control. The time of the Judges is under the suzerain covenant of Sinai in which there may be no other king and in which each member of the people of Israel stands in a direct relationship of covenant and vassalage to YHWH Himself. YHWH's appropriation of the judges as instruments of His judgment is an instance in which they function within this covenant relationship.

5

EHUD

3:12–30

Structure

In terms of the overall movement of degeneration across the entire sweep of the book, Ehud's story reflects a step away from the ideal of Othniel. The time of the people's rebellion has been longer and the discipline of oppression to which they are submitted is more severe than in the previous story. Ehud himself is presented as a faithful representative, though some argue that the trickster pattern of his victory is less honorable than Othniel's military victory, a judgment that is not self-evident. What seems more obvious is that Ehud cannot depend on other Israelites joining him to fight against Moab until he has first assassinated Eglon, showing that their courage and the will to resist conquest has decreased since Othniel led them into battle against Cushan.

In terms of both the chiastic structure and the parallels between the judges, Ehud is set in contrast to Jephthah. Like Jephthah, Ehud begins his defense of Israel with an act of diplomacy. For Ehud this appears to be a ruse, whereas for Jephthah it appears to be a sincere effort to avoid conflict. Ehud is therefore more obedient to YHWH, understanding that there is to be no appeasement for YHWH's enemies who live in the land. Ehud successfully recruits the tribe of Ephraim to join in his battles, maintaining the unity of Israel. Jephthah ends up at war with Ephraim, and a large part of his story consists of the details of this civil conflict. More importantly, both Ehud and Jephthah offer a human sacrifice to YHWH. Ehud sacrifices Eglon, "the little calf," in a way that is obedient; Jephthah sacrifices his daughter in a way that is disobedient.

Gregory Mobley has illustrated the tightly structured nature of the inner section of the Ehud narrative, so that the structure of the story mimics the geography of the story, leading us into an inner chamber at the center (2005: 78–91). Although Mobley does not diagram his conclusions, this is my diagrammatic summary of his article:

A   Eglon and the Moabites go across the Jordan and <u>smite</u> the Israelites (3:13).
  B   Ehud goes to Eglon with tribute <u>in his hand</u> (3:15b).
    C   Ehud turns back at the <u>stone idols</u> (3:19).
      D   Eglon's guards exit from his presence (3:19b).
        E   Ehud enters Eglon's presence (3:20a).
          F   Ehud extended his left arm and drew the blade from his right thigh and struck a blow into Eglon's belly (3:21).
          F′   The hilt entered after the blade and the fat closed behind the blade because Ehud did not pull the sword out of Eglon's belly (3:22).
        E′   Ehud exited Eglon's presence (3:23–24).
      D′   Eglon's servants enter Eglon's (dead) presence (3:24).
    C′   Ehud goes past the <u>stone idols</u> (3:26).
  B′   YHWH has given them <u>into your hand</u> (3:28).
A′   The Israelites capture the Jordan and will not let the Moabites cross back; they <u>smite</u> the Moabites instead (3:28–29).

The structure underscores the great reversal that occurs in the course of the story. In the first half, the Moabites are in power, Ehud arrives with tribute in his hands, and Eglon is very much alive. In the second half, Eglon is dead, Ehud has the Moabites in his hands, and the Moabite army is defeated. The key moment around which the story turns is the execution—or, perhaps better, the sacrifice—of Eglon. This act of courage and obedience on Ehud's part turns the story upside down. Dorsey points out that at this center moment Ehud is delivering a "message from God," which turns out to be judgment and death (1999: 109).

Mobley also shows how Ehud is described in a set of three stair-step descriptors:

3:15 Ehud: son of Ger
son of the Right-hand [region]
a man impeded in his right hand (Mobley 2005: 89)[1]

These three descriptors are parallel to another set of stair-step descriptors describing the army of Moab:

3:29 **to a man** stout
and **every man,** a battler
but escaped no **man** (Mobley 2005: 89)

In each case, the third line is a surprise. Ehud's designation as the son of Ger, the Right-hand, does not prepare us to hear that he was impeded in his right hand. The Moabites' designation as stout battlers does not prepare us to hear that not one of them escaped. Ehud is introduced as surprisingly weak, whereas the Moabites leave the story as surprisingly defeated and surprisingly dead. In the event, Ehud is not weak but a great warrior; he really is just "differently abled." As a left-handed man, his strength comes from an unexpected direction and so catches Eglon by surprise. First Chronicles 7:10–11 lists Ehud as one of the mighty warriors of the house of Benjamin. Even in the midst of the battle against Benjamin in Judg. 20, the narrator acknowledges the military prowess of a special force of "seven hundred picked men who were left-handed; every one could sling a stone at a hair, and not miss" (20:16). It seems likely that Ehud was a member of this elite band. It is not a surprise that his people select him to guard and deliver the tribute that they are offering to Eglon, nor that his story reads rather like a special forces operation.

Sternberg observes, "Each of the three participants introduced, two human and one inanimate, is deviant in some respect. Ehud is left-handed, the sword is short and double-edged, Eglon is very fat" (1985: 331). As it will turn out, each of these oddities contributes to the providential unfolding of the story. Initially, however, the reader's impression is of oddness. "The undersized sword thus contrasts with the oversized king, while its 'two mouths' (the Hebrew for 'two edges') slyly brings to mind the source of his corpulence: to get so fat would require more than a single mouth. Nor is the hero himself excluded from the punning composition"

---

1. Mobley also includes the Hebrew, which I have omitted, though in each case there are recurring Hebrew words that reinforce the three steps as a literary unit.

(332). Since Benjamin means "son of the right hand," there is a good deal of wordplay in identifying Ehud as a Benjaminite who is weak in the right hand. Sternberg continues, "And to cap it all, it is 'by his hand' that the Israelites send their tribute to Eglon—a left-handed tribute indeed" (332). As a result of all this description, the Ehud story is especially memorable. We are given distinctive and memorable identifiers for Ehud, his sword, and Eglon. It is also significant that they are presented in that order, the order of a sentence: Ehud is the subject, the sword the verb, and Eglon the object of that verb.

Even though we can see what's going to happen—that Eglon is going to be conquered by YHWH's appointed savior—the story is not at all boring or predictable in the way it unfolds. As Sternberg says, "There remain impenetrable enigmas, opacities, ambiguities" (1985: 334). This results in what Sternberg calls a "double gain": on the one hand, the uncertainty of events makes it seem highly unlikely that good can triumph, thereby underscoring God's activity behind the scenes of the story, for His "leading role shine[s] through the drama of indeterminacy"; on the other hand, Ehud is presented as a competent deliverer, chosen by God but also equipped with some impressive skills, so that the story also makes sense on a human level (334). The description of the action that follows underlines this, for all the characteristics mentioned in the introduction to the story (Ehud's left-handedness, the sword's shortness, Eglon's fatness) contribute to the unfolding of Ehud's victory.

In the story's conclusion, Ehud and Eglon are seen as synecdoches of their respective peoples. "The battle . . . reenacts the private scene on a national scale. It opens with Ehud's cry to his troops that God has delivered the enemy 'into your hands,' ends with the notice that Moab was subdued that day 'under the hand of Israel,' and consists in the destruction of the whole Moabite army, ten thousand 'stout' men (with the same ambiguity between 'fat' and 'strong' as in English)" (Sternberg 1985: 337). The biblical pattern is to give relevant descriptive information *before* the relevance is obvious, rather than after, so that we are set up to see the inevitability of outcomes rather than given causal explanations after the fact (Sternberg 1985: 338). Such descriptions are connected to action, not to internal character. It is the action that then reveals character. Sternberg contrasts this way of describing reality with Anthony Trollope's "poetics of lucidity, with its exhaustive portraits and static portraitees, [which] launches a one-way movement from character to the action that both follows and follows from it in dramatic shape." In his famous novel *Barchester Towers*, Trollope draws such vivid portraits of all the key players—the gentle Mr. Harding, the conniving Mr. Slope, and the cosmopolitan archdeacon Dr. Grantly—that their decisions and conflicts flow naturally from their characters. In contrast, biblical poetics may be understood as "the poetics of ambiguity," in which the movement of understanding moves forward and backward, so that character is understood retroactively on the basis of action (Sternberg 1985: 344). We discover Ehud's character by watching what he does.

Just War?

Contemporary readers of this story are sometimes offended by what they see as Ehud's treacherous behavior in assassinating King Eglon. It is certainly true that in our world when two states are at war with one another, assassination is against international law and is defined as a war crime. But those who would apply such a standard to ancient Israel appear to be under the impression that this rule about assassination is a natural law that should be known to all people everywhere, whereas in fact making laws about warfare is by no means natural. Nor is it self-evident that sending two armies of citizens who have been drafted into war into a battle in which hundreds or thousands will die on each side is somehow more moral than preemptively executing the people who are giving the command for such a battle. Moral discussion of these issues throughout history has not always reached the same conclusions. In his essay "The Tenure of Kings and Magistrates," John Milton points to the example of Ehud to justify the execution of Charles I. He argues that being a legitimate ruler does not put one beyond the threat of punishment but rather raises the responsibility that a king has to act justly. In Milton's eyes, both Charles and Eglon fail to do this, thereby justifying the decision to execute them.[2] John Calvin expressed more discomfort with the idea of private resistance. "Calvin was quite traditional in denying private persons any right to take up arms against an oppressive ruler, but he exhorted them to repent over their own sins and to pray for deliverance. Calvin was less traditional, however, in allowing a qualified right on the part of the lesser magistrates to resist a tyrant when constitutional laws so provided."[3] Calvin bases the idea that resistance is justified for those who hold some sort of office especially on the example of Abraham, who went to war

2. John Milton, "The Tenure of Kings and Magistrates," in *The Student's Milton*, rev. ed., ed. Frank Allen Patterson (New York: F. S. Crofts, 1946), 760–61. Milton also evokes the example of Samuel's execution of Agag, which Samuel justifies because Agag has "made women childless" by his sword.

3. John L. Thompson, "Patriarchs, Polygamy, and Private Resistance," *Sixteenth Century Journal* 25, no. 1 (1994): 15.

to rescue Lot. The argument is both that Abraham received authorization from the Holy Spirit to do this thing and that Abraham was not acting as a private citizen: because God had already promised him the land of Canaan, Abraham had standing to act against tyranny when he experienced it there. Calvin explicitly draws a parallel between this example of Abraham and the rule of the judges.[4]

Even under contemporary international law, there are times when assassination may be considered legal—when a great crime has been committed and there is no way to bring a perpetrator to trial, for instance. It is under such reasoning that the assassination of Osama bin Laden has been defended as a legal action. Even more clearly, assassination may be legal in situations of insurgency, where a people have been conquered and are attempting to regain their liberty. Many war tactics that would be inappropriate between two sovereign nations are considered justifiable in a case where power and resources are out of balance in this way.[5]

In the Ehud story, this is the situation. Under Eglon, the Moabites have conquered the Israelites and oppressed them for eighteen years. The people of Israel are now required to send tribute to Eglon as a sign of their ongoing capitulation. They commission Ehud to take their tribute, apparently intending that he would use his fighting skills to guard the treasure on the journey. There is no indication that any of the Israelites expected Ehud to reject his role as a diplomatic courier enacting their submission. But in refusing to surrender, Ehud is obeying the commands laid on the Israelites by YHWH when they first entered the land. Ehud's story thus forms an interesting contrast to that of Othniel. Whereas Othniel led an army from the tribe of Judah into open battle against his enemies, Ehud of necessity operates as a spy and an assassin, for his people have lost the courage to resist conquest.

Even so, once Eglon has been assassinated, Ehud has no trouble rallying an army. His people may have been too discouraged to resist the Moabite conquest initially, but once they have been given some reason to hope for a victory, their distaste for their conquerors motivates their resistance. Mobley observes on this subject:

> The degrading rhetoric and use of sacrificial terms [in the Ehud story] may reflect Israelite revulsion toward the practice of paying tribute to foreign powers. . . . Tribute

4. Thompson, "Patriarchs," 18.
5. Michael L. Gross, *The Ethics of Insurgency: A Critical Guide to Just Guerrilla Warfare* (Cambridge: Cambridge University Press, 2015); Louis René Bees, "After Osama Bin Laden: Assassination, Terrorism, War, and International Law," *Case Western Reserve Journal of International Law* 44, no. 1 (2011), http:// scholarlycommons.law.case.edu/jil/vol44/iss1/8; Whitley Kaufman, "The Ethics of Assassination," International Society for Military Ethics, JSCOPE Conference Proceedings 2004, http://isme.tamu.edu /JSCOPE04/Kaufman04.html.

delivery to a foreign power was not only economically and socially onerous but, for Israelites, blasphemous since Yhwh alone was their sovereignty and the *minḥâ*, in its sacerdotal sense of "offering," belonged only to Yhwh. Against the background of other narratives in Judges, such as Gideon's destruction of an altar of Baal (Judg 6:25–27) or Samson's destruction of a temple of Dagon (Judg 16:23–30), the theological dimensions of Ehud's heroics come into focus. The heroics of Israel's deliverers and judges, inspired and raised up by Yhwh, were understood as directed against rival deities as well as rival warriors. (2005: 85–86)

This is a holy war, not just a political war. Mobley also notes the fact that Ehud controls the keys: "Here in the Moabite stronghold, in the place where Ehud should be in danger and Eglon invulnerable, Ehud escapes safely and Eglon does not. Note all the language in reference to Eglon being closed in and shut in . . . Ehud, the Israelite, locks Eglon, the Moabite, in a box" (2005: 92). At the end, all the soldiers of Moab are locked in.

There is also a scatological tone to this story, which many commentators highlight as contributing to the humor of the story. When Eglon is killed, excrement comes out, and the smell serves to confuse his servants, who think that the reason he is slow to come out of his chamber is that he's on the toilet. Furthermore, Ehud kills Eglon with his left hand, the hand that in many cultures around the world is associated with uncleanness, because it is used to clean oneself after defecating. James Jordan points out that all this imagery is not merely for the sake of amusement. According to the law, latrines or toilets were to be kept "outside the camp," not in the area of the camp where YHWH Himself would walk (Deut. 23:12–14). The scatological imagery thus serves to underline that the Moabites are unclean, which is why they are to be removed from the land, for everything in the land is to be holy to YHWH (Jordan 1999: 64–66).

One recent book about how to preach Judges expresses dismay about the "ethnic humor" of this story, suggesting that the preacher must be clear about how unacceptable such humor is, recognizing that the Israelites were indulging in a wrong sort of gloating over their enemies here.[6] I think this is wildly misguided. Throughout the scriptures, YHWH Himself laughs at His enemies and encourages His people to laugh at them as well. Martin Luther famously suggested that laughter is a potent weapon against Satan, and generations of oppressed people throughout the world have found laughter to be a useful tool in maintaining dignity and sanity under oppression. In scripture, such humor is often found in situations

6. Joseph R. Jeter, *Preaching Judges* (Atlanta: Chalice, 2014), 43–44.

in which "there is a contrast between a party possessing overwhelming power and a party lacking all such power, perhaps best demonstrated in the stark opposition between the foreign king and the midwives" during Israel's enslavement in Egypt (Exod. 1:15–21).[7] Cheryl Exum suggests that the trickster quality of the Ehud story is echoed yet more strongly in Jael's assassination of Sisera in chapter 5.[8] And of course Gideon tricks his enemies, and Samson is something of a trickster too, so this trickster/deception motif, introduced with Ehud, does not end with him. There is no indication in the book of Judges or more widely that we are supposed to be disapproving of making a fool of one's enemies as a step toward conquering them.

Ehud's Message

However much of a trickster Ehud may be, he doesn't at any point in the story tell a lie. He informs Eglon that he has a message from God for him, which is not a lie. The text tells us that Ehud was "raised up" by YHWH to be a deliverer for the people of Israel (3:15). It is in response to this calling that Ehud initially prepared his special double-sided short sword, with the intention of executing Eglon. Still, Ehud does not act when he first comes into Eglon's presence. Perhaps this is because the Israelites who had been carrying the treasure were still present, and he did not wish to endanger them, or he thought that they might impede his actions. I am inclined to think he was still indecisive. Whatever the barrier to action, it was removed after he went as far as the standing stones of Gilgal and then turned back. After turning back, he begins to act with swiftness and certainty.

The stones at Gilgal were set up by the people of Israel at Joshua's direction as they were entering the land for the first time, preparing to take the city of Jericho (Josh. 4:1–13). The armies of Israel passed between those standing stones on their way to that unconventional first battle. Joshua told the people that the stones were to serve as a remembrance, and it is after passing the stones that Ehud's memory of the mandate to take the land and drive out the Canaanites appears to have been refreshed. The stones have functioned for him as they were supposed to, and so when he tells Eglon, "I have a secret message for you, O king" (3:19) and again, "I have a message from God for you" (3:20), he is telling the truth. It is a message of judgment.

7. Robert C. Culley, "Themes and Variations in Three Groups of OT Narratives," *Semeia* 3 (January 1975): 9.
8. J. Cheryl Exum, "The Centre Cannot Hold: Thematic and Textual Instabilities in Judges," *Catholic Biblical Quarterly* 52 (1990): 416.

It is thus not surprising that his sword is described as "double-mouthed." The message is to be "spoken" by the sword. Eric Christianson says that for Ehud "violence is simply a tool with which to deliver the word of God."[9] And Joshua Berman demonstrates that this connection between the word of God and a sword is a common biblical theme. "The term 'double- (or, multi-) edged sword' appears in two other occurrences in the Hebrew Bible (Prov. v 4; Ps. cxlix 6), three times in the Christian Bible (Heb. iv 12; Rev. i 16; ii 12), once in the Apocrypha (Sir. xxi 3) and once in the Pseudepigrapha (Ahiqar, col. vii 100b). Whether the language is Hebrew, Aramaic or Greek, the term reads in all of these texts, literally, 'a sword of mouths.' In nearly exclusive fashion it may be seen to be a metaphor for the potency of speech."[10] Berman explains that the edge of a sword was conventionally likened to a mouth not because of its shape but because of its function: devouring the flesh of the one it attacks.[11] Out of this usage grew the convention of using the sword as a metaphor for speech or words. Berman's conclusion is that it is appropriate and not anachronistic to assume that Ehud's two-mouthed sword is also indicating something about his use of language with a double meaning. By extension, from a Christian viewpoint, we may also read the story to point forward to the use of the word of God to divide and distinguish good from evil, the right culmination of Adam and Eve's misdirected desire. This is precisely what Ehud does in removing what is unclean from the holy land: he keeps the land pure from contamination.

Sacrifice

As already noted, there is a contrastive parallel between Ehud's sacrifice of Eglon and Jephthah's sacrifice of his daughter. Marc Zvi Brettler says, "The story as a whole plays on the notion of sacrifice. While pretending to bring tribute/offering to Eglon, it is actually Eglon, 'the calf,' who becomes the offering."[12] The language used in 3:17–18 for the paying of tribute is not the normal language for such a transaction; instead, the verb used here is normally used for bringing a sacrifice.[13]

9. Eric S. Christianson, "A Fistful of Shekels: Scrutinizing Ehud's Entertaining Violence (Judges 3:12–30)," *Biblical Interpretation: A Journal of Contemporary Approaches* 11, no. 1 (2003): 53.

10. Joshua Berman, "The 'Sword of Mouths' (Jud. III 16; Ps. CXLIX 6; Prov. V 4): A Metaphor and Its Ancient Near Eastern Context," *VT* 52, fasc. 3 (July 2002): 292.

11. Berman, "'Sword of Mouths,'" 299.

12. Brettler, *The Creation of History in Ancient Israel* (New York: Routledge: 1998), 81, cited in Mobley (2005: 85).

13. Brettler, "Never the Twain Shall Meet?," *Hebrew Union College Annual* 62 (January 1991), 294–95.

The name Eglon signifies a calf, and the language of the text thus suggests that Eglon is being sacrificed by Ehud.[14] The war against the people of the land more generally can be understood as sacrifice. This is the logic behind the call to cleanse the land of the Canaanites and their ways. But Eglon individualizes this theme of sacrifice via warfare.

Furthermore, the language used to describe Ehud's assassination of Eglon has sexual overtones, suggesting that Eglon has been "feminized" in some way. In the context of the entire book, we can see that this is not just for the sake of mocking the leader of Moab but to underscore the parallel with the story of Jephthah, who also offers a person as a sacrifice. The feminization of Eglon serves to underline his role as a contrast character for Jephthah's daughter. This indirect reference to Jephthah's daughter is the only way in which this story even hints at the role of women in Israelite society, making it unusual among the stories within the book.

The rabbis teach that because Eglon stood when told that Ehud had a message from God, thus showing respect for the divine, he was judged worthy to be an ancestor of Ruth, and through her of Solomon. "The Holy One said that because Eglon honored God by rising from his throne, his descendant (Solomon) will sit upon the throne of God."[15] The suggestion that Eglon is thus also an ancestor of Jesus is an interesting one, though highly speculative. Even if he is not in a direct line with Ruth and so with Jesus, the people of Moab are represented in Jesus's genealogy. In contrast, Ehud is from Benjamin, which is the tribe of Saul as well as the tribe that is almost eliminated by the end of the book. So in the longer picture it may be Eglon, not Ehud, who is blessed by God.

---

14. Brettler, "Never the Twain Shall Meet?," 294–96.

15. *Ruth Rabbah* 2, in A. J. Rosenberg, ed., *Judges: A New Translation: Translation of Text, Rashi and Commentary*, trans. Avrohom Fishelis and Shmuel Fishelis (New York: Judaica, 1983), 23.

6

DEBORAH

4:1–5:31

Structure

On the through-structure reading of the book of Judges, we would expect the Deborah story to show some degeneration in the state of Israel compared to the story of Ehud that precedes it, and indeed the disobedience and the oppression of the people of Israel have both intensified. This time they have been oppressed for twenty years, which is longer than the oppression under Eglon, but the time of rest for the land at the end of the Deborah story is only forty years, as opposed to eighty years after Ehud's victory. Whereas the Ehud story presented a unified Israel opposing the enemy, here we see signs of fracturing between the tribes, as some are reprimanded for not having responded to Barak's summons (5:15b–17). Barak himself is slow to respond to Deborah's call.

In terms of the sequence of six judges as two parallel sets of three, Deborah is set up to be a foil to Samson. In terms of the chiastic structure of the major leaders of Israel, Deborah is contrasted with Abimelech. In all three stories, a male warrior is conquered by a woman utilizing a common domestic implement to strike his head: Jael puts a tent peg through the head of Sisera, an unnamed woman drops a millstone on the head of Abimelech, and Delilah takes a razor to Samson's hair. This is sufficiently specific that we must be intended to notice. The attack on the head reminds us of the promise in Genesis that the seed of the woman will "strike" the head of the serpent (Gen. 3:15). In Deborah's story the embodiment of the serpent is Sisera, a Canaanite, but in Abimelech's story it is Abimelech himself, the son of Gideon, and in Samson's story it is Samson himself, a judge in Israel. Israel's progressive internalization of the character of the serpent is a sign of Canaanization. In both the case of Sisera and the case of Abimelech, that the agent of death is a woman is explicitly presented as a sign of God's judgment against the one slain. The logic of the text is that when women function as successful warriors, conquering trained and capable male generals, the only possible explanation is that God equipped them to do this work. As Paul says, "God chose what is weak in the world to shame the strong" (1 Cor. 1:27). Being vanquished by a woman in battle is the equivalent of being shamed by God, and so it is evidence of particularly severe judgment. Again, what is notable is that whereas in the story of Deborah this judgment is directed against a Canaanite attacker, by the time we get to Abimelech God's judgment has turned on an Israelite.

Deborah is also contrasted with both Abimelech and Samson in terms of her success at leading the army of Israel against the enemy in obedience to YHWH—something neither Abimelech nor Samson achieve. Like Othniel, she makes progress in reversing the curse on the land and the curse between men and women, though her progress is more qualified than his. The Samson comparison yields additional fruit in terms of the different ways women function in these two stories. This is a large theme in each story and will be discussed in detail in the thematic section of this chapter and the chapter on Samson.

John Stek has analyzed the structure of the prose section of the Deborah story, demonstrating that it consists of a frame around three parallel subsections, each arranged concentrically. The frame consists of 4:1–3 and 4:23–24, 5:31b.

A. And the Israelites again did evil in the eyes of Yahweh (episode initiating): v. 1.
   B. And Yahweh sold them into the *hands of Jabin king of Canaan*: v. 2.
      C. And *the Israelites* cried to Yahweh: v. 3.
      C′ And God subdued . . . Jabin king of Canaan before *the Israelites*: v. 23.
   B′ And the *hand* of the Israelites bore down ever harder on *Jabin king of Canaan*: v. 24
A′ And the land enjoyed peace forty years (episode closure): 5:31*b*. (Stek 1986: 55)

Notice that, on Stek's reading, the poem of Deborah and Barak is wrapped into the structure of the whole by this last concluding verse. The frame is common to most of the narratives of the major judges, drawing its structure from the paradigm established in chapter 2.

The first subsection (4:4–10) begins with a prologue (4:4–5) introducing Deborah, telling us that she is a prophet (therefore validated by YHWH) and a judge. There is then another concentrically symmetrical pattern.

  A. Deborah summons Barak to Kadesh: v. *6a*.
    B. Deborah transmits Yahweh's commission to Barak: v. *6b*.
      C. Deborah transmits Yahweh's promise of victory: v. 7.
        D. Barak, hesitant, negotiates: v. 8.
      C′ Deborah commits herself to accompany Barak as an earnest of Yahweh's promise but qualifies the promise: v. *9a*.
    B′ Deborah goes with Barak to carry out Yahweh's commission: v. *9b*.
  A′ Barak summons the tribes to Kadesh: v. *10a*. (Stek 1986: 56; bold added)

On this reading, the central point of the first subsection is Barak's hesitant response to YHWH's message. Deborah has told Barak that he must summon or draw together his army on Mount Tabor and that YHWH will then draw or summon Sisera's army to the Kishon River. YHWH is promising to deliver Sisera to Barak, to take charge of the battle and guarantee its outcome. It is unclear whether Barak's doubt is, like Gideon's in the next narrative, rooted in general skepticism about YHWH's involvement in Israel, or whether it is rather a doubtful response to Deborah's reliability as a prophet of YHWH. The way the promise is subsequently qualified suggests the latter. Stek observes, "He responds to Deborah, not to Yahweh. He has heard Deborah, not Yahweh. Deborah has said . . . Let Deborah act on her words" (1986: 64). Barak has doubted the prophetic credentials of a woman, and therefore a woman will take the honor of military victory from him. Barak's name means "lightning," a name that appears ironic at this point in the text given his unwillingness to act. In contrast, Deborah now springs into action. "Indeed, *arose* marks such a turning point that her claim in the victory song that the nation had been in straits 'till I, Deborah, arose, arose a mother in Israel' (5:7) reads, by virtue of this echo from the narrative, as a statement of fact rather than a piece of credit grabbing" (Sternberg 1985: 274).

The second subsection (4:11–17) also begins with a prologue, this time introducing Heber. The prologue is linked to the last line of the previous section by a reference to Kedesh. Heber is a Kenite, descended from Moses's father-in-law, and the Kenites have historically been allies of Israel. However, Heber has allied himself with Jabin in this fight, perhaps because—as a smith—he found working for Jabin's army, with its many iron chariots, more profitable than an alliance with Israel. In any event, he has relocated in order to be closer to his new ally. The parallel to the previous section is underscored by the reference to the oak of Zaanannim (Josh. 19:33) set in parallel to the palm of Deborah.

After the prologue, we again find a pattern of concentric symmetry.

A. Sisera is informed (by Heber): v. 12.
  B. Sisera summons his army from Harosheth Haggoyim to the Kishon River: v. 13.
  *Deborah sends Barak into battle: v. 14a.
  C. Barak descends from Mount Tabor to do battle: v. 14b.
    D. Yahweh overwhelms the enemy: v. 15a.
  C′ Sisera descends from his chariot to escape the battle: v. 15b.
  B′ Barak pursues the fleeing enemy to Harosheth Haggoyim and destroys Sisera's army: v. 16.
A′ Sisera flees to Heber's encampment: v. 17. (Stek 1986: 57; bold added)

This structure clearly shows the exchange of power between Sisera and Barak. "It also highlights (by asymmetry) the role of Deborah as Yahweh's spokesperson and (by centering) the role of Yahweh Himself as the great victor" (Stek 1986: 57). The asymmetry of Deborah's sending highlights that her exhortation of Barak is superfluous, or should be. If Barak had not been hesitant to obey the word of YHWH, there would have been no need for Deborah to urge him on in this way. The structure contrasts Barak's indecision in the first subsection, not with Deborah's action as before but with the action of YHWH Himself. The placement of YHWH's victory over the enemy at the center of the central section makes clear that the entire story is held together by His actions. The section begins by telling us "Heber had separated" and ends by telling us "Sisera had fled."[1] These two characters, Heber and Sisera, are both tools in YHWH's hand, contributing to Israel's victory over Jabin, even though each man believes he is opposing Israel.

When the two subsections are set side by side, Deborah is seen as Sisera's opposite and primary opponent, since they are the principle actors in points B and C of each section. Barak does not speak in this section; indeed, his only speech

---

1. Deborah's command to Barak echoes Ehud's command to his troops in 3:28 (Sternberg 1985: 281).

in chapter 4 is his doubting speech in 4:8. However, Sisera does not understand his opponent. In 4:12 he is told only that "Barak son of Abinoam had gone up to Mount Tabor." He does not know about the presence of a prophet, nor does he realize that YHWH is directing all the action, including Sisera's own actions. He does not know that Deborah is commanding the action as YHWH's spokesperson (Sternberg 1985: 276). Although Barak is now obedient, he is not in fact the leader of his troops, since YHWH Himself has gone out before him. YHWH is the real general here; Barak is along for the ride.

The way YHWH "overwhelms" the enemy is told in more detail in the song of chapter 5. But even the simple language here in chapter 4 is evocative. "'*Wayyāhām Yahweh*,' says the author. The verb occurs thirteen times in the Old Testament, in all but three with Yahweh as subject. Of these, eight speak of Yahweh the Warrior overwhelming His enemies, and in six of these He does so by attacking out of the thunderstorm. . . . The picture is clear. Yahweh goes forth in storm cloud before Barak; then down from Mount Tabor comes Barak, Yahweh's 'lightning' weapon" (Stek 1986: 68). The significance of YHWH's presence in the storm is especially striking when we remember that the sin for which Israel was being punished was worship of the storm god Baal. YHWH claims authority over all parts of life, even those associated with other deities.

The third and final subsection (4:18–23) is linked to the last line of the previous section by the reference to Jael. Jael is introduced in verse 17 as "the wife of Heber," just as Deborah was introduced as "the wife of Lappidoth," underlining their complementary roles in this narrative while also offering "the thematic irony that both husbands are conspicuous by their absence throughout except in the titles of their heroic spouses" (Sternberg 1985: 281–82). This subsection begins and ends with Jael "going out to meet" someone—first Sisera and last Barak. The central event in this subsection is 4:20, which details Sisera's attempt to take control when he directs Jael to stand at the tent door and tell anyone who asks that there is "no man here." Just as Sisera was blind to Deborah's presence on Mount Tabor, so he is now blind to Jael's presence as a threat (Sternberg 1985: 282). Stek summarizes, "The three centers—Barak's speech, which betrays his irresolution; Yahweh's vanquishing of the enemy; and Sisera's speech, in which he unknowingly speaks the truth about himself—together characterize the two opposing field commanders and focus narrative attention on Yahweh's decisive action. That in the first episode Deborah and in the last Jael dominate the action surrounding the centers structurally reinforces a major theme in the narrative and evenly distributes the honor for victory between these two redoubtable women" (Stek 1986: 59). Jael's assassination of Sisera reminds us of Ehud's assassination of Eglon, making connections between this narrative and the previous one. Like Ehud, Jael has sometimes been criticized for behaving unethically in her defeat of Israel's enemy, but the analysis of such criticism that we considered in defense of Ehud applies here as well.

Levitical Warriors

Barak is identified as being from Kedesh, in Naphtali. Kedesh is the city that Naphtali dedicated to the Levites in the book of Joshua (21:32). So although Barak lives among the tribe of Naphtali, his city is the Levitical city in that territory; he is a Levite, the first Levite to appear in the book of Judges. There is nothing in the way that he is introduced to suggest that he has been in the habit of leading a military life. But the war against the Canaanites is a holy war, and it is appropriate for the priests and Levites to play a role. In the battle against Jericho, the priests carried the ark around the city. Phinehas the priest used a spear to execute YHWH's judgment against Zimri and Cozbi in Num. 25:1–15, and later in Numbers Phinehas leads the army of Israel into battle carrying the vessels of the tabernacle (31:6). There is a tradition of priestly leadership during times of war, and Barak is summoned to fill this role.

Some think that Barak's refusal to go into battle without Deborah is a mark of his wisdom, in that he wishes to have YHWH's emissary present and guiding him. But if this were the case, we should not expect Deborah to chastise him. The response, "I'll go if you go," is especially a sign of degeneration when we consider what Sisera's mother has to say about the battle tactics practiced by Sisera and his soldiers, in which rape is a standard act of war (5:30). By bringing Deborah into battle, Barak is failing to measure up to the standard set by Caleb and Othniel in chapter 1 about the treatment of women. Barak the Levite is foreshadowing the Levite of the second epilogue who tosses his concubine out the door to protect himself from harm. In *The Lion, the Witch and the Wardrobe*, C. S. Lewis has Father Christmas tell Lucy that "battles are ugly when women fight,"[2] a perspective that is shared by the narrator of Judges. The women who fight (Deborah, Jael, the unnamed attacker of Abimelech) are never blamed for fighting, but their participation in battle is a sign of disorder.

If Barak's desire to have Deborah with him were in fact rooted in his recognition of her prophetic authority, this would be rather like insisting on having the

2. C. S. Lewis, *The Lion, the Witch and the Wardrobe* (London: The Folio Society, 1996), 103.

ark go into battle: it would be a superstitious attempt to manipulate YHWH's presence. But as noted in the exploration of the story's structure, it seems instead that his demand is rooted in doubt about her authority, that he is in essence issuing a challenge or a dare, saying that he is unwilling to recognize her message as a word from God unless she risks herself to defend it. Either way, whether Barak is simply being cowardly or is rather doubting Deborah's authority to make military recommendations and the reliability of her prophetic gift, he is certainly not contributing to her flourishing by bringing her onto the field of battle against an army that uses the rape of women as one of its principal weapons. Against the benchmark of Caleb and Othniel, Barak falls short.

Once he is persuaded to act, Barak and Deborah together go to Kedesh and recruit an army from among the tribes of Naphtali and Zebulun. Assembling an army of ten thousand men and moving them all to the battle site that YHWH had chosen for them would have taken some time. In the song in chapter 5, Deborah sings of the time "when locks are long in Israel, when the people offer themselves willingly" (5:2). Apparently, the soldiers of Zebulun and Naphtali had taken Nazirite vows when they were recruited into the army of Israel, and so their hair was long by the time they fought Sisera. The army at least recognized the holy nature of this battle.

Free Will

As noted earlier, Sternberg points out that the biblical narrative operates under what most writers would consider a handicap: the end of the story is almost always known ahead of time. God's complete and sovereign control is central to the theology of the Bible, and this control is typically demonstrated (as in this story) by telling the outcome before it happens to establish that God knows what He is going to accomplish and then accomplishes it. The threat is therefore that the narrative will become very boring, but in fact this is not the case. The question of just how God's promises will come true remains open, and the promises are often subject to reinterpretation, since we may have misunderstood what has been foretold to happen (Sternberg 1985: 275–76). The overall effect is therefore "license amidst constraint" (275).

The narrative thus reflects the nature of reality. God genuinely is in absolute control, and we really do already know the end of our story. We know that we are living in a comedy, not a tragedy; that death and sin have already been definitively conquered, even though the battle is not yet over; that our final destination on the "path of life" is "fullness of joy" and "pleasures forevermore" (Ps. 16:11). But on the way to that destination, where might the path take us? And how much freedom do we have in determining our direction? For Jesus, the path of life led through hell (Acts 2:25–31); we trust that because he has gone there, we need not. But his example suggests we should not expect any exemption from pain and suffering. Nor should we expect to be treated as automatons. Sisera experienced himself as a free person, making free decisions, even though we know that God was drawing him into battle, that God was controlling Heber's change of alliance and Jael's continuing loyalty to YHWH, and that God was directing Sisera's steps when he fled the battle. The Westminster Confession tells us (in harmony with many other sources) that the authority of God as primary cause in no way limits our freedom as secondary causes but rather is the ground of such freedom.[3]

This dynamic of divine sovereignty combined with openness and freedom is brought to the fore in this story by YHWH's direct command over the battle. It is the Lord who has "marched out" at the head of His army (5:4). He has fought commanding the stars in the heavens as His army and using the Kishon River as His weapon (5:20–21). The outcome of the battle was never in doubt because YHWH Himself was the warrior fighting against Sisera. And yet Sisera is a free agent who is rightly judged for his free actions. This interaction between sovereignty and freedom is seen throughout Judges, but with special clarity in this story.

Deborah and the Role of Women

Theodoret of Cyrus, who wrote an early commentary on the book of Judges, asks the question, "Why did a woman prophesy?" His answer is surprising for his era, or at least surprising to us, given our prejudices about his era: "Because men and women have the same nature. As you know, the woman was formed from Adam and, like him, possessed the faculty of reason. Hence, the apostle says, 'In Christ Jesus there is neither male nor female.' Thus, Moses was called a 'prophet,' and Miriam a 'prophetess.'"[4] The existence of a woman who speaks with the authority

3. "God from all eternity did by the most wise and holy counsel of his own will, freely and unchangeably ordain whatsoever comes to pass; yet so as thereby neither is God the author of sin; nor is violence offered to the will of the creatures, nor is the liberty or contingency of second causes taken away, but rather established." The Westminster Confession of Faith, *Book of Confessions: Study Edition* (Louisville: Geneva, 1999), III.1, p. 177.

4. Theodoret of Cyrus, *Questions on the Octateuch*, vol. 2, *On Leviticus, Numbers, Deuteronomy, Joshua, Judges, Ruth*, ed. John F. Petruccione, trans. Robert C. Hill (Washington, DC: Catholic University of America Press, 2007), 329.

of a prophet and acts with the authority of a judge has troubled many readers who assume that women should not hold either role, but the text is completely calm about Deborah's function. The story of Deborah has often featured in debates about the role of women in the contemporary church. Should women be teachers? pastors? priests? These are vexing questions for many Christian denominations today, and Deborah is invoked by people on all sides of these issues to support their position.

The story of Deborah is certainly relevant to this debate. The question of God's design for women within the covenant community requires looking at the full sweep of scripture, and the story of Deborah fits within the trajectory of the overall story. In the introduction we already considered Eve's creation as a priest to Adam, the "help (*ezer*) fit for" Adam because she was bone of his bone, flesh of his flesh. Within the original creation, it is specifically the role of the woman to foreshadow the incarnation of God in Christ, acting as the embodied mediator or representative of YHWH to Adam. I argued in that earlier section that the creational design for woman is to serve as a mediator between YHWH and Adam, just as the creational design for man is to serve as a mediator between YHWH and the natural world. In other words, it is the woman, Eve, whose created nature is obviously priestly.

The curse that followed the fall into sin was also discussed in the introduction as an important background to the book of Judges as a whole. Eve's ability to be a priestly mediator is derailed by her sinful desire for subservience, and the absence of any women priests in the Old Testament is a result of the curse on Eve. For this reason, although Deborah fills the roles of prophet and judge, being authorized both to speak the word of YHWH and to exercise administrative authority, she requires the presence of Barak the Levite to fulfill the priestly role. His reluctance to fill that role means that she steps into it beside him, joining him in leading a holy army into holy war, but the text makes clear that going into war is not supposed to be her job. The question of whether the priestly role is restored to women through the work of Christ can only be answered by looking at the role of women in the post-resurrection community of the church.

Even before the coming of Christ, YHWH works to undo the effects of sin and restore the good creation. The giving of the law includes stipulations protecting women from falling into a state of radical subservience, requiring women to be protected and treated with dignity. The people of Israel are commanded to take the land back from the powers of the serpent and reassert YHWH's rule over it, to function as genuine mediators between YHWH's grace and the land itself, until a state of shalom or creational well-being should be established. But the curse of Eve is also addressed. This new land of Canaan is to be a place where women are named, where women speak, and where women serve as mediators. Deborah does all these things. But just as the occupation of the land fails because of human sin, so too the restoration of women fails because of human sin. Ultimately, it requires the recapitulating work of Jesus to undo the effects of sin and make us—both male and female—into new creations. This is seen in that the role of women expands throughout the trajectory of scripture, with women in the New Testament being enlisted as witnesses to the resurrection, leaders of house churches, teachers, and evangelists. Even the famous pastoral prohibition—that women may not teach but must learn in all submission (1 Tim. 2:11)—fits within this trajectory, since the "submission" that women are to demonstrate when learning is the submission of a student of the Torah before the teacher. In other words, Timothy is told that women are now to be allowed to learn the scriptures, the necessary prerequisite for becoming true teachers. The rabbis taught, "Better to burn the Torah than to teach it to a woman." For women, the door to learning opens in the New Testament. In place of the disordered and needy subservience to a husband, women are to learn the rightly ordered subservience to God Himself.

Some commentators disagree, suggesting that Deborah fills the roles of judge and prophet only because the men in Israel are not stepping up to do their duty, so the presence of a female leader is a disordered situation that should serve as a judgment on male abdication of leadership. One such scholar is Michael J. Smith, who asserts:

> The first three judge stories, Othniel (3:7–11), Ehud (3:12–30), and Shamgar (3:31), set the stage for coming stories by providing normative male roles and leadership, with only the beginnings of signs of decline. The story of Deborah, Barak, and Jael (chaps. 4–5) introduces a reversal of roles as Barak failed to step up to the challenge of leadership as the designated judge and thus lost the honor of killing the enemy commander. In his place, God used Deborah, a "mother in Israel," and Jael, a non-Israelite wife, to play key roles in delivering Israel. Judges 5 is unique in that the narrator inserted a psalm of Deborah, in which she taught Israel about the Lord and His victory—something the men should have done.[5]

5. Michael J. Smith, "The Failure of the Family in Judges: Part 1, Jephthah," *Bibliotheca Sacra* 162 (July–September 2005): 281–82. Other scholars don't even bother to make this argument; they simply identify Barak, rather than Deborah, as the judge in the story. See, for example, Jay G. Williams, who in a list of judges with their tribal affiliations says simply "Barak from Naphtali" with no mention of Deborah whatsoever. Williams, "The Structure of Judges 2:6–16:31," *JSOT* 49 (1991): 80. This despite the fact that Deborah is identified as "judging" Israel (4:4), whereas Barak is never so identified.

However, the text does not support this view. Othniel is the paradigmatic judge, and each of the three judges immediately following Othniel instantiates that paradigm in a particular way, in each case including some quality that readers may find unexpected, or at least distinctive. So Ehud is left-handed, the minor judge Shamgar is not an Israelite, and Deborah is a woman. Ehud's story does not support an assertion that left-handed people are only allowed to be leaders if all the right-handed people abdicate their responsibility and refuse to take leadership positions. Shamgar's non-Israelite status does not support an assertion that God only welcomes non-Israelites into leadership within the covenant community when all the children of Abraham refuse to do their duty. And Deborah's story does not support an assertion that female leadership is a disordered concession to male irresponsibility.

Before Barak is ever on the scene, before he has had any opportunity to accept or reject a position of leadership, Deborah is introduced as a prophet (*nebiah*) who is judging (*shaphat*) Israel (4:4). Neither role is presented as at all problematic. There is no suggestion that any men have refused to serve in these roles, nor was either role ever offered to Barak for him to decline it. The stories both before and after show that there were indeed men being called into this office, so Deborah is not serving as a judge as some sort of judgment on men. Neither is her role of prophet presented as a judgment on men. It is only her role as a military commander that is presented as problematic in this way. She goes into battle as a direct result of Barak's cowardice, as an accommodation to his failure. But the other two roles are seen as normal. So, harking back to our original three questions, the role of military commander is presented as an exceptional adaptation to an unusual circumstance, but the roles of judge and prophet are presented as normal and acceptable roles for a woman to fill, even apart from Christ's redemptive work.

Deborah is not the only woman in this story; there are two others, though neither is obviously relevant to the question of women in leadership within the covenant community. First, we consider Jael. Jael's role in the story is sometimes held up as a violation of hospitality rules, but, as Victor Matthews makes clear, it is Sisera who violates the code of hospitality (2004: 68–73). Rather than going to Jael's husband to ask for refuge, he goes directly to her tent, bringing down on her the possibility of being accused of immodest or even unfaithful behavior. Furthermore, hospitality rules dictated that once he had accepted hospitality, Sisera was not to ask for anything, since doing so insulted the host. Sisera asks for water and so violates this norm. He also tries to take charge, giving Jael directions, telling her to stand in the doorway and instructing her about what to say to anyone who passes by. Again, he violates the hospitality code by suggesting that his hostess will not meet all his needs without being prompted. "Sisera's insistence is both an unnecessary statement and in fact an implied threat against his hostess. At that point, if previous blunders had not already released Jael from any obligation to him, she is free to take action against him. By pressing his point and asserting a status other than guest, Sisera falls back into the role of hostile stranger" (Matthews 2004: 73). Sisera's arrogance in dispensing with the courtesy due to his allies is directly connected to his death at Jael's hand.

A good deal of language in this episode is susceptible to sexual interpretation. Fewell and Gunn demonstrate that this language is used to illustrate Sisera's transformation from a domineering man to a child.

> With this verbal play and visual display, the narrator constructs a symbolic picture in which the tent and its opening become uterine and vaginal images respectively. Sisera, like a man penetrating his lover, has entered, upon invitation, a woman's sphere. Now, like a child in a womb, Sisera lies sleeping in Jael's tent. On this reading, one might even hear the narrator's humor dancing behind Sisera's order to the woman, "Stand at the opening . . . and if anyone comes and asks you, 'Is there a man here?' say, 'No.'" For Sisera, the answer "No, there is no man here" is intended to be a lie, but for the reader attentive to irony, the answer "no" reflects the truth. The mighty man has become a vulnerable child; the virile man lies impotent.[6]

Having reduced Sisera to the status of a child, Jael then feminizes him, taking the male role of the one who penetrates when she drives her tent peg through his head. To those who persist in questioning the morality of Jael's actions, Bruce Waltke answers, "Is Jael an honorable and heroic assassin or a dishonorable, treacherous murderer (4:18–22)? The *prophetess* Deborah (4:4) resolves the ambiguity in 5:24 'Most blessed of women be Jael'" (Waltke 2004: 42). Jael decides to side with YHWH and the people of Israel rather than collaborate with Jabin and Sisera, a decision honored in Deborah's prophecy.

The third woman in the story is Sisera's mother. In her song of victory, Deborah describes herself as "a mother in Israel" (5:7), contrasting herself with Sisera's mother, who cheerfully sends her son out to rape and pillage other people. Deborah is a mother who defends Israel from such attacks. Sisera's mother anticipates the triumphant return of her son, even as he is lying dead in disgrace. *The Iliad* makes

---

6. Danna Nolan Fewell and David M. Gunn, "Controlling Perspectives: Women, Men, and the Authority of Violence in Judges 4 and 5," *Journal of the American Academy of Religion* 58, no. 3 (Fall 1990): 393.

a similar observation about Hector's wife, after the death of Hector: "She called out through the house to her lovely-haired handmaidens / to set a great cauldron over the fire, so that there would be / hot water for Hektor's bath as he came back out of the fighting; / poor innocent, nor knew how, far from waters for bathing, / Pallas Athene had cut him down at the hands of Achilleus."[7] Just as Hector's wife is dismissed as a foolish woman, so Sisera's mother is also foolish. Contemporary readers are sometimes struck by the switch to her perspective, thinking this is a moment in which the biblical text recognizes a plurality of perspectives on reality.[8] However, Deborah's tone is more exalting than sympathetic. Sisera's mother thinks of a woman or two for each man, calmly considering the certainty that her son is raping foreign women. One of the reasons the death of Sisera is justified is that this is how he has used his power in the past: to rape and dominate the helpless. And Sisera's mother thinks of this approvingly. She is in fact a beneficiary of his harsh treatment of other women. The ironic reality is that he has not taken two women by rape, but rather two women have cooperated to kill him.

The Heroism of Holy War

It is significant that both Deborah and Barak sing. Barak has spoken only once in chapter 4, and that was to voice doubt and skepticism. But here he is willing to sing alongside Deborah, to join in praising YHWH for victory, no longer concerned with getting proper credit or with being disgraced by submitting to the commands of a woman. Athalya Brenner suggests that in the prose section of the story Deborah and Barak, "the champions of Israel," are set against their Canaanite opposites, Jabin and Sisera, and that a third duo—YHWH and Jael—interacts with both. In that story the two triangles are the commanders (Deborah, Jabin, and YHWH Himself) and the soldiers who execute the commanders' orders (Barak, Sisera, and Jael).[9] However, Brenner thinks that the structure and the theme of the poem in chapter 5 are quite different from the structure and theme of the prose account in chapter 4. The structure consists of two contrasting triangles. The first triangle is among three women: good mother Deborah, bad mother of

7. Homer, *The Iliad*, trans. Richmond Lattimore (Chicago: University of Chicago Press, 2011), 469.
8. A colleague of mine reported just such a reaction from his adult education class when they were studying Judges together at his church.
9. Athalya Brenner, "A Triangle and a Rhombus in Narrative Structure: A Proposed Integrative Reading of Judges 4 and 5," in *The Feminist Companion to Judges*, ed. Athalya Brenner, Feminist Companion to the Bible 4 (Sheffield: Sheffield Academic, 1993), 99–102.

Sisera, and the mediating Jael. The second triangle is between Barak and Sisera with YHWH mediating in a more explicitly supernatural way in the poem than in the prose description of chapter 4. Deborah and Barak form a pair on one pole, with Sisera's mother and Sisera on the other.[10] Much as YHWH's direct intervention reverses Sisera's expectations, so Jael's intervention (as an instrument of YHWH) reverses Sisera's mother's expectations: she thinks Sisera is out raping women, but in fact he's dying in Jael's bed.

> The sphere of milk and female activity is depicted in the poem as separate from the sphere of water and male activity. The two worlds are different and distinct. Yet they reflect each other—hence the parallel structure. One cannot operate without the other. It is not enough that the female sphere is maternal, private, apolitical. In order for the military-political conflict to be resolved, a certain cooperation between the male and female social spheres is required. This is achieved through the intervention of the female principles—sex and motherhood, Jael and the milk she serves—in the male world of battle, [in much the same way] as through the use of water (the miraculous flood from high above) with the male ("real") world of public life. The combination of the usually distinct gender-and-role worlds is essential for the victory.[11]

If Brenner is correct, we may read the prose section of this story as especially focused on the taking of the land but the song as especially focused on the reconciliation and reintegration of men and women. Barak and Deborah singing together about a victory that was achieved by men and women working together is a hopeful sign that this reconciliation may be possible. The hope will be crushed by the end of the book, but for this moment it is still living. Note that the genre of poetry is different from the genre of prose, and that the expectations about historical fidelity are also different. "It makes no sense, therefore, to . . . dovetail every reference in Deborah's paean with the foregoing tale of the victory" (Sternberg 1985: 247).

What are we to make of the mingling of warfare and religious commitment that we find in this song? YHWH Himself is portrayed as a warrior, and the members of Israel's army are portrayed as Nazirites, going into battle with uncut hair, vowed to God for a holy work. This is a hymn to the glories of holy war led by a warrior God. As noted in our discussion of the second prologue, contemporary people are undoubtedly uncomfortable with such talk, particularly in a world in which we face the prospect of *jihad*. One solution is to move immediately to

10. Brenner, "A Triangle and a Rhombus," 102–4.
11. Brenner, "A Triangle and a Rhombus," 105.

a spiritualized or allegorical reading of the text. However, in the history of the church, the allegorical, anagogical, and tropological readings of texts (i.e., the three spiritual readings) are to be built on the literal. Reading this song as praise for spiritual warfare is fine, but it does not let us off the hook when it comes to literal warfare, since that is clearly the context of the song. Again the book of Judges challenges us to think about warfare in a less cynical way, recognizing that when an oppressed people free themselves from oppression by violent resistance, there may be something courageous, honorable, and even heroic in the effort.

7

GIDEON

6:1–8:35

Structure

Looking at the larger canvas of the book of Judges, we will find that the stories of Deborah, Gideon, and Abimelech form a triptych in the center of the book, and that both the Deborah story and the Abimelech story have three major subsections. Deborah's story focuses strongly on the (failed) attempt to undo the curse on Eve and reconcile men and women. Abimelech's story focuses strongly on the yet more obvious failure to undo the curse on Adam and repair the alienation from the land—understood both as alienation from creation in general and as alienation from the divinely promised homeland of Canaan. Gideon's story is not focused on either of these themes but on the overarching question of YHWH's kingship.

On an even larger scale, we will see that there are three major judges prior to Gideon and three major figures (Abimelech not being a judge) after Gideon. The three prior are all presented as exemplary followers of YHWH. In the first three stories, there is disintegration within Israel but not within the leadership that YHWH raises up. Gideon changes that as a transitional figure leading into the dark period of Abimelech, Jephthah, and Samson—all three of whom are deeply flawed. The story of Gideon is therefore the hinge at the heart of the book.

Within the structure of the downward spiral of the book that moves from beginning to end, Gideon's story is important in that he is the first judge to manifest doubt, cowardice, and idolatrous impulses. Gideon is a far more ambivalent character than those who have preceded him, signaling a step into deeper darkness. After Gideon, the judges are largely ignorant of God's law, complicit in Canaanite religious practice, and incapable of offering consistent moral guidance. Gideon marks the shift from one kind of leadership to another. We also see that the suffering of the people of Israel is intensifying as we move through the book; the damage credited to Midian is greater than anything we have heard of up to this point. Under Ehud, the people of Israel were required to pay tribute to their oppressors; under Deborah, they lived in fear of random acts of violence. But now they are left destitute. The Midianites do not merely take from the Israelites; they actively destroy the land. The land is meant to be a place of fruitfulness, but under the Midianites it has become barren because of their intentional and senseless destruction of its fruitfulness. It is not only the people who are suffering, but the land itself is suffering. The irony is that the children of Israel are worshiping the fertility gods Baal and Asherah, and this very worship is driving their land into barrenness.

Gideon can also be seen as starting the second series of three major judges, putting his story in parallel with Othniel's. One sign of this new beginning is found at the start of the chapter, which follows a familiar pattern. We have heard this pattern for each of the major judges already, and we will hear it again (3:7–8; 3:12–14; 4:1–3; 10:6–9; 13:1). There is one difference, however, in that the introductions to Ehud and Deborah say that the children of Israel *continued* to do what is evil in the eyes of YHWH, whereas this introduction returns to the wording that introduced Othniel. This suggests that Gideon's story is in some way a new beginning for the book, that we are starting a new section (Bluedorn 2001: 57). This approach to the book's structure is further supported by the fact that Israel suffered only seven years under Midian before Gideon was raised up by God. Up until this point in the narrative, the time of suffering has increased before each judge. Othniel was raised up after eight years of suffering under Cushan-rishathaim, Ehud after eighteen years under Eglon, and Deborah after twenty years under Jabin. The move back to only seven years of suffering under Midian signifies a reset of the book's trajectory for the second half of the narrative. Jephthah is raised up after eighteen years under the Philistines and Ammonites, and Samson after forty years under the Philistines. We will see that this second series of three judges has parallels to the first series, though in each case the sin of the Israelites is greater, whereas the saving work of the judge is less faithful and so less effective. Just as Othniel is the paradigmatic righteous judge, Gideon is the paradigm of disobedient and faithless leadership, a paradigm that will be followed by both Jephthah and Samson.

Finally, the third way of reading the book (the chiastic reading) takes into account the added story of Abimelech, which then makes Gideon the central leader in a series of seven, preceded by three good judges (Othniel, Ehud, and Deborah) and followed by three very questionable judges/kings (Abimelech, Jephthah, and Samson). On this reading, Gideon's story is the center point of the great chiasm of the book. Given the centrality of this story, we should expect to see the theme of the Gideon narrative as central to the entire book, and indeed it is. In 8:22–23 the people of Israel ask Gideon to become their king, but he declines, saying, "The LORD will rule over you." However, he goes on to take both kingly and priestly power to himself, establishing a dynasty and (more disturbingly) an alternative center of worship for the people of Israel, which becomes a "snare" for the people, leading them into syncretism. Finding this tension at the heart of the book tells us that the question of what it means for YHWH to be king—over a nation, over a territory, and over individuals—is the central question of the book of Judges. Israel's lack of faithfulness to YHWH's kingship, both politically and in worship, is the central problem.

Paul Tanner has argued that the Gideon narrative itself is also a chiasm. By his count, the entire Gideon narrative has twenty sections, which can then be grouped into five sections; the five sections are then arranged as follows:

A   6:1–10 (A B pattern within this section)
  B   6:11–32 (A B A′ B′ pattern within this section)
    C   6:33–7:18 (A B C C′ B′ A′ pattern within this section)
  B′ 7:19–8:21 (A B C A′ B′ C′ pattern within this section)
A′ 8:22–32 (A B pattern within this section)[1]

Tanner has gained some impressive support for this theory,[2] and I find parts of his analysis quite convincing. However, he fails to account for a clear inclusio linking 6:11 to 7:25, with a thematically connected conclusion found in 8:1–3. There

1. J. Paul Tanner, "The Gideon Narrative as the Focal Point of Judges," *Bibliotheca Sacra* (April–June 1992): 150–51.
2. Notably Bruce Waltke and Charles Yu, *An Old Testament Theology: An Exegetical, Canonical, and Thematic Approach* (Grand Rapids: Zondervan, 2007), 601.

is another clear inclusio linking 6:11 to 8:27. Neither of these linkages works within Tanner's structure. Perhaps more significantly, the tone of the narrative shifts radically beginning with 8:4, when YHWH's role in the drama changes. I think there is a sharp break in the structure at that point, which Tanner's proposal does not recognize. I therefore suggest that the structure of the Gideon narrative is more complex than Tanner's model. Here is the structure as I see it:

6:1–10 Double prologue (echoing the double prologue of the book)

   A 6:11–18 Gideon's call, threshing in the winepress in Ophrah
     B 6:19–24 The first test
       C 6:25–32 Gideon's task: establish right worship in Ophrah
         D   6:33–35 Summoning the army
     B′ 6:36–40 The second test
         D′ 7:1–8 Sifting the army
     B″ 7:9–15a The third test
       C′ 7:15b–22 Gideon's task: reflect the glory cloud to Midianites
         D″ 7:23–25 Expanding the army
  A′ 8:1–3 The harvest and the vintage are both complete
              X   8:4–7 Approach to Succoth
                Y   8:8–9 Approach to Penuel
                   Z   8:10–12 Capture of Zebah and
                      Zalmunna
              X   8:13–16 Vengeance on Succoth
                Y   8:17 Vengeance on Penuel
                   Z   8:18–21 Vengeance on Zebah and
                      Zalmunna
  A″ 8:22–35 False kingship and false worship in Ophrah

(double conclusion also echoes the double prologue)

When we reach 8:3, everything is on the verge of the proper ending, which—according to the pattern established thus far—should be something along the lines of the land having rest for forty years. It is therefore startling to discover that in 8:4 we start a new cycle, a cycle in which YHWH is no longer the initiator or even a genuine actor, though Gideon occasionally invokes Elohim—that is, God in a generic sense. Only once after 8:3 does Gideon use the covenant name

YHWH. The remaining section of the Gideon narrative shows Gideon wandering away from the pattern established with Othniel, Ehud, and Deborah. Here we see that the structure of the story is underlining Gideon's role as the hinge or pivot toward a darker set of stories. The disintegration in Israel's social fabric accelerates from here on out. That this disruption of the pattern is intentional, part of the rhetorical design, seems clear. There is an anti-structure of three villages— Succoth, Penuel, and Ophrah—each damaged in some way by Gideon, which runs parallel to the three tests of the earlier part of the narrative. The Gideon story ends back in Ophrah, forming a second inclusio with 6:11, the beginning of his call narrative. But this time Gideon is not establishing right worship in Ophrah, nor is he reflecting God's glory beyond Israel to the people of Canaan. Rather, he is establishing a false cult that will serve as a trap for his family and all Israel for generations to come.

Seeing God's Glory

In contrast to all the other judge narratives, the Gideon narrative includes extensive conversation between Gideon and YHWH. Gideon's inner life of faith and doubt, fear and courage, is a part of the story in a way that is not true with any of the other judges. This is part of what makes the Gideon story so compelling for contemporary readers used to a more psychologically oriented style of storytelling. It is no accident that this is true only of Gideon, because as the central story in the book Gideon's story is in some ways the entry point to the book.

The initial exchange between Gideon and the Angel of the Lord (6:11–18) centers on the question of God's presence. The Angel (whom we first met during the first prologue, at Bochim) first greets Gideon by saying "the Lord is with you," a claim that Gideon immediately disputes. He has come to doubt the presence of YHWH with his people. It is therefore not surprising that he is also revealed immediately as a coward, hiding his wheat from the Midianites, thereby also disputing the messenger's claim that he is a "mighty warrior." Joshua commanded the Israelites to be courageous (Josh. 1:6, 7, 9), and in chapter 2 in this volume we considered the causal chain implicit in that command: being steeped in the law leads to an awareness of YHWH's constant presence, which then results in strength and courage (see chap. 2 under "Worship").

Gideon's cowardice can be traced backward down this chain. We first see him as cowardly, then hear him doubt God's presence, then discover his ignorance of the law. In the course of the story it will be clear that Gideon's knowledge of the law is spotty at best. He has certainly not been meditating on the teachings of Moses; instead, he and his family have been indulging in Baal worship. Indeed, his father has an altar to Baal and an Asherah pole built in the center of their compound. It also seems likely that the oak tree belonging to Joash had some cultic significance, since trees were often part of the shrines for Baals and Asherahs. Both Isaiah and Hosea identify oak trees with idol worship (Isa. 1:29–30; Hos. 4:13). This may also be an intentional contrast with the Deborah story, since Deborah's home is also marked by a tree, but it is a tree under which she dispenses the word of YHWH.

Since he is not living within the law of YHWH—not meditating on the law, nor allowing the law to shape his thought world, nor submitting his actions to its guidance—Gideon is not aware of YHWH's presence. This is an immediate source of conflict with the messenger of YHWH, who claims that the Lord is with Gideon. Gideon's first words are to dispute this claim. Having come to doubt that God is with him, Gideon is ill-equipped to act with strength and courage. In all this, Gideon—as is true for both of the subsequent major judges—embodies Israel's situation in microcosm. In some way, he stands in for Israel, for his situation of disobedience leading to lack of faith leading to lack of courage is precisely the situation of the people as a whole.

YHWH's approach to this problem is to convince Gideon of His presence, which He does with patience and repetition. Eventually Gideon becomes convinced that God is with him, and in the strength and courage that comes from this awareness Gideon is able to conquer the Midianites. However, his courage quickly turns in a wrong direction, so that as soon as the Midianites are conquered, Gideon turns his strength against other Israelites, prosecuting vengeance for having been disrespected by them during the earlier war. He is not defending God's honor but his own. Strength and courage built not on disciplined meditation on the law but solely on an emotional experience of God's presence do not last. The seed of YHWH's self-revelation has been sown in shallow soil, and by the end of the story it is no longer bearing fruit. In this respect, the Gideon story is a microcosm of the book as a whole, which also turns in a wrong direction toward warfare within Israel in place of the cleansing of the land.

This encounter with the Angel of the LORD is a call narrative, bringing to mind several other such scenes throughout scripture. In the history of Christian interpretation, Gideon's call has often been seen as similar to other call stories, including Moses's call at the burning bush and the annunciation to Mary in Luke 1. Certainly the messenger's greeting to Gideon with the promise of God's presence is reminiscent of the annunciation to Mary, and the calling to save the people of

Israel is reminiscent of the call to Moses at the burning bush. Gideon's protest of his unworthiness also sounds like Moses's. But neither Mary nor Moses is the model for Gideon's cynical reply to the messenger's greeting: "If the LORD is with us, why then has all this happened to us?" (6:13). Gideon's initial response is one of skepticism, not faith. When Moses encountered YHWH at the burning bush, he "hid his face, for he was afraid to look at God" (Exod. 3:6). The Angel who comes to Gideon is also a divine manifestation, as Gideon finally realizes in 6:22; however, Gideon is unimpressed by the Angel's initial appearance and greeting.

As we will see throughout the story, Gideon is incapable of understanding the transcendent. He has been enculturated into the worldview of Canaan, in which the gods are beings within the same sphere of reality as humans, and in which divine action can be measured, predicted, and evaluated using the same tools as those used to measure, predict, and evaluate human action. Gideon consistently interacts with YHWH as if YHWH is a peer of Baal's, an alternative local deity who may perhaps prove capable of defending Israel against the Midianites but who is not a fundamentally different kind of being. Gideon has no understanding of YHWH as the maker of heaven and earth, the ground of all existence, the one who exists beyond the chain of being, beyond what can be investigated, experienced, and controlled. Whereas the previous stories have focused on rescue from oppression, Gideon's story will focus on this conflict between YHWH and the worship of other gods, especially Baal (Bluedorn 2001: 69). Again, the central nature of this narrative for the book as a whole is significant, for even in those stories in which the theme of idolatry does not surface explicitly, it is always present under the surface.

The meeting with the Angel of the LORD also strongly suggests parallels to Abraham's encounter with YHWH in Gen. 18. The messenger to Gideon comes to sit under the oak at Ophrah, whereas "the LORD appeared to Abraham by the oaks of Mamre" (Gen. 18:1). In both stories there is fluidity in reference to the messenger or messengers, who sometimes are presented as angelic beings, sometimes as human messengers, sometimes as YHWH Himself. Both Abraham and Gideon prepare extravagant meals as offerings for their guests. Abraham prepares three measures of choice flour, a calf, and curds and milk. Gideon prepares one ephah of flour, a kid, and broth. Both meals involve a grain offering, a poured-out offering, and a sacrificial animal. The quantity of flour is the same, though Abraham, who is encountering YHWH manifested in three messengers, is described as preparing three measures of flour, whereas Gideon, who is encountering YHWH manifested in one messenger, is described as preparing one ephah. In other ways, however,

Abraham's offering is clearly more costly. He offers *choice* flour, which Gideon does not. He offers a calf rather than a goat, curds and milk rather than broth.

Abraham's encounter is a prelude to his conversation with YHWH about the destruction of Sodom. YHWH is preparing judgment against a wicked city, but Abraham says, "Will you indeed sweep away the righteous with the wicked? Suppose there are fifty righteous within the city; will you then sweep away the place and not forgive it for the fifty righteous who are in it? Far be it from you to do such a thing, to slay the righteous with the wicked, so that the righteous fare as the wicked! Far be that from you! Shall not the Judge of all the earth do what is just?" (Gen. 18:23–25). Eventually Abraham gets YHWH to agree not to destroy Sodom if there are but ten righteous in the city. Given the clear and obvious parallels between Gideon's encounter and Abraham's, it would seem natural to hear the subsequent section of the Gideon story in light of this conversation between Abraham and YHWH. Abraham is raising a moral question about the appropriateness of sweeping away an unrighteous people, which is also a great moral question in the book of Judges. Abraham recognizes YHWH as the Judge, the one with the right to pass judgment, but also as the one who is invested by His very nature in the pursuit of justice. Gideon never attains this ability to understand YHWH's character.

Gideon's conversation with YHWH is not immediately about the destruction of the Midianites but rather about tearing down his father's altar to Baal. Gideon takes ten men with him to perform this action, suggesting that there are yet ten righteous men within Israel—at least righteous enough to tear down an idol. Following the destruction of the altar, the people of Ophrah form a mob and appear at the house of Gideon's father, Joash, demanding that Gideon be brought out and executed. This scene is reminiscent of the mob in Sodom who come to Lot's door demanding that he deliver to them the strangers lodged at his house, or the mob in Gibeah who murder the Levite's concubine in Judg. 19. Joash is more effective than Lot or the Levite's host as a defender, telling the townspeople that they should allow Baal to fight his own battles. So on balance, the town of Ophrah looks to be less iniquitous than Sodom, though not by a lot. There are some righteous people here, but there are more who are not righteous. Joash is a defender of Gideon's mission, but he is also an idol worshiper who has been maintaining Baal worship in his home and in his town. And even his defense is flawed in that it suggests that YHWH and Baal can fight things out to discover who is the stronger god, as if these two beings are peers existing on the same playing field. In Joash we see how syncretistic the Israelite understanding of YHWH has become.

Joash renames his son Jerubbaal, one who contends with Baal. This is an interesting contrast with Jacob, who is renamed Israel, one who contends or struggles with God. Even if Gideon is resisting Baal, his new name tells us that Baal—not YHWH—is the one who defines the terms of Gideon's struggle. Gideon's two names reflect the duality of the story: Gideon cannot find his way to integration as a whole person before YHWH; Baal is always plucking at his sleeve, demanding attention, and leading him into wrong patterns of thought. By the story's end, Gideon is referred to only as Jerubbaal. Daniel Block says that in this conclusion to the story he "find[s] the real legacy of Gideon. His real name is Jerubbaal, and the god after whom he was named has taken up the challenge proposed by Joash (6:31–32) and, sad to say, has apparently successfully contended for himself and won."[3]

Putting Out a Fleece

While Gideon's call story is sometimes compared to the annunciation to Mary, it is even more common to compare the annunciation to the story of the fleece. For instance, the Briçonnet Hours, a late fifteenth-century prayer book, includes an illumination of Gideon praying over the fleece opposite an equally lavish illumination of Mary praying over the scriptures while the dove of the Holy Spirit descends to her. Both Gideon and Mary are accompanied by angels, but both are too focused on their prayers to pay attention to the angelic visitor.[4]

Such a comparison was especially prompted for early Christians by the image of dew, which was connected with fertility. This was not just fanciful. Throughout the Old Testament, dew is used as an image of God's renewing and life-giving presence. In Gen. 27, Isaac blesses Jacob by saying, "May God give you of the dew of heaven, and of the fatness of the earth, and plenty of grain and wine" (27:28), whereas the curse on Esau is "See, away from the fatness of the earth shall your home be, and away from the dew of heaven on high" (27:39). A similar understanding appears in Deut. 33:28, where Moses says, "So Israel lives in safety, untroubled is Jacob's abode in a land of grain and wine, where the heavens drop down dew." Psalm 110:3 says, "From the womb of the morning, like dew, your youth will come to you."

3. Daniel I. Block, "Will the Real Gideon Please Stand Up? Narrative Style and Intention in Judges 6–9," *Journal of the Evangelical Theological Society* 40, no. 3 (September 1997): 365.

4. Martha Wolf, ed., *Kings, Queens, and Courtiers: Art in Early Renaissance France* (New Haven: Yale University Press, 2011), 108–9. Catalogue of an exhibit by the same name organized by the Art Institute of Chicago and the Réunion des musées nationaux, Paris, shown at the Art Institute from February 27 to May 30, 2011.

And Ps. 133:3 likens the beauty of brothers living together in unity to "the dew of Hermon, which falls on the mountains of Zion. For there the Lord ordained his blessing, life forevermore." Isaiah makes the same connection between the dew and new life: "Your dead shall live, their corpses shall rise. O dwellers in the dust, awake and sing for joy! For your dew is a radiant dew, and the earth will give birth to those long dead" (26:19). The prophet Hosea reports that God says He will no longer be angry with Israel, but rather "I will be like the dew to Israel; he shall blossom like the lily, he shall strike root like the forests of Lebanon" (14:5). Similar imagery is found in 2 Sam. 1:21; Job 29:19; and Zech. 8:12. YHWH is explicitly credited with being the source of the dew in Job 38:28 and Prov. 3:20. In Exod. 16 the gift of manna that "rains" from heaven (16:4) is described as appearing with the dew: "In the morning there was a layer of dew around the camp. When the layer of dew lifted, there on the surface of the wilderness was a fine flaky substance, as fine as frost on the ground. . . . Moses said to them, 'It is the bread that the Lord has given you to eat'" (16:13–15). Numbers 11:9 also associates the coming of the bread from heaven with the dew. In Deut. 32:2, Moses associates his teaching about the Lord's goodness with the dew: "May my teaching drop like the rain, my speech condense like the dew." The prophet Micah likens the remnant people of Jacob to dew for the rest of the earth (5:7).

Given this pattern of meaning around the image of dew, Jewish compilers and early readers of the story about Gideon and the fleece would surely have interpreted the coming of dew as a symbol of the coming of blessing from God: the blessing of fruitfulness, the blessing of nourishment, and the blessing of divine teaching. Given this pattern of meaning, early Christians naturally associated the dew with the giving of the Spirit, who renews the face of the earth (Ps. 104:30) and who has already taken "possession" of Gideon in 6:34. This then makes the connection with Mary natural enough, since she was also possessed ("overshadowed," Luke 1:35) by the fertile, life-giving Spirit.

That is, the connection would be natural if Gideon had stopped with asking for only one sign—dew on the fleece. The fleece is clearly a symbol of the people of Israel, who are "the sheep of his [the Lord's] pasture" (Ps. 100:3).[5] When Gideon asks to see the fleece covered with dew, he seems to be asking for a sign that YHWH will bless His covenant people. But then he asks for a second sign: that the fleece might be dry and the ground around it wet with dew. I believe that any ancient Jewish reader of this text would have seen this as an obviously bad idea on Gideon's

5. The symbolism of YHWH as the shepherd of his people Israel is pervasive throughout the Old Testament.

part. It is like the moment in a fairy tale when a character who has been granted three wishes asks for a lot of money. Anyone who knows the genre knows that this character has made a bad move and is about to be in serious trouble. Gideon has just made an equivalently bad move: he has asked for a sign that signifies the removal of blessing from Israel and the giving of blessing to the surrounding nations. It is not surprising that astute exegetes in the early church such as Augustine saw the second fleece miracle as signifying the removal of blessing from Israel and the giving of blessing to the Gentiles.[6]

What is Gideon thinking? Of course the text does not tell us, but it would appear that Gideon is thinking like a Baal worshiper. He is using the symbol set of Baalism rather than the symbol set of the Bible. Baal is the storm god, who claims lordship over the dew. In fact, one of Baal's daughters was named "Dew."[7] Gideon wants to know that YHWH is stronger than Baal, particularly since Gideon has now been marked as one who is to "contend with Baal," and so he asks for a demonstration of power. The first demonstration strikes him as too easy, so he asks for a second—something that seems a little more difficult. Gideon's way of thinking continues to be bounded by the empirical and the technical. He does not understand YHWH as the transcendent Creator, and he does not understand the dew as a symbol of YHWH's blessing. He is no longer steeped in the language or tradition of Israel, and so he is deaf to the symbolic meaning of what he asks. He is simply looking for signs of technical prowess, wanting to know that he will be on the winning side in a battle between competing deities.

The irony, of course, is that Gideon gets exactly what he asks for. His story has two parts. In the first part, he is possessed by the Spirit of God and is used to bring signs of YHWH's life-giving kingdom to actuality. This is the part of the story that features in most children's Bible-story books. In the second part, the Spirit seems to leave him as he pursues a very different agenda. Gideon is no longer concerned with conquering the Midianites but rather with exacting vengeance against Israelites who were not sufficiently supportive of his efforts. Rather than being a blessing to Israel, he becomes a source of punishment and pain. Gideon's turn away from God ultimately leads to Israel's apostasy and subsequent oppression under Abimelech and then under the Ammonites and the Philistines.[8] So

6. Gunn 2005: 96. Gunn, of course, dismisses Augustine's interpretation as "relentlessly chauvinistic." But Augustine understands the symbol set of Israel.

7. Robert B. Chisholm, "Yahweh versus the Canaanite Gods: Polemic in Judges and 1 Samuel 1–7," *Bibliotheca Sacra* 164 (April–June 2007): 172.

8. In a lecture on Judges, James Jordan suggests a more positive reading of the two fleece miracles, arguing that whereas the first fleece signifies God's blessing on Israel, the second fleece signifies the

within the story the two fleece signs come to pass: there is a time during which God blesses the people of Israel, followed by a time during which the blessing is taken away. Taking a longer view, the whole book of Judges is in part a prophetic statement about the ultimate fate of the Northern Kingdom, to which Gideon's tribe of Manasseh belongs. This is seen already in the first chapter when Judah is contrasted favorably with Joseph. The blessing of God will indeed depart from the Northern Kingdom when they disappear into Assyria to be heard of no more (2 Kgs. 17).

The location of this scene with the fleece is important. Gideon's action takes place on the threshing floor—which is where he was meant to be at the beginning of the narrative, but he was hiding in the winepress instead. Throughout scripture, threshing floors are often locations for covenant renewal and for worship, probably because they were large, cleared spaces appropriate for gatherings (see, for instance, 2 Sam. 24:18–25). However, as a result, the threshing floor comes to have a symbolic meaning that gives additional resonance to Gideon's testing of God. The act of threshing precedes the act of grinding, which is a euphemism for sexual union. It is not accidental that Boaz agrees to marry Ruth on the threshing floor. YHWH has invited His people into a united, covenantal marriage with him, but—as we hear again and again—they are prostituting themselves with other gods. Gideon has already had a direct experience of YHWH, who has spoken to him face-to-face and received his offering. He has received the Spirit (6:34) in power and seen the results of this infusion in that Israelites from throughout the northern territory have come to follow him. This should be the moment in the story for Gideon to lead that band of Israelites in a time of commitment to and covenantal renewal with YHWH in preparation for their battle. Instead, by testing YHWH with the fleece, Gideon turns the threshing floor into a place of doubt and fear rather than a place of worship and covenantal union. Gideon does not turn to YHWH in genuine worship until 7:15.

Many Christians use the story of Gideon's fleece as a model for seeking God's will. This is clearly a wrong application of the story. For Gideon, any search for God's will is patently unnecessary. God's will is already known to Gideon, or would be if he were doing the job of remembering and meditating. YHWH has given

---

blessing going out from Israel into the world. Jordan thinks this happens in that Gideon's actions testify to YHWH before the Midianites. This is an attractive reading, but I think it fails to account for the two-part structure of Gideon's story and for the overarching prophetic theme of Judges, which points toward the ultimate fall of the Northern Kingdom. James B. Jordan, Old Testament Survey (Martin Bucer Institute for Biblical Studies, Fall 2009), lecture 4, "Numbers through Judges."

a clear command to his people to claim the land. YHWH has given a clear command to his people to worship no other gods. The things that YHWH is asking Gideon to do are not strange or outlandish, requiring validation. This is not like Abraham being asked to leave Ur, which is a more random sort of command that is not directly connected to God's moral will. This is certainly not like the command to sacrifice Isaac, which seems in contradiction to God's moral will. These commands to Gideon are consonant with God's moral will, so Gideon should have no difficulty in discerning that they are legitimate—if only he were aware of the law of the YHWH.

But Gideon is not really concerned with discovering God's will. He wants to know if he is going to win, if YHWH will in fact deliver Israel. That's a very different question. Gideon is only going to be obedient if obedience will lead to immediate success. YHWH is very patient with Gideon here, but already in the framing of this test we see the seeds of Gideon's downfall. Gideon is trying to short-circuit the process, laid out by Joshua, of finding courage in an awareness of YHWH's presence by meditating on the law. Gideon has a charismatic experience of God's presence and of the Holy Spirit's energy, but he does not allow this to be written on his heart, and so he fails to live in conformity with God's law/logos. He seeks miraculous signs rather than doing the normal work of a covenantal partner and thinking about the law, or will, or logos/design of YHWH. An awareness of YHWH's presence cannot be lasting if it is grounded only in experience; it must be grounded in meditation on the law. By refusing to follow this process, Gideon guarantees that his ability to live a life of obedience and courage will be fleeting.

The Glory Cloud

YHWH begins to work on Gideon's obsession with power in the next section of the story, insisting that the number of soldiers in his army be reduced to such a point that there can be no question of a purely military victory. Instead, this will be a battle fought under YHWH's own leadership, as an act of worship. The text does not tell us whether the battle plan—involving no weapons other than torches and trumpets—was given to Gideon by YHWH or whether Gideon devised this plan himself. Given what we know about Gideon, it seems likely that he received instruction. However, if he did devise the plan, he was certainly informed in that design by the story of other battles Israel had fought, especially Israel's first battle with the Midianites back in the book of Numbers, the battle against the Egyptians at the Red Sea, and the battle to capture Jericho.

At the time of the crossing of the Red Sea, the battle against the Egyptians was fought entirely by YHWH. Moses said to them, "Do not be afraid, stand firm, and see the deliverance that the LORD will accomplish for you today; for the Egyptians whom you see today you shall never see again. The LORD will fight for you, and you have only to keep still" (Exod. 14:13–14). The role of the people of Israel was to walk where they were told to walk, to witness to YHWH's work, and to sing in worship when it was all over. YHWH protected the Israelites from the Egyptians with the glory cloud that stood between the two groups. "The cloud was there with the darkness, and it lit up the night" (Exod. 14:20). Similarly here, it is YHWH who does the fighting, whereas the role of the army of Israel is to enact the glory cloud, that is, the signs of YHWH's presence in glory and power. This is the function of the trumpets and the torches, to surround the Midianites with the sudden and terrifying glory of YHWH, as if the cloud of His glory were settling over their camp.

When the Midianites first appear in the book of Genesis, they are seen as relatives of the people of Israel, since they are also children of Abraham, through his wife Keturah (Gen. 25:1–4). It was a band of Midianite traders who bought Joseph from his brothers and sold him into slavery in Egypt (Gen. 37:28). When Moses fled Egypt, he went to Midian, where he married the daughter of a Midianite priest (Exod. 2). Hobab the Midianite came with the people of Israel on their trek through the wilderness (Num. 10). But by the time we come to Num. 22, the people of Midian are in league with the Moabites against the people of Israel. They attempt to pay Balaam to curse the Israelites, without success, so they instead adopt a campaign of religious subversion, promoting intermarriage between their own people and the people of Israel and attempting to interest the Israelites in Baal worship. This plan works well—so well that YHWH is driven to punish the people of Israel with a plague. In Num. 25, Phinehas the priest—still a young man, son of Eleazar and grandson of Aaron—kills Zimri, an Israelite man, and Cozbi, his Midianite wife, in order to turn back this judgment of YHWH from the people of Israel. YHWH's anger is appeased; however, he commands the people of Israel to "harass the Midianites, and defeat them" in order to pay them back for their trickery in enticing Israelites to worship Baal. The war against Midian is described in Num. 31. What is striking about that battle is that Phinehas goes to war with the army, carrying with him vessels from the sanctuary and trumpets to sound the alarm. At the end of the book of Judges we discover that Phinehas is high priest at the tabernacle at Bethel, meaning that when Gideon sets up a new center of worship at the end of chapter 8, he is setting himself up as an alternative Phinehas. It may be that his battle strategy inspired him to a further, and inappropriate, emulation of Phinehas as worship leader.[9]

When Joshua was preparing to go to battle against Jericho, he encountered the mysterious "commander of the army of the LORD" (Josh. 5:13–15)—a figure who is clearly YHWH himself, given that Joshua is commanded to remove his sandals since he is standing on holy ground. Christians have generally taken this figure to be a preincarnate manifestation of the Second Person of the Trinity, as is the Angel of the LORD, and he is the same person who appeared to Gideon before his battle. Joshua was commanded to fight against Jericho by processing behind the priests, who would be carrying the ark and blowing the ram's horn trumpet. On the final day of their procession, the people were to shout in praise to the Lord, who had given them the city. Here the act of war is an act of worship, in which the battle itself is fought by YHWH. By the time the army begins to fight, the battle is already won; they collect what YHWH has already conquered. This is very much the model for Gideon's battle.

So although the strategy of this battle makes little sense from a military perspective, it makes very good sense from a perspective of biblical history. This is how YHWH has led his people into battle in the past. What is interesting in the Gideon story is the absence of any official priestly presence. Barak was the reluctant Levitical presence in Deborah's war against Jabin, and by the end of the book we have two stories about Levites who are not simply reluctant but actively apostate. The absence of Levitical leadership in this battle is a step on that trajectory.

In the event, the battle that Gideon fights against the Midianites requires him to be a worshiping spectator, testifying to YHWH's presence and standing in the glory cloud of YHWH replicated by the torches and trumpets of his army, much as the people of Israel stood in the light of the glory cloud and witnessed YHWH's victory over Pharaoh's army at the crossing of the Red Sea. Gideon has been named a man of valor, but the way he is called to lead the army gives him no opportunity to exercise military ability.

An Unexpected Conclusion

The situation with the Ephraimites shows a disintegration since the Ehud story, in which they were pivotal in the work of capturing the fords of the Jordan.

---

9. Whether this is the same Phinehas or a descendent of Phinehas is not particularly important for the significance of his presence in this book.

It further shows a disintegration since Deborah's story, in which not all the tribes participated, but no one became actively obstreperous. Things will, of course, get far worse. By the time of Jephthah (12:1–6), the Ephraimites will not be as easily appeased as they are here by Gideon. "The progression from full participation to a lesser role and, finally, in the Jephthah narrative to full enmity follows the pattern of going from good to bad through the Book of Judges" (Matthews 2004: 94).

The attention to Ephraim as a problem tribe throughout the narrative is no doubt connected with the role that this tribe will have in the fracturing of the people of Israel into two kingdoms. The Ephraimite Jeroboam rebelled against Solomon and received a prophecy from the Lord that he would become king over ten of the twelve tribes, as a punishment for Israel's idolatry (1 Kgs. 11:26–40). When Solomon's son Rehoboam proved to be an inept ruler, Jeroboam established a northern kingdom, drawing to him people who said, "What share do we have in David? We have no inheritance in the son of Jesse" (1 Kgs. 12:16). Ultimately, of course, the sin of the Northern Kingdom is even more offensive to YHWH than the sin of Judah, and so He hands them over to the Assyrians. The stories of Ephraim in the book of Judges are a prophetic denunciation of the Northern Kingdom.

Most commentators on this interchange between Gideon and the Ephraimites are impressed by Gideon's diplomacy. However, consider what it is that Gideon says: "What have I done now in comparison with you? Is not the gleaning of the grapes of Ephraim better than the vintage of Abiezer?" (8:2). Gideon says that his victory over the Midianites, the victory at which he was a worshiping spectator while YHWH drove the army of Midian to fight among themselves, is not as impressive as Ephraim's far more conventional victory over the fleeing Midianite army. In other words, Gideon discounts the value of a battle fought as an act of worship in the direct and awesome presence of YHWH, suggesting that military prowess is more impressive. His subsequent actions give evidence that this is not just a piece of diplomatic posturing; this is what Gideon really believes. He spends the rest of chapter 8 swaggering about the neighborhood as a military bully. Back at the beginning of the story, Gideon built an altar to YHWH that he called "The LORD is peace" (6:24). And yet Gideon's actions in this last section of the story are all about gratuitous violence against his own people.

The paradigm laid out in chapter 2 of Judges leads us to believe that the story is nearly over when we arrive at 8:4. At this point we should move on to a discussion of how long the land had rest. But this is not what happens. G. E. Moore observes:

In 7:24f. the Midianites are intercepted in their flight by the Ephraimites, and the two chiefs, Oreb and Zeeb, killed. When Gideon, who is in pursuit of them, comes up, the Ephraimites inveigh violently against him because they were not summoned at the beginning, and are only appeased by his flattering comparison of their achievement with his own. . . . The quarrel itself, and especially Gideon's reply, show that the pursuit was over; vintage and gleaning were both complete. In 8:4–21, on the contrary, we find Gideon and his three hundred men following the retreating marauders across the Jordan, with such uncertain prospect of success that the townsmen of Succoth and Penuel scoffingly refuse to furnish the food he needs for his hungry men.[10]

Moore therefore concludes that the passage in 8:4–21 comes from another source and is not compatible with the earlier narrative. This is a conclusion that simply sidesteps the brilliant organizational power of the final author/editor of this book. Nothing in it is random, and the placing of this story here where it disrupts the expected pattern is surely intentional. Moore is quite right to notice the difference in tone between these two sections. Gideon had been responding to YHWH's call; in 8:4–21 he is pursuing a personal vendetta. On the other hand, Moore muses, seeming to change sides, "That Gideon had a wrong of his own to avenge is not incompatible with the representation that he was called of God to deliver Israel from the scourge; the sharp severing of natural and religious motives is more in the manner of the modern critic than of the ancient story-teller."[11] Not really. Gideon's problem is that his motives have never been purely religious, never been purely about obedience to YHWH, but have always been mixed with desires for self-advancement and personal vengeance. Succoth and Penuel are punished for showing disrespect to Gideon, not to YHWH. Schneider notes, "These verses reveal a side of Gideon not yet emphasized; that of a thin-skinned ruler seeking revenge" (2000: 123). The turn in the story is toward disorder and misdirection. Gideon breaks down the tower of Penuel, killing the men of the city; this will escalate with Abimelech, who burns down a tower and kills all the people of the city.

In the interchange between Gideon and the two kings, Zebah and Zalmunna, we find another of Sternberg's intentional "gaps" (1985: 236). The delay in giving us this information—that Gideon has a personal vendetta to fulfill in his war with Midian—is intentional. This is a technique that we see elsewhere in the book, such as when we do not discover the name of the Levite who serves first

10. George Foot Moore, *A Critical and Exegetical Commentary on Judges*, International Critical Commentary (Edinburgh: T&T Clark; New York: Scribner's, 1895), 174.
11. Moore, *Judges*, 176.

Micah and then the Danites until the very end of chapter 18. Schneider points out that the only battle at Tabor thus far was during the story of Deborah, and in that instance the Midianites (Kenites) were fighting on the side of the children of Israel, suggesting that Gideon's brothers were fighting on the Canaanite side. This may help to explain why Gideon refers to them not as sons of Joash but as his *mother's* sons. Since the great sin of Israel has been intermarriage that then leads to the worship of Canaanite gods, and since Joash has clearly fallen into the consequent portion of that sin, it makes sense to postulate that he had also fallen into the sin of intermarriage, such that Gideon's mother was a Canaanite. If Zebah and Zalmunna are being at all serious in saying that Gideon's brothers looked like kings (and they may not be serious; they may either be flattering or taunting), Schneider suggests that perhaps Gideon's mother was even a Canaanite princess (2000: 124–25). Sternberg says of this same exchange in verses 18–19, "The information sprung by this exchange is so unforeseen as to alter our understanding of the whole sequence of events that leads up to it" (1985: 311). He points out that at the beginning of the chapter, when Gideon decided to cross the Jordan in pursuit of the Midianites, there was no explanation of this decision. We as readers naturally fill in the gap, telling ourselves that Gideon is simply trying "to complete his victory," but now it turns out that the reason is quite other.

> Hence the surprise now occasioned by the surfacing of the familial motive for the pursuit—the slaughter of Gideon's brothers, who have so far played no role in the narrative. Gideon, it turns out, has not even entertained any hope of rescuing those brothers. "Where are the men you *slew* at Tabor?" he asks his royal captives.... The very incoherence of the question betrays the questioner's raging pain and indicates vengeance as the mainspring of his actions all along.
>
> The switch from a national to a private motivation not only reopens and closes anew a gap that has long appeared settled. It also impels us to review the intervening developments.... The manipulation of antecedents thus launches a surprise chain reaction from the point of retrospective (dis)closure, whereby Gideon's personality emerges as more complex and less admirable than before. (Sternberg 1985: 311–12)

It is in the encounter with Zebah and Zalmunna that Gideon attempts to make his son Jether into a warrior, already moving toward a dynastic understanding of his role. Jether's timidity reminds us of who Gideon was at the beginning of the story: frightened and hiding. Jether's presence also foreshadows the tragedy that is to come under Abimelech, for the timid Jether will be slain by his resentful and vengeful brother. Gideon is mixing concern with YHWH's honor and concern with his family's honor. The principle laid out by the lord of Bezek in chapter 1 will be seen in the subsequent narrative, when the actions of Gideon bear fruit by coming back on his own head. Gideon's vengeful spirit and obsession with family honor at the expense of obedience to YHWH will also animate his son Abimelech, leading to the eradication of all but one of Gideon's sons.

Who Is the King?

The story culminates with the question of kingship—and indeed this may be seen as the theme of the entire book of Judges.

> When you have come into the land that the LORD your God is giving you, and have taken possession of it and settled in it, and you say, "I will set a king over me, like all the nations that are around me," you may indeed set over you a king whom the LORD your God will choose. One of your own community you may set as king over you; you are not permitted to put a foreigner over you, who is not of your own community. Even so, he must not acquire many horses for himself, or return the people to Egypt in order to acquire more horses, since the LORD has said to you, "You must never return that way again." And he must not acquire many wives for himself, or else his heart will turn away; also silver and gold he must not acquire in great quantity for himself. When he has taken the throne of his kingdom, he shall have a copy of this law written for him in the presence of the levitical priests. It shall remain with him and he shall read in it all the days of his life, so that he may learn to fear the LORD his God, diligently observing all the words of this law and these statues, neither exalting himself above other members of the community nor turning aside from the commandment, either to the right or to the left, so that he and his descendants may reign long over his kingdom in Israel. (Deut. 17:14–20)

Gideon refuses to be made king because he says that only YHWH is king. And yet Gideon takes to himself the trappings of kingship—specifically the trappings that were forbidden in Deuteronomy. He takes the royal crests for the horses of the Midian kings for himself, he marries many wives, and he collects gold as tribute. He certainly does not meditate on the law, as is evident from his violation of the law in the creation of an ephod and the setting up of a self-contained religious center. He names his son Abimelech, which is to say, "my father is king." He is like the crazed Denethor, steward of Minas Tirith in Tolkien's *The Return of the King*, who gives lip service to an absent king while taking royal power to himself. This is the heart of Israel's problem: they have sworn fealty to YHWH in a suzerain covenant, a covenant that does not tolerate any other authority. And yet they are forever claiming the authority that should be YHWH's for themselves or giving it to unworthy claimants.

Given the pro-Judah stance of the book of Judges, it might seem that the absence of a king in this book is meant to point forward to the coming of David as the anointed king, who will fill the leadership void evident in Judges. The later chapters especially suggest that moral relativism was a result of the absence of a king (18:1; 21:25). However, that claim could also be understood to refer to the absence of YHWH's kingship, which had by then been rejected by the people of Israel. In the subsequent book of 1 Samuel, the last judge, Samuel himself, teaches that YHWH's will for His people was the pattern of judges, not human kings (1 Sam. 8; 12), picturing "the kingship as a rejection of God's rule which was only tolerated by God (12.12f)."[12] The office of judge is the office established by God as a way of accommodating the practical demands of organizing His people without abrogating His own authority as the only king and suzerain.

The claim that YHWH Himself is King over His people is deeply rooted in the beginnings of the covenant community. Brevard Childs notes, "First, the kingship of God is presented by the editors of the book of Judges, both in the Gideon story (8.22ff.) and in Jotham's fable (9.7ff.) as long preceding the establishment of Israel's monarchy, and being an eternal kingship.... Secondly, the concept of YHWH's kingship was retrojected back into the Mosaic period at certain crucial points within the tradition (Ex. 15.18; 19.6; Deut. 17.14ff.) in such a way as to make a theological witness to the selfsame kingly sovereignty of God at work from the beginnings of Israel's history."[13] The tension between the prophetic claim that YHWH is King and the establishment of the monarchy is ultimately resolved with the ascension and session of Jesus, who in His human nature is the heir of the Davidic kingship and in His divine nature continues the claim of divine kingship.

There is never any suggestion in the Old Testament of "an eschatological hope in terms of a return to the office of the judge. Rather, the messianic hope of a righteous ruler became firmly attached to the office of the king, of course, as a Davidic figure."[14] We do find the promise, enshrined in the creed, that Jesus will

12. Brevard S. Childs, *Biblical Theology of Old and New Testaments: Theological Reflection on the Christian Bible* (Minneapolis: Fortress, 1993), 150.
13. Childs, *Biblical Theology*, 634.
14. Childs, *Biblical Theology*, 150–51.

return *to judge* the quick and the dead. In the new creation, however, no such accommodation will be necessary, for Jesus will be on the throne as King of kings. Desire for another king than YHWH is linked to the desire for another god—both are expressions of disloyalty, violations of the suzerain covenant by which each Israelite is related to YHWH.

G. Henton Davies suggests that when Gideon refuses the kingship, "his words are to be understood as an acceptance couched in the form of a pious refusal with the motive of expressing piety and of gaining favour with his would-be subjects." Davies furthermore asserts that "his words conceal a determination to exercise a personal and hereditary kingship within Yahweh's kingship, and that, conversely, Yahweh's kingship does not preclude Gideon's kingship."[15] He argues that Gideon is really saying that when he becomes the king, he won't really be the one ruling, since YHWH will be the true ruler. Davies points to other instances of such indirect communication in scripture, but his primary evidence is that Gideon appears to have become a ruler. Gideon's sons talk about their father as a king, and they contest with each other who is to follow him as king. Jotham tells a parable about being a king, and there is no criticism in the parable about kingship. Earlier, in 8:18, Gideon was treated as a king by the kings of Midian. Finally, Davies says:

> Following Gideon's reply he makes a request for the earrings of their spoil (viii 24). It would be strange if Gideon made a request on top of a refusal, for his request is willingly conceded. Is it not better to suppose that Gideon's reply was a veiled acceptance and that the request for the earrings that followed was his first request as king? This links the two narratives. With the gold Gideon makes an ephod. Why did Gideon want an ephod? I suggest that Gideon's ephod was the same kind of ephod as appears in the stories of Saul's kingship, the ephod worn by Ahijah in Saul's presence at Gibeah (1 Sam. xiv 3 and 18 if LXX is correct against M.T.); the ephod brought by Abiathar to David (xxiii 6), and subsequently used by David for oracular purposes (xxiii 9, xxx 7). Gideon like Saul and David sought to show his royal position by possession of an ephod.[16]

In contrast to Davies's interpretation, Gerald Gerbrandt argues that the problem isn't Israel's desire to have a king but rather the desire to have a king *like the other nations*. He points out, "Israel . . . had various institutions which were parallel to those of the surrounding nations, but in each case the institution had been

15. G. Henton Davies, "Judges VIII 22–23," *VT* 13, fasc. 2 (April 1963): 154.
16. Davies, "Judges VIII 22–23," 157.

reinterpreted or adapted so as to fit into her understanding of Yahweh and his covenant with Israel."[17]

These are both interesting interpretations. Following Davies, it certainly seems that by the time of Abimelech everyone in the area understood Gideon to be a king, and so, yes, he had effectively taken the kingship while refusing it. Perhaps this was clear both to Gideon and to his army already as they were giving him their tribute of earrings; perhaps he started out with the claim of being only a judge and gradually accrued the trappings of kingship. In either case, however, I disagree with the contention that there is no condemnation of the assumption of kingship. Gideon may have been disingenuous in his claim that YHWH was the king of Israel, but the narrator is not. YHWH did not anoint Gideon king, and in claiming the kingship Gideon is falling prey to his Jerubbaal nature, behaving like a follower of Baal rather than a follower of YHWH. The folly of Gideon's kingship is made clear in the subsequent story of Abimelech.

Victor Matthews observes that Gideon's request for a gold earring from each of the Israelite soldiers will be more easily accepted if it is presented as a tribute to YHWH than if it is presented as a reward for Gideon. The rhetoric of refusing the kingship helps to make this request for booty more palatable. "The division of spoils after a battle was considered a sacred act by ancient Near Eastern armies. . . . Thus Gideon's request for a portion of the loot (golden earrings weighing 43 pounds) must be couched in such a way that it does not appear that he is infringing on their rightful share. They had freely offered him the kingship, and in refusing them he seems to be asking that they sacrifice a portion of the spoil as an offering to Yahweh, the divine warrior who had brought them the victory" (Matthews 2004: 97). The comparison with the making of the golden calf seems clear. There too the claim was that this was an act of worship, but in fact it was an act of idolatry.

Whether or not Gideon was immediately intent on setting himself up as king, he seems determined to set up a religious center to rival Shiloh, which is where the ark and tabernacle were located at this time. William Koopmans is not convinced that Gideon claimed the kingship, but he observes that Gideon certainly "led the people into temptation in the realm of the priest. Exodus 28–29 describes the priestly garments, including the ephod. These garments were to be part of the attire of the consecrated priests—of Aaron and his sons."[18] The creation of the ephod is

---

17. Gerald Eddie Gerbrandt, *Kingship according to the Deuteronomistic History*, SBL Dissertation Series 87 (Atlanta: Scholars Press, 1986), 110.

18. William T. Koopmans, "Guile and Grief in Gideon's Gold: A Sermon on Judges 8:27," *Calvin Theological Journal* 37 (2002): 100.

Gideon's greatest sin, and it leads the people of Israel deeper into idolatry. This idolatry will be immediately evident in the story of Abimelech, who sacrifices his brothers to Baal. It will be yet more evident by the end of the book when the men of Benjamin are authorized by the other men of Israel to kidnap, rape, and force into marriage the young girls who are participating in proper worship at Shiloh. Gideon was ignorant of YHWH at the beginning of his narrative, and he has made no progress in knowledge since then. He leaves his people no better off as a result of his work.

8

ABIMELECH

9:1–10:2

Structure

In terms of the downward spiral of the book, Abimelech exhibits a major turn for the worse. The story begins with fratricide on a great scale, foreshadowing the civil war at the end of the book. There is nothing redemptive for the people of Israel in the story of Abimelech. Whereas Gideon's claim of kingship was ambiguous, Abimelech's claim is an overt, explicit defiance of YHWH's claim to be Israel's true king, a defiance that is made clear in that he becomes the source of Israel's oppression rather than the deliverer. Gideon already exhibited a turn in this direction; now Gideon's son turns all his violence against his own people. The minor judge Tola is described as one who "rose to deliver Israel," but the only oppressor mentioned from whom Israel needed deliverance at that time was Abimelech himself.

Abimelech's story touches briefly on the relationships between men and women in that he is killed by a woman dropping a millstone on his head. The connections between that event and the Deborah story have already been explored. Abimelech is more concerned with alienation from the land, as already discussed in chapter 1 in this volume. He is characterized by his half-brother Jotham as a bramble, the very emblem of the curse on Adam. Like his father, Abimelech uses fire and thorns to punish those he believes have been disloyal. The process of alienation specifically from the land of Canaan accelerates during Abimelech's time in power, for his loyalty is to Baal rather than YHWH and his energy is directed at undoing the promise of a holy land occupied by a holy people.

In the structure of the six major judges, Abimelech is folded into the story of Gideon, and this narrative is closely related, both thematically and stylistically, to that immediately prior story. In that Abimelech is Gideon's son, his story serves to complete the story of Gideon, showing the long-range consequences of Gideon's unfaithful actions in introducing idolatry at Ophrah and in marrying many wives, at least one of whom was a Canaanite.

Wolfgang Bluedorn has demonstrated that the Abimelech and Gideon narratives have many parallels. These parallels show Abimelech reversing any good that Gideon achieved and furthering any evil that Gideon initiated. The Gideon story is introduced with the by-now-familiar claim that Israel did evil in the eyes of YHWH (6:1); the Abimelech story is introduced with the idolatry of Gideon (8:27, 33–35). The Gideon story includes a prophetic reminder of the covenant with YHWH (6:8–10); the Abimelech story includes a statement of the new covenant between the children of Israel and Baal (8:33). Both stories include statements that the children of Israel have abandoned YHWH, who rescued them from the hand of their enemies (6:8–10; 8:34–35). Gideon reluctantly accepts YHWH's appointment as a military leader; Abimelech eagerly seeks out authority, soliciting the endorsement of Baal worshipers in Shechem. Gideon is appointed to tear down an altar to Baal, while Abimelech appoints himself to execute his brothers as an offering to Baal. Both actions provoke protest. Gideon is defended by his father, Joash, who tells the gathered mob that if Baal is a god, he should be able to defend himself and needs no defense from them. Abimelech is attacked by his brother Jotham with a parable about kingship. Bluedorn takes it that these two statements—Joash's statement about Baal and Jotham's parable about kingship—are the thematic statements of the two narratives. Gideon is clothed with YHWH's Spirit (6:34–35), whereas YHWH sends an evil spirit to stir up betrayal between Abimelech and his Baal-worshiping supporters in Shechem (8:23). Both Gideon and Abimelech delay in encountering their enemies; both divide their force into three companies when they at last go into battle. Gideon is victorious, but Abimelech is defeated (Bluedorn 2001: 184–85).

Other connections show similarity—particularly between the second half of the Gideon story, when Gideon enters into a campaign of personal vengeance in which the people of Israel are the primary victims. Abimelech is a similar sort of ruler. His pursuit of Gaal, like Gideon's pursuit of Zebah and Zalmunna, leads to the destruction of people he should be protecting. The similarity is underscored by the comparison of the tower of Penuel that Gideon breaks down in 8:17 while slaughtering the men of the city and the tower of Shechem that Abimelech burns down in 9:48–49, thereby killing all the men and women who had taken refuge there.

In the great chiastic structure of the book in which Gideon is at the center, Abimelech is understood as a story separate from Gideon's story and set parallel to the Deborah story. Both the story of Deborah and the story of Abimelech include a lengthy poetic prophecy; both have three episodes. The Abimelech narrative is unique among the seven major stories of the book's center in that, within the paradigm set out in Judges 2, Abimelech takes the role not of the judge but of the oppressor into whose hand YHWH delivers His people. So Abimelech's primary counterpart in Judges 4 and 5 is not Deborah but Sisera. In both cases, God's agency is negative. In 4:15 "the LORD threw Sisera and all his chariots and all his army into a panic," whereas in 9:23 "God sent an evil spirit between Abimelech and the lords of Shechem." And, of course, both Sisera and Abimelech are killed by women who deliver a blow to the head using a domestic instrument—a parallel already discussed in the Deborah chapter. In both cases, being killed by a woman is a sign of coming under YHWH's direct judgment, but the change is that now the oppressor has come from inside Israel, being the son of Gideon.

Deborah's leadership serves as a foil for Abimelech's ambition. Like Deborah, Abimelech has a second-in-command, Zebul. Barak was initially skeptical of Deborah's authority, even though her authority came from YHWH himself; Zebul is very loyal to Abimelech, even though Abimelech's authority is illegitimate. Following Deborah leads Barak into a place of victory, whereas following Abimelech leads Zebul to a place of devastation. Deborah's enemies perish in water sent by YHWH. Abimelech's enemies perish in fire that he himself kindles. Like the fig tree in Jotham's story, Deborah is a source of sweetness. She does not assert herself but is drawn into a place of military leadership. Abimelech is the bramble that hurts and destroys those who choose it.

The Apple Doesn't Fall Far from the Tree

There is some debate about the meaning of Abimelech's name, debate that is tied to how one understands Gideon's behavior. Does the name My-Father-Is-King refer to Gideon, or is it a pious name that refers to YHWH? Whatever Gideon's intentions may have been, Abimelech clearly chooses the first meaning of his name, since he claims royal privilege on the basis of being the son of Gideon, not on the basis of being in covenant with YHWH. The ambiguity serves to underline the theme of the Abimelech narrative, which is again the question of whether YHWH's kingship will be recognized by Israel and what will be the consequences if it is not. Similarly, Gideon's other name, Jerubbaal, underscored the theme of the Gideon narrative as the contender with Baal (Bluedorn 2001: 193).

Abimelech is the son of Gideon's concubine. The distinction between a concubine and a wife is not always clear, but the primary difference seems to be that a concubine did not receive a dowry from her father (Matthews 2004: 103). Here we see, though just in passing, the first of a string of women whose fathers have not contributed to their flourishing, or—perhaps better—whose lack of flourishing can be traced at least in part to the lack of care they received from their fathers. The contrast, of course, is with Caleb back in chapter 1, who not only dowered his daughter but who then increased her dowry when it emerged that she had not been given the water necessary for life. Children of a concubine did not have the same legal rights as the children of a wife. They could share in the inheritance only if their father specifically named them as his heirs. Apparently, Gideon had not taken this action toward Abimelech, making Gideon the first of a series of fathers in the book of Judges who fail to contribute to a child's flourishing.

The location of this story of Abimelech's crowning is especially significant because it was at the oak of Shechem that Joshua had renewed the covenant with Israel in Josh. 24:25–26. Here, in the location of covenant renewal, where Joshua had placed a memorial stone and inscribed the law, there is now an idolatrous sanctuary whose income is used to buy mercenary support, and here in this same location a covenant-breaker who has murdered his own brothers is named king over Israel. YHWH's exclusive claims to be Israel's suzerain are violated in the very place where they had been confirmed. Abram had also built an altar at Shechem (Gen. 12:6–7), and it was at Shechem that the sons of Jacob avenged the rape of their sister Dinah by killing the Canaanite inhabitants (Gen. 34:2–26). No such spirit of chivalrous valor resides in Shechem now. The setting thus makes graphically clear the need for the children of Israel to choose between two paths. Abimelech explicitly rejects the path of covenant renewal by taking the false god Baal-berith, or Baal of the Covenant, as his patron and staging his illicit crowning at the site of covenant renewal. Implicitly, therefore, he is choosing to follow the old model of Shechemite behavior, thereby linking himself both with the rapist Sisera from the Deborah story and with the Canaanites who raped Dinah, rather than with the sons of Jacob.

Notice that just as all of Gideon's brothers had been killed by the Midianites, now all of Gideon's sons (except Jotham) are killed by Abimelech. We expect Jotham then to follow in his father's footsteps as the great military savior, since he is also the youngest and sole surviving. But instead Abimelech is Gideon's true heir, setting himself up as king, fueling his kingship from the coffers of Baal-berith. This name, associated with Shechem, suggests a syncretistic religious ritual linking YHWH of the covenant (*berith*) with Baal. Naturally, Baal is not active in the Abimelech narrative in the way that YHWH is active for Gideon, because the narrator does not attribute active power to Baal. Instead, Baal's supporters are active on Abimelech's behalf (Bluedorn 2001: 186).

Note that Abimelech kills his brothers on a single stone and then is killed by a stone himself (Matthews 2004: 101). Mobley says, "Abimelech and the Stones is a morality tale about one, perhaps the central, moral quality or virtue of ancient Israelite society: fidelity to covenant. The emphasis in biblical scholarship on formal political covenants and the way such contracts were used to formulate theological worldviews tends to obscure the significance of covenant in everyday life. In societies without strong central political, legal, and religious institutions, the guards against chaos were faiths made good, loyalties repaid, and promises kept" (2005: 149). Fidelity to covenant is a moral marker. In his prophecy against the people of Shechem, Jotham thus challenges them to self-examination. "If you acted in good faith and honor . . . ," he says (Judg. 9:16), terms used also in the covenant renewal ceremony of Josh. 24:14.

The retribution theme of this narrative is summarized in the chiastic structure of 9:56–57.[1] We have already discussed this concept of retribution, which is not about God meting out punishment but rather about the generative nature of our actions, such that when we do evil, evil is produced and will eventually find its way back to us, whereas when we do good, goodness is produced and will eventually find its way back to us. We are free agents in this process, and yet God controls the entire causal matrix of the process. This is seen earlier in the Abimelech story, in 9:23–24, when we read that God sent an evil spirit between Abimelech and the men of Shechem. This is a way of describing God's providential involvement in our free actions.

In thinking of the retributive nature of this story, Tom Boogaart suggests that the particular evil of Abimelech and the men of Shechem who assist him can be identified by looking at the consequences that return to them. Boogaart's

---

1. Thomas A. Boogaart, "Stone for Stone: Retribution in the Story of Abimelech and Shechem," *JSOT* 32 (1985): 49.

conclusion is that the great evil of which they are guilty is fratricide, since the consequence is that, after having identified each other as "brothers," they then kill one another.

> Abimelech, his hand strengthened by the men of Shechem, killed his brothers, the sons of Jerubbaal. In the opening episode of the story, where the narrator describes the nature of Abimelech's relationship with the men of Shechem, Abimelech addresses the Shechemites [claiming to be their "bone and flesh"]. Moved by this speech, the men of Shechem respond: "He is our brother" (9.3). . . . Yet what happens to these brothers after God sends an evil spirit between them? In the closing episodes of the story, the narrator tells how Abimelech killed the men of the city of Shechem (9.42–45) and burned the people of Migdal-Shechem (9.46–49).[2]

Abimelech's killing of his brothers, the other sons of Gideon, naturally comes back to harm him in a way that fits his crime. He kills his brothers and is killed by those whom he has chosen as substitute brothers. Further, Abimelech's encounter with Gaal mirrors Gaal's own earlier encounter with the men of Shechem. Boogaart summarizes:

> Both the account of Abimelech's encounter with the Shechemites (9.1–6) and that of Gaal's encounter with them (9.25–41) have the following incidents in common:
>
> 1. a man comes to Shechem (9.1a; 9.26a)
> 2. the man is accompanied by his brothers/kinsmen (9.1b–3a; 9.26a)
> 3. the man conspires against the absent ruler of Shechem with a speech delivered at a gathering (9.2–3a; 9.28–29)
> 4. the speech emphasizes that the ties of the conspirator to Shechem are closer than those of the ruler (9.2b; 9.28)
> 5. the Shechemites put their trust in the conspirator (9.3b; 9.26b)
> 6. the conspirator encounters the ruler (9.5; 9.30–42).
>
> It is clear that the account of Abimelech's conspiracy and that of Gaal's, while by no means identical, are structured in the same way.[3]

So Boogaart points out that the episode with Gaal is not an odd interpolation but an episode that contributes to the central theme of the narrative: there is a moral order to the world such that those who do evil have evil done to them, and the evil we receive is typically shaped by the evil we have initiated.

2. Boogaart, "Stone for Stone," 49.
3. Boogaart, "Stone for Stone," 49.

Regarding Abimelech, just as Shechem had conspired with him against its rightful rulers, the house of Jerubbaal, so Shechem later conspired with Gaal against him; just as Abimelech had emphasized his close ties with the men of Shechem at the expense of the sons of Jerubbaal, so Gaal emphasized his close ties with Shechem at the expense of Abimelech. Regarding the men of Shechem: just as they had responded to Abimelech and had revolted against the house of Jerubbaal, a revolt which they carried to a successful conclusion, so they responded to Gaal and revolted against Abimelech. Their second revolt, however, proved to be their downfall, setting events in motion that brought about not only the death of Abimelech, but their own as well.[4]

Finally, there is the detail of the stones. Abimelech put his brothers to death "on one stone" (9:5), sacrificing them to Baal, probably by beheading. He is himself put to death by a stone dropped on his head (9:53).

The structure of the Abimelech narrative underscores these themes. David Dorsey (1999: 111) suggests this structure:

a   **introduction**: Israel's sin (8:33–35)
   - anticipates Israel's sin against Gideon's family
b   **Gideon's seventy sons killed by Abimelech** (9:1–6)
   - setting: <u>town north of Shechem</u>
   - killing involves a <u>stone</u> (and presumably a sword)
   - <u>sons of Gideon killed</u> by fellow Israelites
c   **Jotham's curse upon Shechem and Abimelech** (9:7–21)
   - calls for <u>strife between Abimelech and Shechem</u>
   - prominence of <u>trees</u>
   - speaks from <u>top of the mount</u> (Gerizim)
   - calling for <u>fire</u> to come out from Abimelech and consume lords of Shechem
   d   **TURNING POINT: God intervenes to help**; summary of Abimelech's rule (9:22–25)
c′ **Jotham's curse upon Shechem fulfilled**: Shechem destroyed by Abimelech (9:26–49)
   - <u>strife</u> breaks out <u>between Abimelech and Shechemites</u>
   - <u>trees</u> or <u>wood</u> used against Shechem
   - <u>tops of mountains</u>
   - <u>fire</u> used by Abimelech to destroy Shechemites

4. Boogaart, "Stone for Stone," 51.

b′ **Gideon's son, Abimelech, is killed** (9:50–55)
- setting: <u>town north of Shechem</u>
- killing involves a <u>stone</u> and a sword
- <u>son of Gideon killed</u> by fellow Israelite

a′ **conclusion** (9:56–57)
- looks back on how God punished Shechem and Abimelech for their sin against Gideon's family

The fulfillment of Jotham's curse allows us to think of Jotham as a prophetic figure. The seventeenth-century writer Joseph Hall observes, "There now lies the greatness of Abimelech: upon one stone had he slain his seventy brethren, and now a stone slays him: his head had stolen the crown of Israel, and now his head is smitten" (quoted in Gunn 2005: 124). As has been the case in previous stories, this narrative again centers on YHWH as the central actor, controlling the unfolding of events.

Empty Men

In *The Abolition of Man*, C. S. Lewis talks about men without chests, those who lack the virtue of magnanimity. Citing the twelfth-century theologian Alan of Lille, he explains that the head, or reason, is incapable of controlling the belly, or the appetites, without assistance. "The head rules the belly through the chest—the seat . . . of Magnanimity, of emotions organized by trained habit into stable sentiments. The Chest-Magnanimity-Sentiment—these are the indispensable liaison officers between cerebral man and visceral man. It may even be said that it is by this middle element that man is man: for by his intellect he is mere spirit and by his appetite mere animal."[5] Lewis's argument is that contemporary education no longer educates young people into habitual, stable sentiments that will make right behavior appealing. Instead, the realm of sentiment is dismissed as purely subjective and unimportant, with the result that we have produced a society of "men without chests," people who lack the proper emotional connection to what is honorable and true. "It is . . . defect of fertile and generous emotion that marks them out."[6] Those who lack this quality of the chest will be at the mercy of their appetites.

5. C. S. Lewis, *The Abolition of Man* (New York: Macmillan, 1955), 34.
6. Lewis, *Abolition of Man*, 35.

Abimelech is clearly the victim of a similarly defective education. He appears to have been taught *something* about the law, about YHWH, and about Israel's covenant with Him, for he could not otherwise make such an effective mockery of the religion of Israel. He certainly was not given any love for the law, nor reverence for YHWH, nor any loyalty to the covenant. The emotions that he expresses are bitterness, resentment, and disdain. Given that Gideon's own grasp on the law was so tenuous, it is not surprising that he failed to inculcate honorable sentiments toward the law in his son. Given that Gideon's childhood home was a place of Baal worship and that Gideon himself introduced a new form of idolatry to the people of Israel, it is not surprising that he failed to communicate any duty of reverence toward YHWH to his son. Given Gideon's own disregard for the Deuteronomic requirements of kingship, it is not surprising that he failed to communicate any sense of obligation toward the covenant to his son. Abimelech has been raised as a man without a chest, and that is precisely how he behaves. He surrounds himself with men described as "empty and reckless" (9:4).[7]

When measured against the rules for kingship from the book of Deuteronomy, Abimelech fails even more miserably than his father. First, there is the irony that for the people of Israel the king is to be "your brother," ironic in that Abimelech murders all but one of his brothers, even while basing his claim to kingship on his status as a brother to the people of Shechem. From the beginning of his story, his complete ineligibility to be a king is clear on account of fratricide. Second, YHWH is to do the choosing, but YHWH does not raise up Abimelech. Abimelech's call is purely self-generated. Similarly, Abimelech claims all credit for his military victories rather than recognizing YHWH as the savior of Israel. Finally, Abimelech shows complete disregard for both the law and the covenant. He lives either as if YHWH did not exist or perhaps as if YHWH is to be defied.

Jotham talks as though his father was a ruler to whom some honor and respect was due. His parable tells us that those who want to be king are precisely the ones who will be most destructive in the role. This is the great problem of human authority, the insurmountable problem of human kingship as opposed to divine kingship. The meaning of Jotham's parable is subject to debate. Is the point that good people must accept responsibility to rule, or else bad people will? Or is the point that it is folly to go looking for a king? Is the parable meant to underscore the superiority of the Davidic kingship over other kings, or is it meant to underscore the problematic nature of all kingship? Which way we read this parable

---

7. The translation is from Mobley (2005: 154), who traces this expression through many stories in the Old Testament.

will be connected to the way we read Gideon's call to the kingship in chapter 8. If indeed the point of the pivotal story in the book of Judges is that YHWH is King, as I have argued, then this parable is also undercutting the legitimacy of human kingship.

The midrash *Tanhuma B* reads the trees as symbols of Abimelech and three of the previous judges: "the olive is Othniel, the fig Deborah, the vine Gideon, and the bramble Abimelech" (quoted in Gunn 2005: 122). Since Jotham understands his father, Gideon, to have been a king or kinglike leader, it seems more likely that the three are Othniel, Deborah, and Ehud. But even if the correlations between specific trees and previous judges appear a bit forced, the story does deliberately remind us that thus far in the book all other leaders who could have become kings have declined to pursue that option. Even Gideon pretended that he was not taking kingly authority.

Jotham asks whether the people had acted with sincerity and integrity in making Abimelech their king, recalling Joshua's words at the end of the book of Joshua, when he told the people, "Now therefore revere the LORD, and serve him in sincerity and in faithfulness" (Josh. 24:14). Jotham thereby makes the people of Shechem complicit in Abimelech's later violence and misrule. Those who have chosen the king are responsible for their own fate when he turns on them.

The image of the bramble is continued in Abimelech's use of trees to fuel the fires he lights around the tower of Shechem. The bramble is a symbol of the wilderness and so of chaos, and (as mentioned in chapter 1 in this volume) it is also connected with the curse on Adam in Gen. 3. Abimelech further alienates the people of Israel from the land and becomes an agent of chaos in his kingship (Matthews 2004: 107). This chaos is not confined to the Abimelech story but continues throughout the rest of the book. Of course, judging a tree by its fruits suggests that Gideon was already a bramble, since he too produced violence against the people of Israel. Gideon's departure from YHWH's pattern for a judge led to violence against his fellow Israelites, which is intensified here with Abimelech and which continues to escalate in subsequent stories.

In his prophecy against the people of Shechem, Jotham takes an approach similar to that taken by his grandfather when the people of Ophrah wanted to kill Gideon. In affiliating himself with the Baal-worshiping people of Shechem and in sacrificing his YHWH-worshiping brothers to Baal, Abimelech has not just made a play for the kingship; he has also initiated a war of deities. This is now a conflict between Baal and YHWH. Jotham's prophecy summarizes the theme of this narrative. "If Abimelech and the Shechemites benefit from each other, they have acted correctly in replacing YHWH with Baalism and YHWH is not god; but if they will be destroyed by their Baalist leader and destroy him, they have acted wrongly in replacing YHWH with Baalism because YHWH is god. Hence the following episodes, which illustrate the failure of Abimelech's kingship, demonstrate the failure of Baalism, so that YHWH is god and Baal is not" (Bluedorn 2001: 230).

In fulfillment of this prophecy, YHWH sends an evil spirit to Abimelech (9:22). Here as elsewhere YHWH claims agency not only for the good but also for the bad. Abimelech does not acknowledge YHWH, but YHWH remains in charge, not just of those who worship Him but also of those who defy Him. The extreme action of sending an evil spirit is also found in the stories of Saul (1 Sam. 16:14) and of Ahab (1 Kgs. 22:19–23). This does not excuse Abimelech's subsequent actions any more than Pharaoh is excused because God hardened his heart, or Joseph's brothers are excused because God brought good from their decision to sell their brother into slavery, or Judas is excused because his betrayal of Jesus was prophesied. Speaking of Judas, Jesus says, "The Son of Man goes as it is written of him, but woe to that one by whom the Son of Man is betrayed! It would have been better for that one not to have been born" (Matt. 26:24). The same is true here.

Naturally it is not surprising that those who conquer treacherously find their supporters treacherous. This is the Adoni-bezek philosophy again: you reap what you sow—a viewpoint that makes sense even apart from YHWH's direct intervention in this case. Abimelech's wars are all civil wars; he does nothing to help the people of Israel get free from their oppressors, nor does he do anything toward the taking of the land. All his energy and considerable skill in warfare is turned against other Israelites. The fact that the duration of Abimelech's reign is given at the beginning of his story, rather than at the end, identifies him with the oppressors of Israel rather than with the deliverers (Bluedorn 2001: 231–32).

Near the middle of the Abimelech story, the people of Shechem are partying in the temple of their god, Baal-berith (v. 27), much as the Philistines will party in the temple of Dagon during the Samson story. Whereas Samson destroys the Philistines directly, the people of Israel are slaughtered by Abimelech as a result of their own treasonous plotting against him, which begins at their temple. Indeed, we have three stories in Judges that reflect the mass slaughter of civilians as well as soldiers: Gideon's tearing down of the tower of Penuel (8:17), Abimelech's burning of the tower of Shechem (9:49), and Samson's destruction of the temple of Dagon (16:29–30). Each instance leads to a greater, escalating level of destruction and death.

The story of Abimelech is referenced later in the midst of the David narrative. In 2 Sam. 11, Joab sends a messenger to David with these instructions: "When you have finished telling the king all the news about the fighting, then, if the king's anger rises, and if he says to you, 'Why did you go so near the city to fight? Did you not know that they would shoot from the wall? Who killed Abimelech son of Jerubbaal? Did not a woman throw an upper millstone on him from the wall, so that he died at Thebez? Why did you go so near the wall?' then you shall say, 'Your servant Uriah the Hittite is dead too'" (11:19–21). Clearly by this time Abimelech's death has become proverbial among the military of Israel, so that Joab anticipates being rebuked with Abimelech's example for his decision to send his troops near the wall of the city they are besieging. Arnold Erlich theorizes, "By mentioning the death of Abimelech at the hands of a woman, Joab seemingly reveals David's secret, as if saying, if Abimelech was killed by a woman, Uriah the Hittite died in a similar fashion because he too was killed by a woman: namely, Uriah died because of his wife."[8]

Of course the parallels are not complete, in that Uriah is not being judged by God in his death; rather, David is being judged. Hava Shalom-Guy notes, "The parallel constructed between King David and Abimelech sharpens the negative side of David's behavior; it also serves to effect an ironic lowering of David. True, Abimelech fell at the hands of a woman, but that was at war, whereas David 'fell' at the hands of a woman because he *did not* go to war. He brings about her husband's death in battle to hide his adultery in town."[9] Shalom-Guy goes on to suggest parallels between the death of Abimelech and the story of the siege of Abel in 2 Sam. 20, in which Joab is pursuing David's enemy Sheba. One of the women of the city summons Joab for a conference and agrees to kill Sheba for him to keep him from destroying Abel and killing many of the people inside.

> In Judges 9 the siege is of a "fortified tower," which Abimelech planned to set on fire (vv. 51–52). In 2 Samuel 20 the siege is of the town itself and involved the erection of a siege-mound that stood against the rampart, and Joab's troops were engaged in battering the wall (v. 15). Second, both protagonists—Abimelech and Joab—approach the besieged precinct. Abimelech reached "the door of the tower" (Judg. 9.52); Joab answered the call of the wise woman who asked to speak to him and "he approached her" (2 Sam. 20.16–17). Third, in both accounts a resourceful woman ends the siege by killing a single individual; and both use the root שלך to describe the killing.[10]

8. Arnold B. Ehrlich, *Mikra ki-feshuto: The Prose Books,* vol. 2, *Divre sofrim* (New York: Ktav, 1969), 212, cited in Hava Shalom-Guy, "Three-Way Intertextuality: Some Reflections of Abimelech's Death at Thebez in Biblical Narrative," *JSOT* 34, no. 4 (2010): 425.

9. Shalom-Guy, "Three-Way Intertextuality," 425–26. She references Sternberg (1985: 221–22).

10. Shalom-Guy, "Three-Way Intertextuality," 426.

Given the earlier passage in 2 Samuel, we know that Joab knows that it is dangerous to approach the wall of a besieged city and that a woman on the wall could well be the source of the danger. But he approaches her anyway, a calculated risk that pays off, leading to saving many lives and a peaceful resolution to his difficulties. Abimelech shows no such awareness of danger and no such desire to resolve the situation peacefully; instead, he is bent on escalation. Abimelech is also the only major character in the book of Judges who is not himself a judge. He is the model of illegitimate kingship, and the connection to Saul (also killed by his armor-bearer) is a not-so-subtle way of delegitimizing the Saulide dynasty as well.

Tola and Jair

Structurally, it's possible to understand Tola as the culmination of the Abimelech story. In this instance, YHWH has not sold his people into the hands of a foreign power but rather has sent an evil spirit on Abimelech, and the raising up of a judge who leads the land into a time of rest is thus the function of Tola, who follows Abimelech's three years of mayhem and violence with a judgeship of twenty-three years (10:1–2). There is no promise that the land rested during that time, however, and Tola is not described as having been raised up by God. He simply rose.

Unlike Tola, Jair is described in a way that suggests he had dynastic ambitions, showing another step of decline. Further, Jair is a contrast with Jephthah, who also has dynastic ambitions but dies without any children, having killed his only daughter (10:3–5). Again, YHWH is not credited with raising up Jair, marking a further decline in the nature of the judges.

9

JEPHTHAH

10:6–12:15

Structure

In the downward spiral of the book, the Jephthah story takes a sharp step down in terms of one of the key markers of decline: the treatment of women. So far we have seen Achsah as the paradigmatic woman, whose husband and father cooperate for her flourishing. We have seen Deborah, Jael, and the unnamed woman who drops a millstone on Abimelech all thriving, but no thanks to their husbands or fathers. Now we see a woman who is put to death by her father. It is a sobering measurement of just how dark the book of Judges is that this is not the lowest point in this spiral of mistreatment and suffering.

Notice that the process of disintegration does not show itself in any lessening of Israel's military potential, which is as great as ever. In fact, in terms of pure generalship, Jephthah is the equal of Othniel. But military power is not the standard by which YHWH judges a society.

> Some take pride in chariots, and some in horses,
> but our pride is in the name of the LORD our God.
> They will collapse and fall,
> but we shall rise and stand upright. (Ps. 20:7–8)

Jephthah's military expertise is an ambiguous good. Yet his military prowess and the fact that under his leadership an army of Israel can still drive out an oppressor is evidence that the people of Israel could be obeying YHWH in terms of taking the land, even now. They are kept from obedience by a lack of courage, a lack of faith, and a lack of will—not by a lack of ability. Their defeat is not inevitable.

The standard pattern set in chapter 2 is broken at the beginning of this story. The people fall into apostasy, so YHWH becomes angry and gives them over to an oppressor (in this case, both the Ammonites and the Philistines); they then cry out for help. So far, so familiar. However, this time when the people cry out to YHWH, rather than immediately raising up a judge, He threatens to cut them off entirely. "And the LORD said to the Israelites, 'Did I not deliver you from the Egyptians and from the Amorites, from the Ammonites and from the Philistines? The Sidonians also, and the Amalekites, and the Maonites, oppressed you; and you cried to me, and I delivered you out of their hand. Yet you have abandoned me and worshiped other gods; therefore I will deliver you no more. Go and cry to the gods whom you have chosen; let them deliver you in the time of your distress'" (10:11–14). The story of Jephthah can be understood as an illustration of what happens when God's people do in fact go and cry to pagan gods. Even though Jephthah consistently addresses YHWH, he treats YHWH according to the rules for pagan gods, and his troubles follow from that fact.

By this time in the book, we have seen deliverance after deliverance. YHWH's warning is that there comes a time when the door to grace is shut, when those who have turned away from Him must live with the consequences of their choices. In the New Testament, Jesus warns of a similar closing off of grace, a time after which He will say to those who come seeking Him, "I never knew you" (Matt. 7:21–23; 25:11–13). This is a distinct change in the pattern that has persisted up to this point in the book of Judges.

The people of Israel respond to this ultimatum by confessing their sin and rejecting the "foreign gods" they have been worshiping. It is a return to the repentance at Bochim at the beginning of chapter 2. In the NRSV we then read that YHWH "could no longer bear to see Israel suffer" (10:16), but we are *not* told that he raises up a judge. What does it mean that he "could no longer bear" their suffering? The verb is *qatsar*, which can be translated as "to be impatient, to become intolerant, to be tired of waiting."[1] It is hard to see why this should be translated as meaning that YHWH "could no longer bear to see Israel suffer,"

---

1. Jeremy Thompson, *Bible Sense Lexicon: Dataset Documentation* (Bellingham, WA: Faithlife, 2015).

since He does not give in to the people of Israel. He does not raise up a judge. Webb, Frolov, and others agree on translating this expression as YHWH "became exasperated with the misery of Israel" (Webb 2012: 301; see also Frolov 2013: 209). Of course, exasperation is just as analogical a description of YHWH as is sympathy, but in this case it is a more comprehensible analogy since no deliverance is forthcoming. Webb explains that the verses immediately preceding this one tell us YHWH is no longer impressed by the putting away of idols, since He has seen this many times before (305–6). He has announced that He will not relent; it would thus be very odd if in the next sentence He did relent. Again, this refusal to relent is a significant departure from the previous pattern.

Also departing from the previous pattern, the story of Jephthah's call does not involve any divine intervention. Given YHWH's silence, the people of Gilead take it upon themselves to find a deliverer. YHWH's validation of Jephthah is delayed and at best indirect. It appears that the threat to leave Israel to the protection of their false gods is to some extent being carried out in this story. The people call Jephthah out of Aram to save them, and he brings with him an Aramean understanding of the moral law, divine power, and right worship, with disastrous consequences. He interacts with YHWH as if He is Chemosh, the god of the Arameans, offering the sort of sacrifice that Chemosh would have valued.

In terms of both the series of major judges and the great chiasm, Jephthah's story is placed opposite the story of Ehud. Ehud is a warrior in Israel, one of the elite Benjaminite warriors, chosen to represent his people before a foreign king. Jephthah is also chosen by his people because of his warrior status. In this respect, they appear to be equals. Ehud fought against Moab; Jephthah is fighting Ammon—two nations founded by brothers, the sons of Lot, born of his incestuous relations with his daughters after the destruction of Sodom. Again, they are equals, fighting equal enemies. Both Jephthah and Ehud have diplomatic interactions with a foreign king, and at this point they are not equal. Ehud knows and understands the message of the stones at Gilgal; he knows that he is obligated to conquer any foreign invader. Jephthah's knowledge of the history of Israel is less complete, and what he knows he does not seem to understand. He believes that a peaceful negotiation is an appropriate solution to this threat, either not knowing the command to take the land or not understanding that command as having any continuing relevance. Both Ehud and Jephthah also have dealings with the Ephraimites, and here again Jephthah does not benefit from the comparison. Whereas Ehud leads the Ephraimites into battle against the enemies of Israel, Jephthah fights against Ephraim, continuing the pattern of civil war established by Gideon.

But there is a more significant parallel. Ehud's slaying of Eglon is deliberately presented in sacrificial terms. Eglon is a "calf," and when he is slain, the uncleanness comes out of him, as it would have come out of an offering. Jephthah also offers a sacrifice; he sacrifices his daughter. Many Christian commentators and preachers want to believe that Jephthah's sacrifice consisted simply of dedicating his daughter to a lifetime of service at the tabernacle. The evidence for this is generally thought to be that the Israelites did not practice child sacrifice. But the point of the story is that things have degenerated so much that a judge in Israel does not know he is not supposed to sacrifice his daughter to appease YHWH. I consider that the parallel with Ehud's sacrifice of Eglon combined with the trajectory of death and destruction throughout the book effectively answers the question of whether Jephthah really killed his daughter. Yes, he did. And this sacrifice, unlike the sacrifice of Eglon, was not in harmony with YHWH's will. Ehud removed the uncleanness and shame from Israel, putting uncleanness and shame on Moab instead. But Jephthah takes the shame of Ammon (since child sacrifice is associated with the Ammonite god Chemosh) and brings it into Israel.

Barry Webb demonstrates an interesting structural parallel at the beginning of the story. He offers the following diagram:

Episode 1	Episode 2
The Israelites reject Yahweh.	The Gileadites reject Jephthah.
The Israelites find themselves in a predicament they can't deal with.	The Israelites find themselves in a predicament they can't deal with.
The Israelites seek help from Yahweh, the One they rejected.	The Gileadites seek help from Jephthah, the one they rejected.
Yahweh rebuffs their appeal.	Jephthah rebuffs their appeal.
The Israelites "repent" of their rejection of Yahweh.	The Gileadites "repent" of their rejection of Jephthah.

Source: Webb 2012: 313–14

Webb suggests that this parallel tells us just how insincere the Israelites' repentance before YHWH really is. The parallel tells us that the people of Israel are attempting to negotiate good terms from YHWH in just the same way that they are attempting to negotiate good terms from Jephthah. Neither YHWH nor Jephthah is fooled by this, but Jephthah is in a weaker position than YHWH. Not only is he a mere creature, but he also has no land, no home, and no position. He comes to terms with the people of Israel more quickly than does YHWH. But then, too, this is Jephthah's first such negotiation, whereas YHWH has been down this path many times already (Webb 2012: 314). The Israelites' true indifference to YHWH's authority is seen in that they do not attempt to seek out His will when trying to answer the question of who should lead them into battle. In this way, they contrast poorly with the people of Israel at the beginning of chapter 1, who did ask for such guidance.

Jephthah's story is structured in two main parts, the first centered on his diplomatic responses to the Ammonites, the second centered on his diplomatic responses to the Ephraimites. Dorsey (1999: 112) suggests this structure:

a   **introduction**: Israel's oppression and cry for help (10:6–16)
  • chronological note
b   **diplomacy in response to Ammonite threat** (10:17–11:28)
  • begins: Ammonites called to arms
  • Ammonites cross over to Gilead to fight (11:12)
  • why have you come against me to fight against my land? (11:12)
  • Jephthah first resorts to diplomacy, which fails
c   **Jephthah's vow** (11:29–31)
    d   **TURNING POINT: Yahweh gives victory** (11:32–33)
c′   **Jephthah's vow sadly fulfilled** (11:34–40)
b′   **diplomacy in response to Israelite threat; tragic civil war** (12:1–6)
  • begins: Ephraimites called to arms (12:1)
  • Ephraimites cross over to Gilead to fight
  • why have you come up against me today to fight against me? (12:3)
  • Jephthah first resorts to diplomacy, which fails
a′   **conclusion**: summary of Jephthah's rule; his death and burial (12:7)
  • chronological note

The disastrous oath is right at the center of the story. Serge Frolov points out that the grammar of the oath suggests that it has been shoehorned into the story at this point, that it does not appear to fit. Judges 11:29 describes Jephthah's journeys, ending with "he passed on to the Ammonites," and 11:32 follows naturally from that point, saying, "So Jephthah crossed over to the Ammonites to fight." The vow interrupts this natural flow, both rhetorically and historically. Frolov argues that the editor of Judges created this effect intentionally, making a clear break between the giving of YHWH's Spirit and the oath to sacrifice a burnt offering, in order to avoid the suggestion that the Spirit inspired the oath (2013: 208). It is surely true that the Spirit did not inspire the oath, since the fruit of the

Spirit is never disobedience. The editor has made the vow appear awkward and misplaced within its context because the vow *is* awkward and misplaced when offered to YHWH. It is also significant that the hinge between an obedient war against Ammon and a tragic war against fellow people of Israel is this horrific act of ignorance and disobedience.

Life in the Land of Tob

By this point in the book of Judges, we are accustomed to the sad prevalence of ignorance of the law of Moses, the absence of right worship, the embrace of idolatry, and a failure to grasp YHWH's transcendent otherness as the one Creator. All these things naturally result from the collapse of the covenantal community's ability to pass on a living faith in YHWH from one generation to the next. This collapse is seen in the multiple instances of poor parenting in the book of Judges. Gideon was raised by a Baal worshiper, probably an Israelite who had married a woman of Canaan and adopted her religious practice. No surprise that Gideon made so many mistakes in his efforts to worship YHWH. Gideon himself then had a son with a woman who worshiped Baal, whom he did not receive as a full wife, and his treatment both of his concubine and of his son was such that the boy grew up bitter and resentful of Israel and Israel's God. Now we come to Jephthah, whose mother was not merely a concubine but a prostitute. Victor Matthews points out that the clear statement about Jephthah's parentage—that Gilead was his father, something that Gilead's other sons all knew—is evidence that Gilead must have acknowledged him publicly, since otherwise the father of the child of a prostitute would not be named (2004: 117). However, Gilead had not made sufficient provision for Jephthah under law to give him any protection after Gilead's death. His father failed to provide for him, leaving him with no home or portion within the land of Israel.

Jephthah takes refuge outside Israel in the land of Tob. It is an ironic name, since Tob means "good," but Jephthah fails to learn much about goodness during his sojourn there. Tob is located east of Gilead, and this exile to the east reminds us of Cain, who was sent away east of Eden to make a new life for himself. Jephthah surrounds himself with outlaws, literally with "empty men." This is the same expression used to describe the men who surround Abimelech in 9:4. The emptiness of these men might refer to their characters, but it more likely refers to their lack of property. They are men without inheritance and therefore without standing in the land. They are men who are experiencing the weight of the curse on Adam.

Given all this background, Jephthah is a strikingly noble man. He is introduced as a "mighty warrior," the same expression applied to Gideon in 6:12. Unlike Gideon, Jephthah appears to deserve the name from the beginning. Unlike the outlaw chief Abimelech, Jephthah appears to be making a serious effort to do the right thing. Unlike Barak or Gideon, Jephthah is not reluctant to take responsibility, nor is he cowardly when facing the prospect of leading an army into battle. He has confidence in his ability to be a leader and negotiates to make that a permanent position. The title used is not "king" but rather something like "clan chief," a title that "links him into the traditional hereditary leadership of Gilead. In other words, this exiled, disinherited son of a prostitute is to have his clan rights restored and is to become the highest-ranking leader over all the clans of Gilead" (Matthews 2004: 118–19). It is also a point in Jephthah's favor that he says he will accept this position of chief only if YHWH gives the Ammonites into his hand. Even though the elders of Gilead did not see fit to consult YHWH about their choice of leader, Jephthah still acknowledges that YHWH must have the final say.

Once he has negotiated his return to Israel with his half-brothers, he goes to Mizpah where he "spoke all his words before the LORD" (11:11). Here too Jephthah shows himself superior to those who have preceded him. Not since Joshua has a leader been described as accepting leadership in such an intensely devout way, recognizing YHWH's authority so explicitly.[2] His negotiations with the Ammonites reflect a knowledge of the history of Israel. The conclusion of his negotiation is a recognition of YHWH's authority over both Israel and Ammon: "It is not I who have sinned against you, but you are the one who does me wrong by making war on me. Let the LORD, who is judge, decide today for the Israelites or for the Ammonites" (11:27). Webb reflects on this conclusion, saying:

> The theological summary of his case is primarily for the ears of Yahweh, on whom Jephthah now depends utterly for a favorable outcome. His appeal to Yahweh to judge between him and his adversary *today* . . . expresses a belief that the issue will be settled in heaven (by the decision of the divine Judge) before it is settled on earth (by trial of arms). It is neither Jephthah himself nor his adversary who will have the final say, nor Chemosh or any other god, but Yahweh. At this critical moment Jephthah's belief in the unrivaled supremacy of Yahweh shines through. It is his finest hour. (Webb 2012: 324)

2. Phyllis Trible is more cynical about Jephthah's motivation here, noting that in his negotiations with the Gileadites he mentions YHWH's validation in terms of getting the job of chieftain but does not seem to anticipate any ongoing accountability to YHWH (1984: 95).

At this point in the story, it seems as though we may be able to reverse the direction set by Gideon and Abimelech. Perhaps the mistakes of that family will prove to be exceptional. Perhaps with Jephthah we can return to the sort of judges we saw at the beginning of the book, judges who were righteous and noble and obedient, even though the people they were leading were not consistently any of these things.

Alas, no. Although Jephthah expresses loyalty to YHWH and confidence in YHWH's power, he still appears to think of YHWH as a god among gods—perhaps the greatest and strongest and most likely to win, but still a god among other gods. Jephthah's negotiation with the king of Ammon has a similar logic to Joash's negotiation with the crowd that wanted to kill his son Gideon, or to Jotham's prophetic denunciation of Abimelech before the men of Shechem: let the two gods contend together, and we will see who wins. This is also a theme later in the Bible, when Elijah stages his great showdown with the prophets of Baal on Mount Carmel (1 Kgs. 18). However, the point of Elijah's confrontation is to demonstrate that Baal does not exist, that he is a foolish object of worship. In contrast, Jephthah seems to accept the Baalist worldview insofar as he sees all gods, including the God of Israel, as characters within the known world. Unlike Elijah, Jephthah does not recognize God as transcending the world or as the one Creator of the world. He simply believes, or perhaps merely hopes, that YHWH is stronger than Baal or Chemosh.

Jephthah's faith is strong enough that YHWH now legitimizes him as a leader and as an anointed instrument of judgment by sending His Spirit to come over Jephthah (11:29). Even though YHWH didn't initiate the choice of Jephthah, He recognizes him now. Still, as we observed with Othniel and with Gideon, the giving of the Spirit in the Old Testament does not have the same meaning as the baptism in the Holy Spirit that we find in the New Testament. The giving of the Spirit is not a claim about regeneration but about judgment and being used by YHWH. As has already been seen with Gideon and will be seen with Samson, a judge who has received the Spirit may still take actions that are clearly opposed to God's express will. For Jephthah too, not all of his subsequent actions may be attributed to the gift of the Spirit.

Jephthah decides that he needs to make a bargain with YHWH in order to secure His favor. Webb points out, "The vow is effectively a bribe" (2012: 329). Trible says the vow is "an act of unfaithfulness. Jephthah desires to bind God rather than embrace the gift of the spirit. What comes to him freely, he seeks to earn and manipulate. The meaning of his words is doubt, not faith; it is control, not courage" (1984: 97). Jephthah is behaving like a man from Tob, like an Aramean.

He is offering to YHWH exactly the kind of sacrifice that would have been pleasing to Chemosh. He does not seem to be aware that such an offering is explicitly
forbidden in Israel. No doubt he is attempting to show respect.

There is an illuminating contrastive parallel with Caleb, who also made a vow or
promise of what he would do should there be victory in battle. Both vows involve
a daughter, although in the case of Jephthah he does not know that until it is too
late. Caleb's vow leads to life and flourishing for his daughter—indeed, it was
designed to lead exactly to that end. Jephthah's vow leads to death for his daughter
and was always designed to lead to death for someone. Although we might like
to believe that Jephthah was imagining a goat wandering out to greet him on his
return home, it is far more likely that he envisioned sacrificing a servant. Augustine
says Jephthah surely did not intend to sacrifice an animal, "for it is not the custom
now, nor was it then, for sheep to run out to greet a returning master." Augustine
concludes that Jephthah must have intended to sacrifice his wife.[3] Schneider suggests that, in light of the references to Sisera's mother waiting for his return from
battle, the reader is being led to expect Jephthah's mother as the person who will
come out to greet him (2000: 176). Since it was common for women to greet
victorious warriors with songs and dancing (see, e.g., 1 Sam. 18:6–7), it does seem
likely that he expected to sacrifice a woman.

The victory of the Ammonites is credited to YHWH: "the LORD gave them
into his hand" (11:32), which is precisely the wording of Jephthah's request in his
vow. Although the vow was Jephthah's own initiative, by granting what he asked,
YHWH has become a participant in the vow. The sacrifice will now be made,
and YHWH will be the one receiving it. Jephthah has succeeded in doing what
the Gileadites recruited him to do. He has "subdued" the Ammonites, thereby
securing his position as a chieftain, something that the Spirit had already equipped
him to do before he made his vow. However, the vow being made, the victory that
would have been YHWH's gift to him now comes at a high price.

It is his daughter who comes to meet him, "with timbrels and with dancing"
(11:34). Jephthah rends his clothes at the sight of her. This is not because his vow
forces him to perform a human sacrifice; he was already planning on that. His
repentance is personal and self-interested. His concern is that he must sacrifice his
only daughter. "If Jephthah suffered for the sins of his parents, how much more

3. Augustine, *Quaestiones in Heptateuchum* 7.49.6 (PL 34.812; CCSL 33:361.954–62), cited in
John Thompson, *Writing the Wrongs: Women of the Old Testament among Biblical Commentators from
Philo through the Reformation*, Oxford Studies in Historical Theology (Oxford: Oxford University
Press, 2001), 126.

shall this child bear because of the machinations of her father. Unfaithfulness reaches into the third generation to bring forth a despicable fruit. 'Is there no balm in Gilead?' (Jer. 8:22)" (Trible 1984: 100).

It is possible that his daughter is the first person to meet her father precisely because she knows about the vow. If Jephthah's vow was public, which it may well have been, she may have been courting a heroic role, or perhaps she was saving someone else, such as her mother. On this account, Jephthah's speech that seems to blame his daughter for his sacrifice of her makes some sense: "Alas, my daughter! You have brought me very low; you have become the cause of great trouble to me" (11:35). If the daughter has not sought her role as the sacrifice, this reaction is incomprehensible from a man who has thus far appeared to be as decent and caring as Jephthah. From the daughter's perspective, it would make sense that she claims the right to die for her people, to die as a payment for victory, just as any soldier would. Her reply to his sorrow is immediate: "Do to me according to what has gone out of your mouth" (11:36). Both Jephthah and his daughter display some nobility in this story, though of a pagan variety.

She is not only his daughter; she is his only child, and it seems as the story progresses that in sacrificing her he has also sacrificed all hope of descendants. Why this should be is not explained. Jephthah's own birth gives evidence of how easy it is for a man of whatever age to get children from a variety of women, but Jephthah does not seem to consider that option. Perhaps he is like Jon Snow of the epic *Game of Thrones*, a bastard who has found his illegitimacy so painful that he will never risk bringing another illegitimate child into the world.

Throughout the matter of the vow, Jephthah makes three great mistakes. First, Jephthah tries to negotiate with YHWH the same way that we have seen him negotiate with everyone else. He tries to have a quid pro quo relationship with God, a fair exchange. That is a pagan understanding. In paganism people pay off their gods, because in paganism one's god is contained within the natural order of the world. The gods are more powerful than mere human beings, and yet they are themselves also mere beings. They are simply higher on the chain of being. Negotiating with one's god is not conceptually different from negotiating with one's king or lord. From a pagan perspective, gods have needs that human beings can meet, so there are grounds for negotiation. However, the God of Abraham, Isaac, and Jacob is not just one god among the gods. He is the maker of heaven and earth. He does not need any service or gift from His people.

Jephthah's treatment of YHWH as one deity among others is not that distant from the way many religious people in our pluralist culture speak about our own religious commitments. We present our religious convictions as choices and invite others to make the same choice we have made on purely utilitarian grounds. We market our religious choices to others, saying, "I find this to be an effective religion that works well for me. Why not give it a try?"

Like Ruth choosing to live in Bethlehem, Jephthah has come to live in Gilead and has determined that their gods should be his. This is part of the package of being received back into the fold in Gilead and given the role of chieftain. It is his responsibility to serve the god of this people, and he is doing his best. Whereas Elijah understands YHWH as the true God who is radically unlike any other, Jephthah has never been taught to think of YHWH in such terms. Again, Jephthah is not unique in attempting to worship a being he does not understand, nor is he unique in attempting to domesticate, manipulate, buy, and persuade his god to do things his way.

Jephthah's second mistake is that he thinks a human sacrifice is an acceptable way to placate YHWH. He has no knowledge of the law at all. He does know the history of his people, as is obvious in his negotiation with Ammon. But he doesn't understand what any of it means. He is like the students mentioned above in chapter 1 who could tell any number of Bible stories but had no understanding of Christian faith. Jephthah knows the stories of Israel. He may well have known the story of Abraham's willingness to sacrifice Isaac in obedience to YHWH's command. But Jephthah has drawn the wrong lesson from the story. He has no theological framework that would give him insight and so does not understand why a prohibition of child sacrifice for the people of Israel grew from that event. The fact that Jephthah could think human sacrifice was a good offering that would please YHWH shows the depth of his ignorance. Jephthah is negotiating with YHWH without any understanding of what sort of offering would be pleasing. It seems clear that his efforts to be a faithful worshiper of YHWH are sincere, but they are also pagan efforts, premised on the idea that YHWH desires sacrifice. The prophet Micah recites the same story that Jephthah uses in his diplomatic exchange with the king of Ammon, but he then moves to a very different conclusion. Having reminded the people of King Balak of Moab, he then asks whether the sacrifice of one's firstborn child would suffice to pay for one's sin, and concludes that, no, YHWH desires a transformed life of obedience, conforming to what He has shown to be good (Mic. 6:6–8). The psalmist also repeatedly makes the point that sacrifice is not necessary to God and cannot earn His favor:

> If I were hungry, I would not tell you,
> for the world and all that is in it is mine.

Do I eat the flesh of bulls,
or drink the blood of goats?
Offer to God a sacrifice of thanksgiving,
and pay your vows to the Most High.
Call on me in the day of trouble;
I will deliver you, and you shall glorify me. (Ps. 50:12–15)

Jephthah does not have this idea of YHWH. Although he knows the stories of Israel's military history, he does not know the law.

When the LORD your God has cut off before you the nations whom you are about to enter to dispossess them, when you have dispossessed them and live in their land, take care that you are not snared into imitating them, after they have been destroyed before you: do not inquire concerning their gods, saying, "How did these nations worship their gods? I also want to do the same." You must not do the same for the LORD your God, because every abhorrent thing that the LORD hates they have done for their gods. They would even burn their sons and their daughters in the fire to their gods. (Deut. 12:29–31)

Later, in Deut. 18 (a passage we considered in chapter 1 in this volume) one of the abhorrent practices of the nations is mentioned specifically: "No one shall be found among you who makes a son or daughter pass through fire" (18:10). Jephthah's error is especially dramatic, but what he is doing is very common. Most human beings attempt to bargain with God, and we all find it easier to negotiate with God as if He is a somewhat elevated peer rather than to throw ourselves on His mercy or submit ourselves to living in conformity with His righteousness.

Jephthah's third mistake is that he doesn't know there is a way out of this vow. Even once the horrible consequences of his vow became clear to him, Jephthah does not know how to extricate himself. Leviticus 5:4–6 gives instruction about how to extricate oneself from a "rash oath" by paying the penalty of a female sheep or goat as a sin offering. Leviticus 27 is even more explicit about what to do if one has made an inappropriate vow about another person.

The LORD spoke to Moses, saying: Speak to the people of Israel and say to them: When a person makes an explicit vow to the LORD concerning the equivalent for a human being, the equivalent for a male shall be: from twenty to sixty years of age the equivalent shall be fifty shekels of silver by the sanctuary shekel. If the person is a female, the equivalent is thirty shekels. If the age is from five to twenty years of age, the equivalent is twenty shekels for a male and ten shekels for a female. If the age is from one month to five years, the equivalent for a male is five shekels of silver, and for a female the equivalent is three shekels of silver. And if the person is sixty years old or over, then the equivalent for a male is fifteen shekels, and for a female ten shekels. If any cannot afford the equivalent, they shall be brought before the priest and the priest shall assess them; the priest shall assess them according to what each one making a vow can afford. (Lev. 27:1–8)

Jephthah did not need to do what he did. The law offered him a solution that was pleasing to YHWH. He could have paid ten shekels to the tabernacle and saved his daughter's life while avoiding an act that would in fact be displeasing to the God he was trying to appease. People who are offended by this story in the Bible often ask in outrage why it is that God intervened to save Isaac but not to save Jephthah's daughter. Is the life of a girl worth less than the life of a boy? they ask. But YHWH had intervened. He had given Moses a law that addressed this very situation.

James Jordan points out that the Levitical exemption might not have applied in Jephthah's case, because it is qualified by another passage in Leviticus: "Nothing that a person owns that has been devoted to destruction for the LORD, be it human or animal, or inherited landholding, may be sold or redeemed; every devoted thing is most holy to the LORD. No human beings who have been devoted to destruction can be ransomed; they shall be put to death" (Lev. 27:28–29). But then Jordan believes that Jephthah's vow simply required him to dedicate his daughter to a lifetime of service in the tabernacle, that such consecration would have fallen under the rubric of "destruction" in ancient Israel (1999: 201–3). I disagree with Jordan that Jephthah had any such intention. I believe it is clear from the text and the context that he had vowed to sacrifice a human being. Since such a sacrifice would violate YHWH's clear prohibition, I cannot see that this later section of Lev. 27 applies. The only appropriate application of that section would be to warfare. Rabbinic interpretation agrees. Regarding Jephthah's sacrifice of his daughter, "early rabbinic discussions reflected in Talmudic and Midrashic texts regarded the sacrifice as errant, clearly prohibited by Torah (e.g., Genesis Rabbah, 60:3, and Leviticus Rabbah, 37:4). The Law provided penance for rash oaths (Leviticus 5) and redemption for inappropriately devoted things, including persons (Leviticus 27). Later medieval scholars such as Moses ben Nahman, known as Ramban (1194–1270), maintained this judgment (commentary on Leviticus, 480–81)" (Gunn 2005: 134). If someone vows to commit a sin in YHWH's honor, the fact that YHWH's honor was intended does not set aside the sin.

In 1 Sam. 14, King Saul makes an oath binding his army not to eat until after a day of battle. The text describes this oath as "rash" (14:24), and when his son Jonathan hears about the oath, Jonathan also condemns it, saying that the troops would have killed more Philistines if they had been allowed to eat (14:29–30). By the time Jonathan hears about the oath, however, he has already eaten. There is a long process whereby this fact is uncovered, and Saul decrees that in order to keep his oath he must put his son Jonathan to death. But Jonathan is the hero of the hour, having been the mightiest warrior against the Philistines. The army rebels at the thought of his death. "Then the people said to Saul, 'Shall Jonathan die, who has accomplished this great victory in Israel? Far from it! As the LORD lives, not one hair of his head shall fall to the ground; for he has worked with God today.' So the people ransomed Jonathan, and he did not die" (14:45). The ransom offered by the people is not stated, but it seems likely that it is the ransom specified in Leviticus in the case of rash vows; the soldiers who had fought beside Jonathan chipped in their share of the money so that he would not die. Perhaps the teaching of Samuel had restored some knowledge of the law to the people of Israel.

Or perhaps the practice of virtue had been deeply enough internalized by some members of the army that they could simply see how far away from holiness and righteousness a vow like Saul's really was, even without a knowledge of Leviticus. When a child promises her friends to do something rash and dangerous, her protests to her parents that she must do the thing because she has *promised* are quickly overridden. Some promises are rash, and to lift the keeping of a promise or a vow to the status of an unbreakable law—no matter how it was coerced, no matter how the consequences were unanticipated, no matter how the keeping of it will violate one's honor, and no matter how unrighteous the act might be—that is a rash act indeed.

Even apart from knowledge of the law, Jephthah should have broken his promise. If he believed that breaking the promise would bring down condemnation on his own head, then he should have risked such condemnation rather than execute his daughter. The only reason he went through with his vow was that he did not see it as sinful. He saw it as tragic but honorable. Such a failure in judgment is a sign of being an empty man, not just in terms of land but in terms of moral perception.

In the time of Jephthah, the people of Israel had forgotten the law, and the people of Gilead did not share the impulses of Saul's army. Perhaps their dread of a broken vow was too keen. Jephthah's ignorance of the law is striking, but even more striking is that apparently there was no one in his army and no one in Gilead who could advise him about the law and tell him how easily he could redeem his daughter.

There was no Levite or priest whom he could consult, and in the weeks that his daughter was preparing for her martyrdom, no one in the community of Israel knew enough about the law to produce the information that would have saved her life.

In the early church, Origen commented on Jephthah's daughter and named her a martyr. He did not condone Jephthah's actions, but he did admire the way the daughter went bravely to her death. Unfortunately, Origen's homily on Judg. 11 is not extant; however, John Thompson points to another sermon in which Origen talked about the connection between Old Testament sacrifices and martyrdom, explicitly referencing Jephthah's daughter.

> Old Testament sacrifices were like the deaths of martyrs today, he writes, in that both prefigure the death of the Lamb of God. Though it seems cruel of God to demand martyrdom, Origen insists that these deaths do contribute somehow to the defeat of evil. It is here that he comments on Jephthah's daughter. She too was a martyr, for it was by her willing death that Jephthah triumphed over the Ammonites. . . . No one can accuse Origen of being naive about martyrdom. His own father was martyred when Origen was but a teenager. We are told that the young Origen was stopped from following his father only because his mother had hidden all the boy's clothes. When Origen was fifty, persecution resumed, and he responded by composing *Exhortation to Martyrdom*, perhaps the best-known treatise on martyrdom ever written. And you may know that Origen, too, practiced what he preached: his own life was ended some twenty years later, as an effect of the torture he suffered under Emperor Decius.
>
> What is most remarkable about Origen, however, is his clear denial that martyrdom is a visible triumph of any kind! Martyrs do contribute to the defeat of evil, but this is not something we see. It is something we believe. Indeed, were we to believe what we *see*, we would have to conclude that God enjoys it when Christians suffer cruel and senseless deaths. No, the martyr's crown is visible only to faith: the true significance of these cruel deaths remains, for now, a secret known only to God.
>
> Consequently, when Origen admits that the death of Jephthah's daughter looks and feels senseless, he's not treating her as just a problem to be solved. No: he is filling in the silences, extrapolating from Israel's defeat of the Ammonites and the selfless virtue of the daughter in order to make sense of the story.[4]

Although her death was unnecessary, neither she nor her father knew that. They believed that she was paying for a military victory that had secured the future

4. John L. Thompson, "Preaching Texts of Terror in the Book of Judges," *Calvin Theological Journal* 37, no. 1 (April 2002): 54–55.

of her country, and that conviction allowed her to make her death meaningful. In that sense, we may see Jephthah's daughter not only as a martyr but also as a heroine, much like Iphigenia, daughter of Agamemnon, who was sacrificed by her father to allow his army to escape from Troy. Jephthah's daughter seems to have understood her fate in much that way.

Jephthah is held up as a man of faith in the book of Hebrews, and his daughter should be held up too. Jephthah does what he can with what he's got. But see how his community has let him down. See what happens when this forgetfulness sets in about who God is and how different He is from the gods of the nations. The civil war that follows is connected to this forgetfulness, for the people of Israel no longer remember who they are.

Victor Matthews points out that Jephthah's vow is also in some ways parallel to Gideon's earlier testing of God with the fleece. "In both cases the chosen leader already has been invested with the spirit of the Lord (6:34; 11:29a), and he has begun to raise an army (6:35; 11:29b). At that point both leaders seem to falter in their resolve and attempt to obtain reassurance or even a form of victory insurance from God" (Matthews 2004: 90). Clearly, Jephthah's story is much darker, and the consequences of his insecurity are much more dire. This is further evidence of the degeneration portrayed throughout the book. Matthews says, "There is no response from God to Jephthah's vow. While this divine silence could be interpreted as divine culpability, it is more likely a signal that Jephthah should not be ad-libbing and instead should rely on the instruction provided by the investment of God's spirit" (124).

Barry Webb is more compassionate toward Jephthah. He imagines that Jephthah is speaking out of his experience of rejection, which has taught him that the worthy and the innocent do not always prosper. In his negotiations with the people of Gilead, he has made his position as their head contingent on victory in this battle. He has a great deal to lose if the battle does not go his way (Webb 2012: 328).

Bewailing Virginity

The bewailing of virginity is an instance of a theological shift from Old Testament to New Testament. In the Old Testament, the mark of YHWH's favor is especially seen in the flourishing of the family structure. Those who cannot have children are cut off from YHWH's blessing, and the best way to be a good citizen in Israel was to marry and raise up children to YHWH.[5] This focus on family life can be traced back to the creation of Adam and Eve and the blessing that they would be fruitful and multiply. YHWH's people are built up and His image on earth is multiplied in this family relationship. In the New Testament, however, the truth toward which marriage points is made manifest directly: God's helping presence comes among us in Jesus, who is bone of our bone and flesh of our flesh. He is the Bridegroom, and we his people are his bride. Now that the reality has come, the relationships that serve as pointers to that reality are relativized. Christian marriage remains a good thing—indeed, an even better thing than it was in the Old Testament, since now there is an explicit connection between the relation of husband and wife and the relation of Christ and his church. But the possibility of celibate singleness is now introduced as an equally good thing, or even a preferable good thing. By the time of the early church, when a young virgin went to martyrdom, she did not need to bewail her virginity. Instead, she could go to martyrdom as a bride to her Bridegroom.

The book of Judges ends with the violent abduction of two groups of virgins of Israel—the young women of Jabesh-gilead, spared when everyone else in their town is slaughtered, so that they may be brides for the men of Benjamin; and the young women dancing in the fields outside Shiloh, worshiping YHWH and then snatched by others of Benjamin to be their wives. Those young women were forcibly married to the men of Benjamin precisely so that they would bear children for Benjamin and prevent the extinction of the tribe; however, the structure of Judges, with its spiral into worse and worse behavior, suggests that we should pity them more than we pity Jephthah's daughter. Dying a virgin who has never had the chance to bear children is by no means the worst thing that can happen to a young woman in Israel.

Even more interesting is the assumption voiced by the army of Israel in chapter 21 that it is unthinkable for the men of Benjamin to die without becoming fathers. None of the soldiers of Israel spoke up to defend Jephthah's daughter from death, but they were willing to resort to rape and kidnapping in order to prevent one Benjaminite man from dying childless. Judges ends in a place of disdain for the worth of women and elevation of the needs of men, but the trajectory of the book, including the story of Jephthah's daughter, reminds us that the story of the unmarried men of Benjamin is not meant to be normative; it is evidence of the decline of Israel into ungodliness.

5. See chapter 10 below on Samson for a treatment of barrenness.

War with Ephraim

Jephthah's story continues to disintegrate in the subsequent episode of the war with Ephraim. The Ephraimites were loyal soldiers for Ehud, but they were antagonistic for Gideon, and now with Jephthah they have become genuinely hostile. Jephthah was made the head of Gilead in order to deal with a foreign invasion and fight a dramatic war, which he did well. But the result was that he found himself embroiled in civil war, fighting another tribe of Israel for no real reason. The hostility of Ephraim is especially vicious when they threaten to burn down Jephthah's house. However, Jephthah's tragedy has left him immune to such threats. He has already destroyed his own house; he has burned her himself (Matthews 2004: 129).

The escalating troublesomeness of Ephraim serves the prophetic message of the book, which includes an anti-Ephraim polemic. When Moses established the Israelite encampment, God assigned Judah preeminence on the eastern side of the camp and Ephraim preeminence on the western side. Ephraim was Judah's chief rival for dominance in Israel, as was seen already in the first chapter of Judges, which describes the rivalry in terms of Judah versus Joseph. To the extent that the book of Judges is an apologetic for the Davidic line and the tribe of Judah (and I believe that it is only secondarily such an apologetic), the diminishment of Ephraim is part of the argument.

10

SAMSON

13:1–16:31

Structure

In terms of the book's spiral into sin and misery, Samson is a step down again from Jephthah. Whereas Jephthah attempted to lead the people of Israel in resisting their enemies and retaking their land, Samson at no point is reported as doing anything for the good of his people. Gideon turned to personal vengeance for the dark second half of his story, but Samson spends his entire career in that place. Whereas the first three judges were exemplary leaders demonstrating what the people of Israel were supposed to be like, with the charges of apostasy and collaboration being leveled only against the people at large, Samson embodies these flaws in himself. He is Israel in microcosm: called to a special task and given a special covenantal relationship with YHWH, he disregards the value of this relationship, violates his Nazirite vow, and seeks to marry a Canaanite woman and to sleep with a Canaanite prostitute. His relationship with YHWH is marked by infidelity. He is used by YHWH in spite of himself. He does make a beginning in driving out the Philistines and in taking back the land, but those good outcomes are side effects of his suicide.

In terms of the measurement of society based on the treatment of women, Samson does not come out well. This is underscored by the comparison with Othniel, whom Samson is set against in the great chiasm of the book. It is a comparison that reveals Samson as deeply flawed. Othniel is given leadership and a godly wife as a result of conquering the land in obedience to God's command. Samson claims a Canaanite wife without doing anything to earn her and makes no effort to conquer anyone, being content with individual acts of vandalism, violence, and disorder. Othniel's wife ends up secure in a well-watered land, enjoying the companionship of her husband and good relations with her father. Samson's wife ends up burned to death along with her father and all her family, leaving Samson alone, surrounded by death and parched with thirst. The only woman who may be said to benefit from Samson's career is Delilah, and she is paid by the hand of the Philistines.

In the sequence of six judges, Samson parallels Deborah, for she is the third in the first sequence and he the third in the second. There is an implication in the Deborah story that the soldiers in the army have taken a Nazirite vow upon embarking on their war with Sisera, a vow that they will keep until Sisera is conquered: in the song of chapter 5, the warriors are depicted as riding down the mountain with their long hair streaming out behind them. In contrast, Samson is a lifelong Nazirite, but he is remarkably casual about his vows. Whereas the soldiers of Israel are committing themselves to a different sort of warfare than the Canaanites, a warfare marked by self-control and self-discipline rather than the weapons of rape and looting, Samson exercises neither self-control nor self-discipline but allows the Philistines to provoke him to retaliation. In obedience to a word from YHWH, Deborah successfully leads an army of Israelites against Sisera, resulting in a new time of freedom for Israel. Samson never leads an army against the Philistines but succeeds in being enough of an irritant to the Philistines that the oppression of his people is worsened by his acts. He does nothing to set his people free until his death. Deborah considers the conflict with Sisera from the perspective of his mother, an enemy woman; Samson joins himself to enemy women at every turn. Jael attacks Sisera's head with a tent peg; Delilah attacks Samson's head with a razor. In this last instance, as we saw with Abimelech, the one who is under judgment is now within Israel, rather than without. It is Samson the judge who takes the role of the serpent, whose head is attacked by the woman.

The Samson saga itself is especially complex, not surprising given that it is the longest story in the book (ninety-six verses, followed closely by the Gideon saga at ninety-three). The annunciation to his mother, his ill-fated marriage to the woman of Timnah, his vengeance on the Philistines, the trip to Gaza, the episode with Delilah, and his final imprisonment and death—the connections between these stories are not always obvious, and many commentators question whether they are connected. David Dorsey argues that the whole saga does hold together, following this pattern:

a   Samson's birth (13:1–25)
   b   Samson betrays his secret to his Philistine wife (14:1–20)
      c   Samson visits wife at Timnah (15:1–8)
         d   TURNING POINT: Samson kills one thousand Philistines with jawbone of ass; fellow Israelites reject Samson's leadership and Philistines begin to take the initiative against him (15:9–20)
      c'   Samson visits prostitute at Gaza (16:1–3)
   b'   Samson betrays his secret to Delilah (16:4–22)
a'   Samson's death[1]

This outline has the merit of connecting the story of Samson's birth into the full saga, something not always recognized by commentators. However, it fails to recognize the false ending at the end of point d: "And he judged Israel in the days of the Philistines twenty years" (15:20). The pattern for the judge stories established with Othniel leads us to expect that this summation sentence will be followed by a statement about the land having rest, and then the Samson story should conclude. It would be natural to think that by single-handedly killing one thousand Philistines Samson has indeed fulfilled the destiny prophesied about him and completed his duties as a judge, in much the same way that Shamgar fulfilled his role as a judge by an exceptional act of slaughter (3:31). One might assume that such an act would suffice for Samson to have begun the defeat of the Philistines. However, that is not what happens.

The full conclusion—that Samson was buried in the tomb of his father—is withheld at the end of chapter 15, just as it was withheld midway through the Gideon story. Instead of ending at this point as the pattern of the judge stories leads us to expect, the story restarts. Both the story of Gideon and the story of Samson take a new and unexpected direction just at the moment when an ending seems imminent. In the case of Gideon, a story that was tracking in the direction of obedience veers off in the direction of personal vengeance. Samson's story begins in personal vengeance expressed in ever-escalating acts of strength and violence;

1. Dorsey 1999: 113. Dorsey's outline includes subpoints for each of the lettered points, underscoring more details of the parallelism and giving strong support to this structure.

the story is then redirected by God's grace into a trajectory of failure and growing weakness through which Samson at last achieves his great victory.

Samson's second attempt to live out the destiny promised to him includes parallels to the first. Bruce Waltke identifies a structure of two parallel stories from 13:25 to 16:30, each following the same plot points:

1. Begin with wrong entanglements with Philistine women leading to entanglements with Philistine men and their deaths: 14:1, 19 [cf. 15:1, 8]; 16:1, 30.
2. Prank with display of strength: 14:5–6; 16:3.
3. Coaxing of secret/riddle: 14:15; 16:5.
4. Challenge from Philistine leaders with threat of burning/promise of money: 14:15 (cf. 15:6); 16:5, 18.
5. Manipulation by wife/woman: 14:16; 16:15.
6. Pressured by woman to turning point: 14:17; 16:16, 17.
7. Handing-over by third party: 15:13; 16:19.
8. Response to being bound: 15:14–15; 16:20.
9. Motivated by revenge: 15:3 (wife), 11; 16:28 (eyes).
10. Prayer for life/death: 15:18; 16:28.
11. Concluding stereotypical frame: 15:20; 16:31b. (Waltke 2004: 55)

Cheryl Exum endorses a similar structure. She points out that the two sets of stories about Samson's exploits are framed by an inclusio in 13:25 and 16:31. Between them are two "symmetrical" stories. "The progression of events is similar in both cycles: Samson sees a woman; he is persuaded by a woman to reveal a secret; once directly and once indirectly as a result of a liaison with a woman, he is bound and given into the hands of the Philistines; Samson calls on Yhwh and Yhwh answers Samson's prayer."[2] What is left out of this parallel as Exum sets it forth is the story of the prostitute in Gaza and the ripping out of the city gates. Since that event seems to stand in parallel to the pulling down of the temple of Dagon, this calls her structure into question.

Here is a broad outline of the overall structure that I see in this story. Because the story is so complex, we will consider the details of each section as we move through the narrative, and concentrate here only on some of the elements that unite all the pieces of the saga. The initial "x" section is the false start, initiated by Samson seeing not the LORD but a Timnite woman whom he desires. This disordered desire for forbidden women repeatedly interrupts the proper flow of the story, leading to a narrative of personal vengeance at the expense of the land.

2. J. Cheryl Exum, "Aspects of Symmetry and Balance in the Samson Saga," *JSOT* 19 (1981): 4.

The story restarts in an appropriate, though painful, direction after Samson prays at the end of chapter 15. His prayer is far from ideal, being characterized by entitlement and resentment, and yet it is a catalyst for the tearing out of the gates of Gaza, which is the first turn back into the proper story.

A   Moving from barrenness to fruitfulness—conversations between Manoah, his wife, and the Angel of the Lord regarding Samson's Nazirite obligations
  a   "We have **seen** God" (13:22)
  b   Spirit of the Lord stirs Samson <u>between Zorah and Eshtaol</u> (13:25)
      x   Honey from a corpse—Samson **sees** a Timnite woman; turns away from YHWH and violates Nazirite vow
      y   Betrayed by his bride: Spirit of the Lord rushed on him (14:19); he then kills thirty Philistines and takes their clothes
      z   Bride given to another: <u>burned</u> three hundred foxes, Philistines' fields, and orchards
      z′ Bride and father-in-law <u>burned</u>: killed Philistines "hip and thigh"
      y′ Betrayed by Judah with new ropes: Spirit of the Lord rushed on him (15:14); he then kills one thousand Philistines with jawbone of an ass
  c   Prayer for water (15:18)
B   Ripping out the gates of Gaza. **Saw** a prostitute; ripped out the gates (or **eyes**) of Gaza.
A′ Moving from strength to weakness—conversations between Samson, Delilah, and the Philistines
      x′ Samson's love turns toward Delilah, surrenders Nazirite vow
      z″ Breaks bonds as if "touching fire" (16:19) to attack phantom Philistines
      y″ The Lord has left him (16:20)
  a′ **Eyes** gouged out (16:21)
  b′ Hair begins to grow—renewal of Nazirite vow (16:22)
  c′ Prayer for defeat of Philistines (16:28)
B′ Pulling down the temple in Gaza. Buried <u>between Zorah and Eshtaol</u> (16:31)

This restart is not the same as Gideon's restart in that the darkness has already been manifest in the first section. Samson has never led the Israelites into battle, and—despite killing a thousand Philistines soldiers—at the end of chapter 15 he still hasn't begun the deliverance of Israel from the Philistines. Furthermore, the new beginning does not start with great virtue, since the first thing we discover about Samson is that he has gone to Gaza to visit a prostitute. But there he does perform a feat of strength that foreshadows the destruction of the Philistines: ripping out the gates of Gaza. The restart section is framed by two feats of strength—this breaking out of Gaza and then the destruction of the temple in Gaza. In the end, Samson does fulfill the prophecy, but in his death rather than in his victory.

Barrenness to Fruitfulness

At the beginning of the Jephthah story, the pattern that had held up to that point (the people crying out to God followed by God raising up a deliverer) was broken. The people had cried out to God, but God had declined to help. Now, at the beginning of the Samson story, the people have ceased to cry for help. Not only have the people of Israel not asked for a deliverer; Manoah and his wife have not even asked for a child in their barrenness. And yet God is still preparing a deliverance, for Israel as well as for this barren couple. God's sovereign initiative is seen also in His secret working. His grace is operative even (perhaps especially) when we do not seek it.

Annunciation to a barren woman is a common pattern in the Old Testament. The first instance is Hagar, who is met by an Angel who promises her a son after Sarah has driven her away. Hagar "named the LORD who spoke to her, 'You are El-roi' [God who sees]" (Gen. 16:13). Hagar is comforted to know that God is paying attention to her and also that she is allowed to see Him, that her encounter with the Angel of the LORD has not led to her death. Typically, when people have these encounters with the Angel of the LORD, they first think they are talking to a human person, but by the end of the encounter they think they are talking to God, which also seems to be Hagar's experience. Sarah and Abraham also have an encounter with a divine messenger who announces the birth of Isaac. And, of course, the annunciation to Mary in the New Testament is the annunciation to which all annunciations point. A variation on the annunciation pattern occurs earlier in Judges when Gideon entertains an Angel who announces Gideon's rebirth as a mighty warrior, a story that may in some ways foreshadow the annunciation to Manoah's wife. But the annunciation that is most connected to the story of Samson is the annunciation to Hannah of the birth of Samuel.

We have already discussed the implicit role of Joshua in the book of Judges, claiming that Othniel is standing in for Joshua, who is the true paradigmatic judge at the beginning of the book. In a similar way, Samson is really being compared to Samuel more than to anyone within the book of Judges, though in this case the comparison is contrastive. Samuel is the true last judge. It can be argued that he is the most powerful, the most virtuous, and the most wise, certainly the only one of the judges who can be compared with Joshua in terms of such qualities. Adding his stories to the book of the Judges would completely undermine the saga of descent and despair, and so his stories are told in his own book. Nonetheless, Samson and Samuel share many things, most obviously in that they are contemporaries, both fighting against the Philistine occupation. Whereas Samson begins the deliverance from the Philistines, Samuel helps to complete it.

The two annunciation stories underscore the connection between these men. Waltke summarizes the connections:

> The birth episodes of Samson and Samuel are strikingly similar: Both lived during the Philistine occupation of the Land; both [mothers] are barren; both conceive through divine intervention; both raise their sons as Nazarites; both sons deliver Israel. But Hannah is blessed by an adversary who provokes her to pray and struggles with God, whereas Manoah's wife stoically resigns herself to barrenness and despairs of prayer. Hannah raised a prophet; Manoah and his wife parented a Hercules. Samuel accepted his Nazarite conscription and obeyed the LORD; Samson did neither. Samuel defeated the Philistine; Samson killed them but did not deliver Israel. (Waltke 2004: 54)

The birth of each of them was announced miraculously to his mother. Hannah has the promise of a child directly from Eli, the high priest. Hannah and her husband, Elkanah, are both named, and both are regular attenders at the tabernacle. When Hannah is depressed about not having children, she naturally prays about her concerns. Hannah receives the good news that she is to have a child via the ordinary means of grace: her attendance in worship and her interactions with a priest. Hannah is a devout woman who is happy to dedicate her son to God, and she understands that the right way to do this is to bring him to the tabernacle to be raised there.

By contrast, Samson's mother, who is unnamed, is not mentioned as ever praying for a child; instead, as Waltke notes, she appears to be resigned to her fate, just as the people of Israel are resigned to their oppression. She is not portrayed as traveling regularly to the tabernacle or petitioning YHWH for His favor in giving her a child. Her experience is that a messenger from God appears without warning to talk to her about this. Grace comes to her without her seeking. Her husband Manoah is even more out of his depth in interacting with the Angel of the LORD; they are told that His name is "too wonderful" for them to know. There is no mention of Samson ever going to the tabernacle, a significant gap. There is no indication that Samson was ever taught the law, and unlike Jephthah he never "says his word" before YHWH to make his parents' vows his own. Like Jephthah, Samson cannot share what he has not received and therefore does not teach the law to others.

The Angel has commanded that Samson is to be a Nazirite from birth. The Nazirite vow is explained in most detail in Num. 6. The essence of the vow is that Nazirites are *separated* from others, the meaning at the root of the word. This separation is seen in three ways. First, they may not eat or drink anything that comes from grapes: no wine, no strong drink, no grape juice, no fruit, no seeds, no skin, and no vinegar. Grapes are associated with celebration and feasting, but the Nazirite is not to feast until the vow is accomplished. Second, Nazirites may not cut their hair until the vow is complete. Upon the completion of the vow, the hair is cut and offered up in the tabernacle. This stipulation makes the status of the Nazirite public and observable by other members of the community. This is why some commentators think that Absalom may have taken a Nazirite vow, since there is so much commentary about his hair. Third, Nazirites are to avoid everything unclean, even unclean things that everyone else in Israel must come into contact with. So they may not be in contact with corpses to prepare the body for burial; that needs to be the role of someone else in the family. In this emphasis on remaining ritually clean, Nazirites have much in common with priests.

Samson and Samuel are both unusual in being Nazirites from birth. Most of the Nazirites in scripture are people who make a short-term vow. The apostle Paul makes such a vow in the book of Acts, which he completes at Cenchreae, where "he had his hair cut, for he was under a vow" (Acts 18:18). Jesus takes a Nazirite vow when He is with His disciples at the Last Supper, promising not to drink the fruit of the vine until they are together again in the Father's house. Jesus did not live all his life as a Nazirite; rather, He took a vow the night before He died, a vow that He is still keeping. Only three people are named in scripture who are Nazirites from birth: John the Baptist and this duo of Samson and Samuel. These three do not choose to take this vow; it is made for them by their parents. Samuel grows up to be a teacher of the law and a true judge in Israel, keeping the vow his mother made for him for all his life. Samson regularly breaks his vow.

In thinking about this lifetime Nazirite vow, I am reminded of the sorts of conversations I have with friends who believe in credobaptism and who find my support of paedobaptism confusing. What, they ask, is the meaning of a vow made on your behalf before you have any ability to understand it, let alone assent to it? For those of us in the Reformed tradition, the baptism of infants is efficacious because of the covenant that God has made with his people, a covenant that is concerned not only with individuals but also with communities. The promises of God are not only offered to believers; they are also offered to believers' children.

G. K. Chesterton deploys a metaphor for God's initiative in claiming us that I have always found useful. In one of his Father Brown stories, the priest speaks of a criminal whose confession he has recently heard: "I caught him, with an unseen hook and an invisible line which is long enough to let him wander to the ends of the world, and still to bring him back with a twitch upon the thread."[3] In his novel *Brideshead Revisited*, Evelyn Waugh makes use of that expression—"a twitch upon the thread"—to describe the experience of being brought back to the faith into which one was baptized after a lifetime of running away from it. This is what happens to Samson throughout his story. The Nazirite vow is the covenant relationship with YHWH that has hooked him from his mother's womb. He is given a long line and wanders a long way, but YHWH at last brings him back with a violent twitch upon the thread.

Unlike Samson, Samuel does not wander. He allows himself to be caught. In my imagination, Samson and Samuel are like Orual and Psyche in C. S. Lewis's book *Till We Have Faces*.[4] Orual and Psyche are sisters, one of whom lives life in the darkness of rebellion and unbelief, the other of whom lives in the light of faith. At the end of the novel, Orual has a vision of their parallel lives; they have been pursuing the same tasks, called to follow the same path, moving toward the same goal. But Psyche has been aware of that goal and cooperating with the One who calls her, whereas Orual has fought Him at every step along the way. Their journey has been intertwined and has been working for purposes beyond what they can see. Samson is like Orual, stumbling through his calling, using his gifts of strength and wit and intellect to resist God more often than to cooperate with Him. And yet, in his death, Samson effectively begins the work of defeating the Philistines, a work that Samuel finishes in 1 Sam. 7:3–17.

Jichan Kim shows the strong emphasis on the barrenness of Manoah's wife at the beginning of the story. First the narrator tells us, "And his wife was barren [A], and had not given birth [B]." Then the Angel of the LORD appears to the woman, repeating this information: "Look you are barren [A], and have not given birth [B], but you will conceive [A'], and give birth to a son [B']." After giving her instruction about her dietary restrictions while pregnant, he reiterates the promise of fertility: "For, look, you will conceive [A'], and will give birth to a son [B']." This promise is repeated a third time when Manoah's wife reports it to him, saying, "But he said to me: Look, you will conceive [A'], and give birth to a son [B']" (Kim 1993: 175). The repetition is intentional and effective at driving home both the present state of barrenness and the promise of future fruitfulness.

3. G. K. Chesterton, "The Queer Feet," in *The Complete Father Brown* (New York: Penguin, 1981), 50.
4. C. S. Lewis, *Till We Have Faces: A Myth Retold* (New York: Harcourt, Brace, 1984).

Kim offers this analysis of the structure of the entire annunciation story:

A   YHWH's Promise
    Manoah's wife will <u>give birth to</u> (*yld*) a son; he will become a Nazirite;
    the BOY (*nʿr*) will begin (*ḤLL*) to deliver Israel; thus there is a necessity
    for keeping the Nazirite regimen.
    B   Ignorance of the Identity
        1. She did not **ask** (*šʾl*) <u>where</u> (*ʾy-mzh*) <u>he</u> came from;
        2. the man of God did not tell her his name (*šm*). Report of the an-
            nouncement of the man of God.
            X   Manoah's Prayer
                In answer to Manoah's prayer that God allow the man to
                come again to teach them what (*mh*) [to] DO with the Boy
                (*nʿr*), God allows him to appear again to them.
            X' Manoah's Questions
                In reply to "what (*mh*) will be the rule for the BOY (*nʿr*) and
                his DOING," the man reiterates the same regimen; despite a
                hint Manoah still did not know that he was the messenger of
                YHWH.
    B' Revelation of the Identity
        2' The man retorted: "why (*lmh zh*) do you **ask** (*šʾl*) my name (*šm*)?
            For it is wonderful."
        1' Seeing the man <u>go up heavenward</u> (*yʿl*), Manoah knew that <u>he</u> was
            the messenger of YHWH.
A' God's Promise Fulfilled
    The woman <u>gave birth to</u> (*tld*) a son; the BOY (*nʿr*) grew; the spirit of
    YHWH began (*ḤLL*) to stir him. (1993: 223)

This structure highlights two central questions: What is the boy's rule of life to
be? And who is this messenger who is bringing the news of the promised child?
Manoah's slowness at understanding the answer to these questions moves the
story along.

Kim sees in this story an emphasis on obedience to YHWH, primarily on the
part of the woman who must watch her diet during her pregnancy so that her
unborn child will not be violating his Nazirite vow while in the womb. But the
story also looks forward to the need for Samson's own obedience to the terms of
the vow his parents have made for him (Kim 1993: 225).

The annunciation is made by the Angel of the LORD. This is His third appearance in the book of Judges. By the time the Angel leaves, Manoah is confident that he's about to die because he's seen the face of God, so Manoah at least believes that the Angel is divine. As we have already considered when looking at the earlier appearances, the Angel of the LORD may best be understood as a preincarnate appearance of Christ, the one whose name is Wonderful.

Although Samson's mother is unnamed, the Angel of the LORD persists in addressing her rather than Manoah, refusing to allow Manoah to take over the conversation. If there were no other reason to think that this messenger is Jesus, the way He treats this unnamed woman would suggest He must be. Dorothy Sayers observed long ago that Jesus's treatment of women was unique. She comments on the loyalty of the women around Jesus, who stayed at the cross to watch Him die when other disciples had fled, and who were first at the tomb on Easter morning. Sayers considers such loyalty natural because of how unusual Jesus's treatment of women was. "They had never known a man like this Man; there never has been such another. A prophet and teacher who never nagged at them, never flattered or coaxed or patronised; who never made arch jokes about them . . . ; who took their questions and arguments seriously."[5] Manoah's unnamed wife must have had this same experience with the Angel of the LORD. Although the text gives her no name, Jesus surely called her by name, for He is the Namer who gives each of us our true name (Rev. 2:17); and when He speaks our names, we who are His sheep know His voice (John 10:27). It is a comfort to think that this overlooked woman with the ponderous husband and the promiscuous son had a few moments of conversation face-to-face with the one whose name is too wonderful.

The question remains why, of all the great tragedies that occur in life—warfare, famine, death, despair—it is barrenness that over and over again in scripture elicits a personal visit from the Angel of the LORD to offer reassurance and a promise of fruitfulness. Certainly, it is true that in the ancient world a barren woman faced troubles far beyond an unmet desire to be a mother. In ancient Israel, a woman with no children had little security for her old age and faced a precarious future. Such a woman was also seen as having failed in her duty as a citizen in Israel, for not having children jeopardized the future of the community as well as one's personal future. Behind these economic and social issues was then and is now the perennial problem of feeling that life is barren, meaningless, and bearing no fruit—a problem that recurs in every culture and historical era.

5. Dorothy L. Sayers, *Are Women Human?* (Grand Rapids: Eerdmans, 1971), 47.

The definition of fruitfulness changes in the New Testament with the coming of Jesus, and already in the Old Testament there are prophecies looking forward to that change. The prophet Isaiah offers comfort to the barren woman, saying:

> Sing, O barren one who did not bear;
> > burst into song and shout,
> > you who have not been in labor!
> For the children of the desolate woman will be more
> > than the children of her that is married, says the LORD.
> Enlarge the site of your tent,
> > and let the curtains of your habitations be stretched out;
> do not hold back; lengthen your cords
> > and strengthen your stakes.
> For you will spread out to the right and to the left,
> > and your descendants will possess the nations
> > and will settle the desolate towns. (Isa. 54:1–3)

And again a few chapters later, looking forward to the gathering at God's holy mountain of all those joined to the Lord, Isaiah says:

> . . . do not let the eunuch say,
> > "I am just a dry tree."
> For thus says the LORD:
> To the eunuchs who keep my sabbaths,
> > who choose the things that please me
> > and hold fast my covenant,
> I will give, in my house and within my walls,
> > a monument and a name
> > better than sons and daughters;
> I will give them an everlasting name
> > that shall not be cut off. (Isa. 56:3–5)

The apostle Paul takes some of those prophecies to himself when he tells the Christians in Corinth that he has become their "father through the gospel" (1 Cor. 4:15).

With the coming of Jesus, the whole family structure of His people changes. There is now a new way to understand what it is to be part of the family of God. The broken relationship of Adam and Eve is restored when the one to whom it points, the one who is bone of our bone and flesh of our flesh, comes to live among us as the Bridegroom searching for His bride. Once the Bridegroom has come, all the family structures that had been pointing toward Him become relativized. On the one hand, they take on new significance since they point even more directly to Him and to His relationship with the church. On the other hand, they are no longer necessary. Once we arrive at the destination, signposts showing the way lose much of their significance. The new thing that Jesus introduces is not new patterns of sexual behavior but rather the new life of celibate singleness made possible through the gift of the Holy Spirit, who enables the fruit of self-control.

The desire for fruitfulness that God takes so seriously through the Old Testament continues to be addressed in Jesus, but now the focus is not simply on bearing children. God continues to desire our fruitfulness, but now fruitfulness is primarily seen in how we function within the family of the church. The biological family needs to find its place within the community of the church, for the biological family will pass away after death, while the community of the church persists into eternity. Here in the church, male and female, married and single, childless and those with many children are all fruitful. Not until Jesus comes does the fruitfulness that has always been God's mandate to those made in His image expand beyond the biological family to the family of the baptized. Already in the Old Testament, it is Jesus who appears to all these barren people, promising the coming of children. He is the one who makes all of us fruitful and who continues to be concerned with lives that bear good fruit.

Unequally Yoked

The first thing that Samson says in the book of Judges is addressed to his parents: "I saw a Philistine woman at Timnah; now get her for me as my wife" (14:2b). It is significant that his story begins with his sight of a woman, because his desire for women is what drives him throughout the saga. When his parents protest that he should not be chasing Philistine women but should find a wife among the women of Israel, he reiterates his demand: "Get her for me, because she pleases me" (14:3b), or more literally "she is right in my eyes." The two speeches begin and end with a reference to Samson's seeing, and the second speech foreshadows the depressing refrain of the later chapters in Judges, when each person is doing what is right in his or her own eyes rather than submitting to what is right in YHWH's eyes (17:6; 21:25). We have already seen in other stories how YHWH has arranged the world so that sin brings about punishment that is suited to the offense; it will therefore be no surprise when, at the end of his story, Samson is punished by the loss of his eyes. Samson makes no attempt to resist what pleases him, no attempt at custody of the eyes or at any form of self-control. The Spirit of the LORD has begun to stir in him, but the fruit of the Spirit is power and restlessness, not necessarily virtue. He is being prepared to be an instrument of judgment in the hand of YHWH, but at this point in the story he gives no evidence of any internal regeneration. The LORD also "stirred up" the spirit of Cyrus, king of Persia, but there is no assumption that Cyrus is regenerate (2 Chron. 36:22). The stirring of the Spirit working on Samson is driving him toward a destination that will serve YHWH's work, but Samson may make wrong, sinful decisions on the way to that destination.

In the section on structure, I argued that portions of chapters 14 through 16 are digressions during which Samson does precisely this; he resists the work of YHWH in his life, violates the terms of the Nazirite vow to which he has been bound since before his birth, and allows himself to be led along a path of escalating violence that does nothing to further his assigned task of beginning to deliver Israel from the Philistines. The entire digression begins with the vision of a desirable woman. She is unambiguously off-limits for Samson, since she is a Philistine woman and intermarriage with the people of the land is forbidden for the people of Israel, just as certainly as worshiping the gods of the land in place of YHWH is forbidden.

The text says that Samson's parents "did not know that this [i.e., his desire for the Philistine woman from Timnah] was from the LORD; for he was seeking a pretext to act against the Philistines" (14:4). Some commentators take this to mean that Samson was doing a virtuous act, perhaps even an act of evangelism or missional outreach by seeking to marry a Philistine woman. This cannot be true, given YHWH's clear command against such marriage. It may sometimes be the case that God calls us to specific actions, such as the call to Abraham to move from Ur, an action that could not have been discerned from a revelation of God's moral will alone. However, in the normal course of life, we discover God's will for our lives by studying His word and being obedient to it, and in no instance does God's special revealed will ever contradict His publicly available revelation in scripture. To suggest that YHWH gave Samson a secret message, saying that the law against intermarriage with the Canaanites, applicable to all Israelites, did not apply to him, is a gross misunderstanding of the will of God. It is true that in the Old Testament God did sometimes communicate His will directly to people through signs, visions, dreams, angelic visitation, the casting of lots, the Urim and Thummim, or the message of prophets[6]—but for God's people in the Old Testament, just as truly as for God's people under the new covenant,

6. Bruce Waltke, *Finding the Will of God: A Pagan Notion?* (Grand Rapids: Eerdmans, 1995), chap. 3.

God's word is not sometimes yes, sometimes no (2 Cor. 1:19–20). His standards of goodness do not shift.

In the chapter on Abimelech, we considered the idea that Abimelech remained responsible for his own sinfulness despite the fact that YHWH sent an evil spirit on him, just as Judas remained responsible for his betrayal of Christ despite the fact that his betrayal served God's salvific purpose. In the same way, the fact that YHWH will make use of Samson's transgressions does not turn them into righteous acts. Samson's inability to resist his own impulses, his constant attraction to the world of the Philistines, and his refusal to take YHWH's commandments seriously are all culpable weaknesses that should be resisted. Gideon, Abimelech, and Jephthah are all the children of unequal marriages, and Gideon himself entered into such a marriage, but only after the limits of the story that we have about him in this book. Samson is the first of the judges who contemplates marriage with a Canaanite as part of the account of his service as a judge in Israel.

Eating Honey from a Corpse

On his way to Timnah to visit his intended, Samson encountered a lion, which he was able to kill. The problem with this encounter is not the lion but the fact that Samson was walking through a vineyard when he had the encounter. As a Nazirite, Samson had no business being anywhere near a vineyard. He was not taking his vow seriously. The next time he went down to Timnah, he intentionally took a detour into the vineyard to look at the lion's carcass, another strange action for a Nazirite, who is supposed to avoid unclean things, particularly dead bodies, as well as vineyards and all grape products. The carcass turned out to be full of honey, but before telling us about the honey, the text mentions the presence of a swarm of bees. Jichan Kim points out, "Bees are mentioned only four times in the OT. The other three occurrences (Deut. 1:44; Ps. 118:12; Isa. 7:18) all allude to their irritable, vindictive nature and their painful sting, as symbols of Israel's enemies" (Kim 1993: 243). The bees should have warned Samson away from the honey, even if the dead and rotting body itself was not enough to do that; however, Samson chose to eat the honey that he found in the carcass, something that would be considered disgusting and unclean for any Israelite but is doubly offensive for a Nazirite. The sweetness of the honey was contaminated by death, but Samson was undeterred. He scraped the honey from inside the dead lion. He even shared the honey with his parents without telling them where he found it, thereby involving them in uncleanness as well. This becomes a potent symbol of how Samson approaches life: he delights to pursue his desires into the place of uncleanness and death. As a Nazirite he is meant to be set aside for holiness, but holiness is beyond him; he cannot even keep himself in a state of cleanness. Just as he cannot resist the lure of honey, even though it is embedded in a dead body, so he cannot resist the lure of the Philistines, who are supposed to be equally off-limits to him, no matter how much they sting. There is a deadly sweetness in the idolatrous culture of the Philistines that attracts him and that he makes no effort to resist, even though it is poisonous.

In his novel about Samson, *Prelude to Delilah*, the early Zionist author Vladimir Jabotinsky explores Samson's story as an allegory for the experience of Jews attempting to regain Israel while it was under British rule. Throughout the novel, Jabotinsky likens Samson's attraction toward all things Philistine to the way many Jewish settlers were drawn to the British, seeing them as cosmopolitan and clever, wanting to share in their rich cultural lives and receive acceptance and affirmation from them as fellow intellectuals, even while the British were interfering with the Zionist project of reclaiming Israel. Jabotinsky thinks Samson needs to learn to be proud of being Jewish rather than seeking approval among the Philistines.[7] The sweetness of the Philistines is like the sweetness of the occupying British—an apparent cultural superiority and a sophistication that draws and flatters those who surrender to it while it threatens assimilation and loss of identity.

When Samson goes to Timnah for his wedding, he is surrounded by thirty Philistine men acting as his attendants. Thirty attendants seems excessive, Kim argues, pointing out that "the usual number of friends who were to keep the groom company was seven" (1993: 251). The Philistines appear to be indulging in some intimidation. Daniel Block thinks that the excessive number points to a group of bodyguards or soldiers hired to keep Samson in line (1999: 432). Samson attempts to win over his attendants by engaging them in a battle of wits but finds that, despite his intelligence and his strength, he is no match for the solidarity of the Philistine community against him, a solidarity that requires his wife and her family to take the side of the Philistines against him as well. Samson's anger at his new wife's betrayal and at the underhanded methods of his "attendants" breaks out in his first recorded act of violence against other people: the murder of thirty random Philistine men so that he can steal their clothing to pay off his wager. This act of violence may seem to share in the trickster quality of Ehud's attack on Eglon, but Ehud was attacking the enemy king, thereby removing the head of the occupying force and preparing the way for an Israelite uprising and

7. Vladimir Jabotinsky, *Prelude to Delilah* (New York: Bernard Ackerman, 1945).

victory. Samson has no such strategic end in view, nor does his murder of thirty men in order to rob them in any way undermine the Philistine's power over Israel. This is a purely personal matter of vengeance, and those whom he kills are not even the same men as those who disrespected him.

Not surprisingly, this sets Samson on a trajectory of escalating violence. The Philistines, including his father-in-law, take his slaughter of thirty of their countrymen as a sign that he is repudiating his wife, and she is given in marriage to someone else. When Samson discovers this, he considers himself justified in a further attack and undertakes his "prank" of capturing three hundred foxes, tying them to one another by their tails, then setting them on fire and sending them running through the Philistines' wheat fields. This stunt only appears funny at first glance; if one thinks about it for more than a few moments, the humor quickly disappears. This is a profoundly cruel, anti-creational way to achieve vengeance, in which the primary sufferers are not the offensive humans who have mocked and disrespected Samson but animals toward whom Samson, as a human being in the lineage of Adam, owes care and stewardship. It is a sign that the alienation from the land named in the curse on Adam is not being lifted.

In retaliation for the burning of their fields, the Philistines burn Samson's wife and her father to death. The contrast with Othniel, explored in chapter 4 of this volume, is strengthened here. Marriage to Samson has led this young woman to a fiery death rather than to a secure home in a well-watered land. Samson escalates the violence further, determined to take revenge by killing Philistines "hip and thigh with great slaughter" (15:8). The result of this is to intensify the Philistine oppression of the people of Israel. Nothing that Samson has done up to this point in the narrative has been of any benefit to the people of Israel. He has pursued nothing but personal vengeance as retaliation for being disrespected, and although he has created a good bit of mayhem, he has not yet begun the work of delivering the people of Israel from the Philistines. His actions are reminiscent of the vengeful period of Gideon's story, in which Gideon is led astray from his mission by his thin-skinned need to punish those who have treated him without the respect he demands.

The threats of the Philistines lead three thousand men of Judah to come after Samson so as to turn him over to the Philistines, who are threatening them with violence. If Samson were functioning as a proper judge, he would lead those three thousand men of Judah along with men from other tribes in an uprising against the Philistines to win their freedom. Gideon delivered the Israelites from the Midianites with only three hundred men, and here Samson is engaged in a parley with ten times that number. But he makes no attempt to rally them or lead them into battle. He makes no attempt to encourage them to resist the Philistines themselves. He exhibits no solidarity with the people of Israel; his only concern is his personal war with the Philistines. Most commentators fault the men of Judah in this story for their cowardice in turning Samson over to the Philistines, and their passivity is certainly a falling off from the victories of Judah in chapter 1. But given how Samson has been acting, why should they do anything else? He has certainly not presented himself as a leader of men who might be able to command them in a battle against their oppressors. He has presented himself as an unstable, unpredictable creator of chaotic violence directed against anyone who fails to show him proper respect. He is a far cry from Jephthah.

After he has been tied up and turned over to the Philistines by the men of Judah, the Spirit of the Lord comes on Samson so that his bonds melt away. He then takes advantage of an unconventional weapon, the jawbone of an ass, to kill one thousand Philistines in a great slaughter. But when that slaughter is over, he finds himself alone in the desert, parched with no water in sight, surrounded by heaps of corpses. These corpses have no honey in them; the sweetness has disappeared, and all that is left is death. Samson, whose conception was a miracle of fertility in the midst of barrenness, now finds himself in a place of barrenness. His wife is dead; he has no children; he is surrounded by dead bodies; he is parched with thirst. And yet he has not conquered the Philistines. The army remains powerful and more determined to capture him than ever. At this moment, for the first time in the story, Samson offers a prayer. It is not a very good prayer. It is a prayer of resentment and entitlement, but it is at least an acknowledgment of temporary dependence on YHWH.

At the beginning of chapter 16, the story resets. It is not that Samson begins living a blameless life; he does not. But the trajectory of the story reverses. Whereas the story of chapters 14 and 15 has followed a trajectory of increasing violence and increasing slaughter, accompanied by increasing barrenness with no resultant victory, the trajectory that begins in chapter 16 leads to increasing weakness, helplessness, and blindness, but also to the accomplishment of Samson's mission.

Strength to Weakness

The story restarts, though with no obvious advantage initially. Indeed, the visit to a prostitute is a further descent into degradation, evidence that Samson remains captive to his impulses. And yet the primary event in this first story is the ripping up of the gates of the city of Gaza. Here at last is a genuine assault on the center

159

of Philistine power, an act that might increase the likelihood of an Israelite resistance against the Philistines. It remains a matter of personal vengeance, but it is an act with high symbolic and strategic value. The capital of the Philistines now lies open and vulnerable. More than that, for a brief moment Samson has broken free of the Philistines; he has walked away from Gaza, carrying Philistine power on his back, and placed himself and the symbols of that power facing Hebron, the city where David was to be anointed king.

Throughout much of Christian history, this episode has been understood as a type of the victory of Christ over death, with the gates of Gaza understood as symbols of the gates of hell. What seems more obvious to me is that Samson is a microcosm of the people of Israel. He was brought to birth through a direct intervention of YHWH, dedicated to YHWH's service from the beginning of his existence, and given extraordinary gifts beyond his deserving to be used in the service of YHWH. YHWH has given Samson His Spirit of judgment and power, but Samson has been unwilling to launch an all-out attack on the Philistines. He lashes out at them in wounded pride and anger while simultaneously courting them, seeking their approval and respect. He is drawn to the Philistines and has not truly wanted to drive them out, only to wound and punish. He has squandered his gifts, broken his vows, and pursued unfaithful relationships, but he is still equipped to do what YHWH has commanded: claim the land for YHWH's people.

"After this he fell in love with a woman in the valley of Sorek, whose name was Delilah" (16:4). This is the first time that Samson is described as "falling in love." His attraction to his bride was an attraction based only on seeing, but here something more is happening. Samson is not only attracted to Delilah; he actively loves her. There was a time when social scientists believed that the phenomenon of falling in love was a social construct devised in western Europe during the Middle Ages as a chivalric conceit, and that prior to that time it was unknown. This foolish idea has been widely discredited by anthropology and psychology alike.[8] Not every culture connects the experience of romantic love to marriage, but people have been falling in love with each other since the creation of human beings. This is how God made us.

In American popular culture, the experience of falling in love is considered self-justifying. It is seen as bigoted and narrow-minded to suggest that this experience

<hr />

8. Laura Smit, *Loves Me, Loves Me Not: The Ethics of Unrequited Love* (Grand Rapids: Baker Academic, 2005), 272. Also see R. F. Baumeister, S. R. Wotman, and A. M. Stillwell, "Unrequited Love: On Heartbreak, Anger, Guilt, Scriptlessness, and Humiliation," *Journal of Personality and Social Psychology* 64 (1993): 377–94.

is not a sufficient basis for morally admirable commitment. However, the Bible does not see romantic attraction as possessing this kind of authority. It is not self-justifying, but must be examined as to whether it is a love that is fitting for one of YHWH's people. The apostle Paul warns against being "mismatched with unbelievers" (2 Cor. 6:14), demonstrating that the warning against marriage with Canaanites or with any who are not part of the covenant community is not simply an Old Testament prohibition tied to the expansion of the nation of Israel. When we fall in love with someone and surrender to that experience, we will be shaped by the one we love. God designed romantic love to work this way so that our commitments to God-honoring romantic relationships will be strengthened, drawing us closer to God's will for our lives and helping us become the God-glorifying people He designed us to be. Romantic attraction can have positive power when the person with whom we have fallen in love joins us in loving God and wishing to serve Him. However, our sin regularly leads us to love unworthy things and inappropriate people, to be drawn away from God by our loves. God forbids intermarriage with the Canaanites not because He wants His people to be unhappy but because such entanglements will inevitably lead to idolatry. We may believe that our love will change the other person, and if our love is mutual, perhaps it will; but it will also change us. This is what happened to Solomon: "His wives turned away his heart after other gods; and his heart was not true to the LORD his God, as was the heart of his father David" (1 Kgs. 11:4).

In a case where there is no indication that the love is mutual, there is reason to expect that the one who feels most will be most influenced. Such appears to be the case with Samson's love for Delilah. His love for her makes him more vulnerable than he was to his Timnite wife or to the prostitute of Gaza. Love is a great good, but when it is a directed to an unworthy object, it becomes a twisted good in the service of the diminishment of the self. As Henry Scougal famously observed, "The worth and excellency of a soul is to be measured by the object of its love. He who loveth mean and sordid things, doth thereby become base and vile; but a noble and well-placed affection, doth advance and improve the spirit into a conformity with the perfections which it loves."[9] It is precisely because love has power to remake us into the likeness of its object that YHWH places such importance on not marrying outside Israel. Marriage with an idolater has the power to make a worshiper of YHWH into an idolater. "Do not intermarry with them [the people of the land], giving your daughters to their sons or taking their

9. Henry Scougal, *The Life of God in the Soul of Man* (Boston: Nichols and Noyes, 1868), 40.

daughters for your sons, for that would turn away your children from following me, to serve other gods" (Deut. 7:3–4).

Samson's love of this woman shapes him into her likeness, and it is possible that she is also shaped by him. The Sorek valley is in Israelite territory, and it may be that Delilah was an Israelite woman. If so, however, she is a collaborator, since she is in the pay of Philistines. Possibly Samson found that he could only be drawn to an Israelite woman who shared his fascination with the Philistines, or perhaps Samson finally turned away from the Philistines to love an Israelite woman only to bring the Philistines with him, so that she was enmeshed in their culture because of him. Either way, this love bears bad fruit and should have been resisted.

A wrong love is best resisted by cultivating a stronger love for a worthy object, and the best love to cultivate is a love for God. Turning again to Scougal: "First, I say, love must needs be miserable, and full of trouble and disquietude, when there is not worth and excellency enough in the object to answer the vastness of its capacity. So eager and violent a passion, cannot but fret and torment the spirit, where it finds not wherewith to satisfy its cravings. And, indeed, so large and unbounded is its nature, that it must be extremely pinched and straitened, when confined to any creature; nothing below an infinite good can afford it room to stretch itself, and exert its vigor and activity."[10] We have been made with the capacity to love God Himself, and when that love becomes dominant in our lives, lesser loves fall into their proper position. Loves for lesser goods are put in their right place, and loves for what is not good grow weaker and lose their hold on us. Samson's primary problem is that he gives no evidence of having such a love for God, and so the lower loves, those loves that are fueled by appetite and by the senses and by physical desire, have no check on their dominance in his life.

Samson's interactions with Delilah follow many of the same patterns as his interactions with his bride in Timnah, but without the spirit of vengeance or the escalation of violence. Here too he has a secret, which she pesters him to share over many days. Here too she is under pressure from the Philistines to betray him and does so. Here too he ends up bound and handed over to the Philistines. The new thing that Delilah offers is that she is so transparent; over and over she reveals that she will do to him whatever he tells her will weaken him. The repeated appearance of the Philistines also makes clear that she is sharing information with them. This raises the question asked by every Sunday school class

10. Scougal, *Life of God*, 45.

and Bible study group that has ever looked at this story: How stupid is Samson that he tells her his secret?

Samson is not stupid. He is impulsive, thin-skinned, and lacking in the ability to manage his anger. But he is not stupid. Indeed, throughout these stories he is shown as being very clever. So why would he tell Delilah his secret? Some think that—as with his wife in the earlier story—he was simply worn down by her persistence, but unlike his wife, Delilah has shown clearly that she will test whatever answer he gives her. He knows full well that she will cut his hair. So why? First, it is possible that he is surrendering. He is in love with Delilah, and for most of his life he has also been entranced by Philistine culture more generally; perhaps he is just giving in. He is admitting the superiority of the Philistines and changing sides in the struggle between the Philistines and Israel. The problem with this view is that when he awakes and finds that his hair has been cut, he does not think to himself, "Well, that's done then." Instead, his first thought is to fight off the Philistines. "When he awoke from his sleep, he thought, 'I will go out as at other times, and shake myself free'" (16:20). If there had been a passing thought of surrender, it did not last.

Second, it is possible that Samson was ready to stop being a Nazirite, and a Nazirite vow ends with the cutting of the hair. Perhaps he thought that the great feats of strength he had already performed were enough, that he would like to call an end to this covenantal relationship with YHWH. His mother had been told that he would be a Nazirite until his death, but most Nazirite vows are not lifelong; they are defined by a particular task or promise, and once the task is finished or the promise kept, the vow is over. Perhaps Samson had decided that he had done enough to count his vow as completed. Again, his reaction upon waking does not fit well with this possibility, since it suggests that he expected to continue being a strongman, continue leaping into brawls with Philistines, and continue doing all the things he has done up to this moment.

In my view the only explanation that makes sense is that he no longer believes his strength has anything to do with the Nazirite vow, or with his hair, of even with YHWH. He has violated the terms of his vow over and over again with no consequences in terms of his strength or power. He has been in contact with vineyards and corpses; he has dallied with Philistine women; he has broken the two great commands to the Israelites as they settled in the new land by marrying a Philistine and by not resisting the Philistine occupation in any organized way, which means he has failed to pursue the calling for which he was born: he has done all this, and he is as strong as ever. He has come to believe that his strength is his own. He does not believe that cutting his hair will make any difference.

In truth, the strength is a gift from God, and if his hair had been cut against his will without his collaboration, and if at the same time he had been firmly and intentionally committed to his covenanted relationship with YHWH, Samson would not have lost his strength. The account that he gave to Delilah—that his hair was the source of his strength—was not true. Samson's hair did not make him strong, and articulating the story in that way is to move into a place of superstition. The hair is a sign and symbol; one might even call it a sacrament. But it is not the thing signified. The hair is a sign of the vow that unites Samson to YHWH. Given that his relationship with YHWH is already broken and his vow is already purely nominal, the maintenance of his long hair had indeed become the last vestige of the vow, and when it was taken away, there was nothing left. "He did not know that the LORD had left him" (16:20b), but he is to discover that absence soon enough. The Philistines proceed to gouge out his eyes, yet this is the moment when Samson at last sees truly. That moment of the Lord's absence and his own weakness is the twitch on the thread.

Eyeless in Gaza: Triumph in Death

In his poem *Samson Agonistes*, John Milton imagines Samson speaking to a visitor when he is imprisoned by the Philistines. He thinks back on his miraculous birth and wonders why he was identified as separate and special with a high divine purpose if in fact he was destined to end up here, a slave of the Philistines, doing animal labor by pushing a millstone. "Promise was that I / Should Israel from Philistian yoke deliver; / Ask for this great Deliverer now, and find him / Eyeless in Gaza at the Mill with slaves, / Himself in bonds under Philistian yoke."[11] This moment of dereliction is an expression of Israel's current state of life; it is also the moment in the book of Judges at which one of the judges is most Christlike, though I would not go so far as to call him a type of Christ. Samson will find the ability to fulfill his calling through this experience of weakness, an experience that drives him to reenter his relationship with YHWH, this time correctly.

For the text of Judges tells us that here, enslaved by the Philistines, "the hair of his head began to grow again after it had been shaved" (16:22). The point is not that his hair is magical, for it is not the hair that gives him power. The point is that

---

11. John Milton, *Samson Agonistes*, lines 38–42, in *Complete Poems and Major Prose*, ed. Merritt Y. Hughes (New York: Macmillan, 1957), 552.

he has recommitted to a Nazirite vow. By facilitating the cutting of his hair, he had disavowed the vow made on his behalf at his conception; now he has renewed that vow. For the first time in the story he is committed to doing what he was made to do, which is to begin the defeat of the Philistines. He is an eyeless slave, and it is by no means clear how he will be able to do such a thing, but for the first time he is focused in the right direction. As Paul says regarding the "thorn" that was such a trial to him, of which he had asked to be relieved, "[The Lord] said to me, 'My grace is sufficient for you, for power is made perfect in weakness.' . . . Therefore I am content with weaknesses, insults, hardships, persecutions, and calamities for the sake of Christ; for whenever I am weak, then I am strong" (2 Cor. 12:9–10). As for Paul, so for Samson. This time of apparent weakness will be the occasion for his greatest display of strength.

When the Philistines seek to humiliate Samson yet further by making him "entertain" them (exactly how is not specified), he prays for the second time in the saga. It is still not a wonderful prayer, since he is still asking for personal vengeance, but for the first time Samson recognizes that YHWH is the source of his strength and that he will succeed or fail at YHWH's pleasure. Samson understands that he can no longer hope to fulfill God's purpose for his life—the destruction of the Philistines—without also destroying himself, since his life is so enmeshed with theirs. He chooses death, though as a path to life. Hebrews 11 names Samson as a hero of faith, and we must assume that it is on the basis of this last prayer, for nothing earlier in his life gave evidence of much faith. This mention gives us confidence that God greeted Samson's sacrifice with mercy.

Cheryl Exum points out that YHWH answers prayer in all three sections of the saga. In the birth narrative, Manoah's prayer is answered, though not exactly in the way that he wanted. YHWH remains free and in control of the situation. Similarly, both of Samson's prayers are answered but in ways that "underscore divine freedom and grace."[12] At the end of chapter 15, Samson appears triumphant and full of the Spirit, but then—unexpectedly—he reveals weakness and dependence that drive him to prayer. YHWH's answer reinforces that Samson is indeed dependent on him for life. At the end of chapter 16, Samson appears abandoned by YHWH, but then—unexpectedly—Samson's prayer brings him YHWH's renewed presence. It also brings death. "Answered prayer reverses the outcomes we expect on the basis of the other two types of theological references. It reminds us of Yhwh's freedom to alter the course of events and willingness

---

12. J. Cheryl Exum, "The Theological Dimension of the Samson Saga," *VT* 33, fasc. 1 (January 1983): 39.

to respond to human need."[13] These moments in which YHWH responds to prayer are unlike the moments when YHWH works secretly behind the scenes in ways that the actors cannot know, for in these responses the petitioners are aware of YHWH's presence. Answered prayer is also different from the coming of the Spirit, since the Spirit's presence comes at YHWH's initiative, not at Samson's request.

> The one who answers prayer is the true center of attention in each cycle. In xv 18–19 we see who is really powerful—Yhwh, not Samson. In xvi 28–30 we see who is really God—Yhwh, not Dagon. When Samson brags and baits, Yhwh manifests power with no assistance from Samson. Divine response in xv 19 serves to undercut the hero's boastful claim. When, on the other hand, Samson turns directly to Yhwh for help, Yhwh accepts him as an instrument through which to carry out the divine plan, xvi 30. At no point does the narrative pass judgement upon Samson, either for baiting the deity in his request for life, ch. xv, or for his prayer for vindication and death in ch. xvi. The decision both for life and for death rests with Yhwh, who has been controlling all—at times behind the scenes, at times through the spirit, and, preeminently through answered prayer.[14]

YHWH's complete control over life and death is again asserted in the Samson saga, as it has been asserted throughout the book of Judges in YHWH's claim that He has the right to judge which nations live and which nations die.

In *The Tree of Life*, Bonaventure references Samson as a type of Christ precisely at this moment. In the section of the work "Jesus, Triumphant in Death" he writes:

> Now that the agony of the passion was over, and the bloody dragon and the savage lion thought they had obtained victory by murdering the Lamb, the power of divinity began to shine forth in His soul descending into hell. Through this power, our strong *Lion of the tribe of Juda* [*sic*], rising against His fully armed foe, tore away its prey, broke down the gates of hell, and shackled the serpent. *Disarming the Principalities and Powers, He displayed them openly, leading them away in triumph.* Now Leviathan has been led about with a hook, his jaw pierced by Christ Himself. Thus Satan, who had no power of the Head he had assaulted, lost also any power he had seemed to have over the body. It was then that the true Samson destroyed by His death a whole army of enemies; then, that the immaculate Lamb delivered His prisoners *by the blood of His testament*, and *sent forth* His *prisoners out of the*

13. Exum, "Theological Dimension," 40.
14. Exum, "Theological Dimension," 42.

pit wherein is no water; then, that the radiance of a new light long expected shone upon those *that dwelt in the region of the shadow of death.*[15]

Jesus teaches that this pattern of a seed dying in order to bring forth life is the pattern of life for all his disciples, not a pattern unique to Him.

---

15. Bonaventure, *The Tree of Life*, in *The Works of Bonaventure*, vol. 1, *Mystical Opuscula*, trans. José de Vinck (Quincy, IL: Franciscan Press, 1960), 132.

11

THE FIRST EPILOGUE

17:1–18:31

Structure

This epilogue stands parallel to the second prologue, which was focused on the sin of idolatry and the apostasy of Israel in falling prey to that sin. This epilogue considers the same theme. The idolatrous worship that was already evident in Judg. 2 has become much worse, more explicitly and unapologetically idolatrous, and so the slide into radical infidelity to YHWH that was predicted at the beginning of the book has been realized as we near its end.

This first epilogue is tied to the second epilogue by the well-known refrain that "in those days there was no king in Israel." The refrain appears twice in this epilogue (17:6; 18:1), twice in the next (19:1; 21:25). The first and last of those four occurrences add the information that "all the people did what was right in their own eyes." The epilogues are also connected in that both involve as the central character a Levite who is living in Ephraim but is from Bethlehem. Although it seems likely that the historical events behind these stories involved different Levites, the editor of Judges has collapsed them into one composite character, a strategy that contributes to the prophetic message that these stories are meant to express. It is also important to remember that in the book of Judges the stories are arranged not by chronology but by theme. The stories in these two epilogues may have occurred earlier than the Samson and Samuel stories, since they involve a grandson of Moses and a grandson of Aaron as principle actors, though there is also an argument from the fate of the Danites and the rootlessness of the Levites that the historical events behind the stories occurred much later, perhaps even after the separation of the Northern Kingdom (Webb 2012: 420). Webb points out that "there is no way, finally, of adjudicating between [these possibilities]. What is clear, however, is that whatever their original provenance and purpose may have been, these two narratives now form a most appropriate epilogue to Judges" (2012: 420).

Dorsey suggests the following structure for this first epilogue:

a Micah sets up an <u>idolatrous shrine</u> for his private use (17:1–6)
  b Micah secures services of Levite (17:7–13)
    c Danite spies visit Micah's house in peace (18:1–6)
      d TURNING POINT: Danites carry out their mission and return to propose hostility (18:7–10)
    c′ Danite spies visit Micah's house in hostility (18:11–17)
  b′ Micah loses services of Levite (18:18–26)
a′ Danites set up an <u>idolatrous shrine</u> to serve their entire tribe (18:27–31)[1]

Although the story seems at the beginning to be primarily about Micah and his mother, and then seems to be primarily about the wandering Levite, the scope of the story quickly expands and turns out to be centered not on one idolatrous family but on an entire tribe that is abandoning its assigned place in the land and setting up an alternative center of worship to compete with the ark and the tabernacle.

The pattern established in Judg. 2, which has governed the judge stories to this point, is now broken. The pattern of disobedience followed by foreign domination, cries for deliverance, and the raising up of a judge ends with Samson. In these epilogues there is no need for foreign domination; the conflicts are all between Israelites. And there are no more judges to deliver.

The recurring conflicts with Ephraim come to a head in this epilogue. The Ephraimites cooperated with Ehud, complained of mistreatment from Gideon, and rebelled against Jephthah—moving from fighting with zeal against the enemies of YHWH to creating strife within Israel. Now Ephraim is the center of

1. Dorsey 1999: 116. This is a simplified version of his schematic, which involves detailed subpoints that are also in parallel.

an alternative religious practice, which also tears the people of Israel apart. The secessionist king, Jeroboam, was of the house of Ephraim (1 Kgs. 11), and so the religious division created in this story foreshadows the political division that will be created then. The subsequent leaving of the promised land of Canaan by the Danites foreshadows the disappearance into exile of not only the Danites and Ephraimites but all the tribes of the Northern Kingdom.

Apostasy

Micah and his mother are so dysfunctional as to be almost funny. The story begins with Micah confessing to his mother that he has stolen 1,100 pieces of silver from her. Presumably, he is motivated to confess because she has laid a curse on the unknown thief. His desire to have the curse lifted is the only motive suggested, even indirectly, for his confession. Having confessed, he returns the money to his mother, and she is so happy to receive her money back that she celebrates by deciding to use all (or perhaps only part) of the money to make "an idol of cast metal" (17:4). The fact that the story centers on 1,100 pieces of silver—the very amount that Delilah was paid for her services by each of the five Philistine lords—connects this story to the story of Samson. In terms of history there is surely no connection, but literarily there is a strong connection. Micah's mother is not literally Delilah, and Micah is not literally the son of Samson, and yet the character of Micah is precisely what we should expect to proceed from Samson's life. Micah is Samson's spiritual heir, even if not his biological son. This link between the stories also suggests that the money being used for the making of an idol and the founding of this new religious center is blood money, like Judas's pieces of silver, in addition to being stolen money, making the idol that is created with it exponentially more unclean.

Micah's mother says she's dedicating all 1,100 pieces of silver to the LORD, but she then only gives 200. This sort of distorted piety characterizes the entire story. She also says that she is "consecrat[ing] the silver to the LORD" (17:3). As we considered when looking at the Jephthah story, there are laws about the irrevocability of things and people that have been consecrated to YHWH; however, that does not remove the guilt for what she is doing. Consecrating idolatry to YHWH is a nonsensical thing to do, just as the consecration of a human sacrifice to YHWH was a nonsensical thing for Jephthah to do. As Jesus says, "Not everyone who says to me, 'Lord, Lord,' will enter the kingdom of heaven, but only the one who does the will of my Father in heaven" (Matt. 7:21). Setting up idol worship in one's home does not become a good thing because one says that it is consecrated to the Lord.

YHWH doesn't act in this story. He is invoked by the mother, and of course her theory is that the whole sanctuary is to His glory, but He has become conspicuously silent at this point in the narrative. Since throughout the book YHWH has been very active, claiming responsibility for everything, this silence is ominous and significant. The worship that is being established here by Micah is not of YHWH: not properly directed toward Him and not authorized by Him. It is irrelevant to Him.

It seems likely that Micah and his mother are both well intentioned. There is evidence throughout scripture that some Israelites thought it was possible to borrow the imagery of the Canaanites to reinforce or support their faith in YHWH. They would have said that they were not in fact making new gods when they made idols, but were simply crafting a symbol of YHWH that could be a focal point for worship. This is the same logic that dominates many parts of the Christian tradition throughout history, in which the hope is to make worship more relevant to the surrounding culture or to give Christians for whom interaction with the word of God is difficult visual supports for their faith. However, God has already revealed Himself using authoritative images—the pillar of fire, the cloud of smoke, the tabernacle, and the ark in the Old Testament; the bread, the wine, and the font in the New. We tend to think that innovation is always a good thing, even in the language and imagery that we use to speak of God, but in scripture the emphasis is not on inventing new images or new language. Rather, the emphasis is on conforming to the revealed language and restricting oneself to the use of authorized, revealed images.

Good intentions and sincerity of belief do not guarantee righteousness. It is quite possible to be sincerely wrong. C. S. Lewis explains:

> Having allowed oneself to drift, unresisting, unpraying, accepting every half-conscious solicitation from our desires, we reached a point where we no longer believed the Faith. Just in the same way, a jealous man, drifting and unresisting, reaches a point at which he believes lies about his best friend: a drunkard reaches a point at which (for the moment) he actually believes that another glass will do him no harm. The beliefs are sincere in the sense that they do occur as psychological events in the man's mind. If that's what you mean by sincerity, they are sincere. . . . But errors which are sincere in that sense are not innocent.[2]

2. C. S. Lewis, *The Great Divorce* (San Francisco: HarperSanFrancisco, 2001), 38.

The problem with attempting to make our worship accessible or relevant to our context is that the influence does not go only from our religious commitments into the culture; in fact, the influence is more likely to go the other direction, with the new accommodation reshaping our understanding of God. Jephthah was sincere, but his worship of YHWH was tainted with the patterns of Tob. As we attempt to be relevant, we also begin to search for approval from those we are addressing, the very people from whom we are called to separate. Samson longed for the respect and the approval of the Philistines, and for most of his life he suppressed his true calling in hopes of gaining their acceptance. As we attempt to devise new ways of worship, we may find that those new ways become, as Gideon discovered, "a snare." They entrap us, tangling our minds in concepts about God that are inadequate and inaccurate, preventing us from an encounter with His reality.

John Calvin acknowledges that God did use signs to signify His presence throughout the history of Israel, but he suggests that these signs were deliberately designed to prevent speculation and to convey the transcendent otherness of God. "For clouds and smoke and flame, although they were symbols of heavenly glory, restrained the minds of all like a bridle placed on them, from attempting to penetrate too deeply. . . . The mercy seat from which God manifested the presence of his power under the law was so constructed as to suggest that the best way to contemplate the divine is where minds are lifted above themselves with admiration. Indeed, the cherubim with wings outspread covered it; the veil shrouded it; the place itself deeply enough hidden concealed it."[3] Calvin goes on to say that human nature is "a perpetual factory of idols," precisely because the human mind wants "to imagine a god according to its own capacity."[4] He points to the creation of the golden calf as just such an event. The people of Israel were not trying to invent a new god; they were trying to worship YHWH according to their own capacity, in a way that was accessible and under their control. The fact that they intended the sign of the calf to point to the God of Abraham, Isaac, and Jacob, just as Micah intended the sign of his ephod to point to YHWH, does not diminish their sin. That intention is itself blasphemous because it reduces YHWH to the level of the worshiper. In Ps. 50, YHWH addresses His wayward people, saying, "you thought that I was one just like yourself. But now I rebuke you, and lay the charge before you. Mark this, then, you who forget God, or I will tear you

3. John Calvin, *Institutes* 1.11.3, in *Institutes of the Christian Religion*, 2 vols., ed. John T. McNeill, trans. Ford Lewis Battles (Philadelphia: Westminster, 1960), 1:102.
4. Calvin, *Institutes* 1.11.8 (Battles, 1:108).

apart, and there will be no one to deliver" (Ps. 50:21–22). YHWH will not be domesticated, captured within an image or a figurine.

Of course, idolatry is unavoidable, even for the most iconoclastic of us. In his poem "He Whom I Bow To," C. S. Lewis speaks to God of his own inevitable idolatry, since every time he thinks of God or addresses Him in prayer, he is always addressing "meanings" that cannot be who God is, something that Lewis knows even as he prays. He concludes, "All prayers always, taken at their word, blaspheme," because all of us are "self-deceived," speaking not to God Himself but to the nonexistent being of our imagining. Our only hope is that God will "divert" the randomly fired "arrows" of our prayers toward Himself, beyond anything that we deserve.[5]

The law is meant to place a bridle on our idolatrous impulses by limiting our inventiveness in worship and by directing our prayers and confessions into divinely sanctioned channels. Here toward the end of the book of Judges, those controls have fallen away and the impulse to idolatry is unresisted; it is given free rein and full expression. Micah is creating his own religion in competition with the worship that is still being conducted at Shiloh, where the tabernacle is established and the ark is housed. In Josh. 24, Joshua challenged the people of Israel, saying, "Now therefore revere the LORD, and serve him in sincerity and in faithfulness; put away the gods that your ancestors served beyond the River and in Egypt, and serve the Lord. Now if you are unwilling to serve the LORD, choose this day whom you will serve, whether the gods your ancestors served in the region beyond the River or the gods of the Amorites in whose land you are living; but as for me and my household, we will serve the LORD" (Josh. 24:14–15). Micah demonstrates that the choice has been made. There is no middle ground between serving YHWH and idolatry, and to seek the middle ground is to choose against YHWH.

The great difference between the experience of Israel in the Old Testament and our own experience in the twenty-first century in the West is that everyone in the ancient Near East of whatever nation believed in the supernatural. The absence of explicit religious practice, so common in our own culture, was not an option. And yet the difference is not as great as it might seem. The "supernatural" in which the gods of the nations operated was supernatural vis-à-vis our reality, but it was not an ultimate or different way of existing. The gods of the nations

---

5. C. S. Lewis, "He Whom I Bow To," in *The Collected Poems of C. S. Lewis: A Critical Edition*, ed. Don W. King (Kent, OH: Kent State University Press, 2015), 225. A different version of this poem appears under the title "Footnote to All Prayers" in C. S. Lewis, *Poems*, ed. Walter Hooper (New York: Harcourt, 1992), 129.

behaved much as human beings do, but with more power. They could be bribed and placated and manipulated in the same ways as human beings can be. The gods were often connected to natural powers, such as storms and rain, the sun and the moon. When YHWH says to His people, "For my thoughts are not your thoughts, nor are your ways my ways" (Isa. 55:8), He is emphasizing that He is not like these other gods. The worship of such gods is a form of technology, an attempt on the part of a human being to control and manipulate the world. Micah is falling back into a technological approach to religion, rather than the sort of encounter with the holy I AM of Israel that made the people at Sinai tremble in fear. Such an encounter calls the worshiper to surrender control rather than assert it. The goal of right worship is not to manipulate and transform the world around us according to our desires but rather to have our desires transformed according to God's will.

Micah's efforts go beyond setting up a personal altar in the corner of his home. He is setting up a shrine, probably one that he expects to open to the public, a shrine that will raise the profile of his town in the area and make it an important center. He is making an ephod, which means that people will come to his priest to receive answers to their questions. He even goes so far as to consecrate one of his sons as the priest of this shrine. Since Micah is presented as an Ephraimite, such an appointment shows a high disregard for the Levitical law. "The priest that Micah appointed was just as makeshift and irregular as everything else in his shrine" (Webb 2012: 425). In Hebrew the shrine is called a *bet elohim*, which could mean "the house of God" (as Elohim is often used as the non-covenant name for YHWH) or "the house of *gods*." Webb suggests that this ambiguity

> captures and completes the satirical irony of the entire passage: Micah's "house of God" is in fact a "house of gods," but neither Micah nor his mother seems to be able to tell the difference. The body of the book has shown us the nation of Israel vacillating between faithfulness to Yahweh and going after other gods, but at least able to know they were doing so (as, e.g., in 10:15–16). The present passage shows us that, at the domestic and village level, even this ability has been lost. The man whose name means "Who is like Yahweh?" can become the owner and patron of a house of idols! It is an episode of complete religious chaos. (Webb 2012: 426)

In the Pentateuch, people who assert themselves in worship are typically punished, and the first hearers of this story might naturally have expected to hear of Micah and his son coming to a grisly end, being consumed by fire from heaven perhaps. Instead, the first statement of the refrain follows immediately after the explanation of what Micah has done: "In those days there was no king in Israel; all the people did what was right in their own eyes" (Judg. 17:6). The punishment now is not, as with Nadab and Abihu, death by incineration (Lev. 10:2). The punishment is worse: it is the absence of YHWH. The King has withdrawn from His people, leaving them to their own devices.

The Levite

At the end of the story, we are told that the Levite who comes to serve as Micah's priest and then goes off with the Danites is Jonathan, the grandson of Moses. Given the flagrant idolatry of the story, this is a startling word. The other named person in these epilogues is Phinehas, the grandson of Aaron, but he is not tainted as is Jonathan. The descendent of the lawgiver has thrown away the law. The law that was given through Moses to the people of Israel at Sinai was not simply a list of rules; it was a guide for conforming oneself to the nature of reality as revealed by the Maker of all reality. For pious Israelites, the law involves all of YHWH's design for the heavens and the earth. It is a pattern of order and beauty that invites meditation and praise as much as obedience. For Jonathan, the grandson of Moses, to join in doing what is right in his own eyes, rather than conforming himself to the revealed will of YHWH, is more than simply breaking rules; it is a rejection of the claim that YHWH is the creator of heaven and earth, the designer of the cosmos, the one who orders reality. It is a rejection of the claim that YHWH has a plan for His people, a destination that He has implanted in them toward which He is drawing them. That is to say, it is a rejection of teleology. Instead, it is the assertion that human beings can and should write their own stories, shape their own destinies, and chart their own paths. Each person should do whatever is right in his or her own eyes, because the only destination for a human life is the one each person sets for himself or herself.

The Levite appears on the scene as one who has been "sojourning" in Bethlehem and who is now traveling about in order "to sojourn in whatever place he could find."[6] Webb notes that to *sojourn* is "living as a landless foreigner" (2012: 428). Naturally, as a Levite he was to be landless, but not as a foreigner, since the Levites were to be at home in the land, caring for the people of Israel as priests. YHWH had told Aaron that he and his children would have a different

---

6. Translation of 17:7–8 from Webb (2012: 427).

portion than land: "Then the LORD said to Aaron: You shall have no allotment in their land, nor shall you have any share among them; I am your share and your possession among the Israelites" (Num. 18:20). And this was true not only for Aaron but for all the tribe of Levi. "The levitical priests, the whole tribe of Levi, shall have no allotment or inheritance within Israel. They may eat the sacrifices that are the LORD's portion but they shall have no inheritance among the other members of the community; the LORD is their inheritance, as he promised them" (Deut. 18:1–2; Ps. 16:5–6). The sacrifices of the people were also counted as the "portion" of the Levites, which was supposed to be a tithe of the bounty of the Israelites, so this was not a calling to intentional poverty. Only the sons of Aaron were allowed to offer sacrifices (Num. 18:8), but all the Levites performed service in the tabernacle (Num. 18:23), and it appears that the service Jonathan is performing for Micah is this sort of service in the "holy" place, since there is no mention of an altar nor of sacrifice.

The fact that Jonathan the Levite is wandering about with no clear direction is a graphic demonstration of the breaking of the tie connecting the people of Israel to YHWH, a tie established when Abram first responded to YHWH's call and set off from Ur to parts unknown. Always they have been drawn toward YHWH; always He has set their direction and their course. But Jonathan no longer has a destination in view.

Jonathan's need for stable employment is a sign that the troubles of this story are systemic, not individual. The failure of the people of Israel to maintain worship at the center of their life is leaving Levites with not enough to do. But then the people's failure may well be the result of Levites such as this one who lack any real commitment to or knowledge of YHWH and so are incapable of leading the people into a robust life of worship, considering themselves free to leave their assigned posts and improvise a new line of work for themselves.

The Migration of Dan

The expansion of the story with the arrival of the Danites shows just how systemic the sin in Israel has become. One might expect that Israelites traveling through the land would be more aware of right worship practices than Micah, who is somewhat isolated in the hill country, and that the presence of a false shrine in the territory of Ephraim would be greeted with shock and disapproval. There is no shock, only envy. By this point in Israel's history, Micah's apostasy is not exceptional but is the story of Israel in microcosm.

The migration of Dan to Bashan is a fulfillment of Moses's prophecy: "Dan is a lion's whelp that leaps forth from Bashan" (Deut. 33:22).[7] Dan's migration to Laish is initiated without any consultation with YHWH. The people of Dan do not like the land they have been allotted and decide to go find some place easier to live. It is not surprising that people with such a mindset also decide that their religious life should be customized to meet their needs. This, of course, is not how YHWH works. He expects us to be customized to Him. However, the Danites decide that every new village needs a religious center, so they offer the Levite a position. In recognizing the voice of the Levite (18:3), it is highly unlikely that they recognize him specifically; it's more likely that he's chanting or reciting set prayers or psalms in a Levitical manner, which is what they recognize. Although they are rejecting the content of the law, they choose to hold on to its trappings, reducing the right worship of YHWH to a nostalgic veneer over their idolatrous practice.

The Danites first send out spies to investigate the land they are thinking of invading. The process of sending the spies reminds us of the spies who were sent into Canaan after the Israelites had been wandering in the wilderness. In that case, the investigation was in the service of bringing the people of Israel home to the promised land. In this story, however, the Danites are reversing the exodus. They wish to leave the land of promise, where they have had difficulty conquering the native peoples (something we saw already in Judg. 1), and instead they wish to conquer a land of safe and complacent people, who will surrender quickly. In so doing, they have left obedience behind, and their conquest of Laish is done without the authorization or blessing of YHWH. The reference in this story to "the camp of Dan" (Mahaneh-dan, 18:12) contrasts with the right worship that the Israelites conduct in the camp of YHWH (1 Chron. 9:19; 2 Chron. 31:2).

"In Those Days There Was No King"

"In those days there was no king in Israel; all the people did what was right in their own eyes" (17:6). This refrain unifies the two epilogues and offers a commentary on the disturbing stories of idolatry and violence that we find at the end of the book of Judges. The claim that each person in Israel did what was right in his or her own eyes strikes us as a description of a disordered and lawless situation. But Yairah Amit points out that this is only because of the context. "In other words,

7. Meredith G. Kline, *Treaty of the Great King: The Covenant Structure of Deuteronomy; Studies and Commentary* (Grand Rapids: Eerdmans, 1963), 147.

had the preceding and subsequent material provided us with information which conformed with positive biblical norms, there would be a tendency to interpret this statement as advocating a regime where there was no king."[8] Jean-Jacques Rousseau wrote a prose poem about a story in the second epilogue (*Le Lévite d'Ephraïm*, written in 1762) in which he construed the refrain as a beautiful and positive statement. His version goes like this: "In those days of freedom when no one man reigned over the people of the Lord, there was a time of liberty when each man, recognizing neither magistrate nor judge, was himself his own master and did all that seemed right to him. The nation of Israel, spread out over the fields, had no large towns, and the simplicity of its ways made law superfluous."[9]

But Rousseau's egalitarian, libertarian vision (at least egalitarian for men, since Rousseau was inclined to highlight a defense of patriarchy in the Levite's story) has little to do with the scriptural vision. The book of Judges is concerned not so much with the absence of a human king as with the lack of recognition for YHWH's kingship. The vision of Judges is never one of autonomy or radical equality but rather one of radical dependence on a sovereign God. Those who are doing whatever is right in their own eyes are putting their own judgment in the place of God's judgment. As Shakespeare said, "Take but degree away, untune that string, / And, hark, what discord follows!"[10] The relationship between God and His creatures can never be one of equality but must be a relationship of sovereignty on His part and submission on ours.

8. Yairah Amit, "Hidden Polemic in the Conquest of Dan: Judges XVII–XVIII," *VT* 40, fasc. 1 (January 1990): 6.

9. Cited and translated by Thomas M. Kavanagh, "Rousseau's *Le Lévite d'Ephraïm*: Dream, Text, and Synthesis," *Eighteenth-Century Studies* 16, no. 2 (Winter 1982–83): 150. "Dans les jours de liberté où nul ne régnait sur le peuple du Seigneur, il fut un temps de licence où chacun, sans reconnaître ni magistrat ni juge, était seul son proper maître et faisait tout ce qui lui semblait bon. Israël, alors épars dans les champs avait peu de grandes villes, et la simplicité de ses mœurs rendait superflu l'empire des lois."

10. William Shakespeare, *Troilus and Cressida*, act 1, scene 3, lines 109–10, in *The Complete Signet Classic Shakespeare*, ed. Sylvan Barnet et al. (New York: Harcourt Brace Jovanovich, 1972).

12

THE SECOND EPILOGUE

19:1–21:25

Structure

This gruesome and violent story begins to come into focus when we remember the chiastic structure of the book of Judges, which places this final conclusion in parallel with the first prologue. That first prologue was about the taking of the land, Israel's task of removing the Canaanites so that the land might be a holy place dedicated to YHWH. In this parallel epilogue we see that, instead of the land being made holy, the Israelites have been Canaanized. The Jewish town of Gibeah echoes the behavior of the paradigmatically evil town of Sodom. There is no longer conflict with the Canaanites, since the people of Israel have been culturally assimilated.

Also in the first prologue we were introduced to the story of Achsah, which was dropped into the midst of a story of battles with no clear rationale for its placement there. Now we see the rationale. That story about a woman, her husband, and her father stands in parallel to this story about a woman, her husband, and her father. The differences are illuminating.

To begin with, whereas the first chapter was full of interesting names, not only for Achsah, Othniel, and Caleb but for many other characters, this epilogue concerns unnamed people. The only person who will be named between now and the end of the book is Phinehas, who is serving before the ark at Bethel. This anonymity is a sign of falling away from God. In the Genesis creation story, God gives the power of naming to Adam. This is one way Adam reflects God's own logos-nature, for God has created everything by the power of His word. The loss of a name is a symptom of the slide backward from the creation into which we have been called toward nonbeing. The people of chapter 19 are thus less real than the people of chapter 1—not in a literary sense, but in an ontological sense. They are living more and more in the parasitic world of sin, illusion, and lie, rather than in the reality with "firm foundations" that is God's creation. This is what Augustine refers to as "the mass of perdition," out of which we must again be called by the gracious naming of the Logos, Christ.

A second difference: Achsah is described as a wife, whereas the unnamed woman in chapter 19 is a concubine. The exact status of a concubine is not always clear in the Old Testament, but at least one possible distinction between a wife and a concubine is that a wife receives a dowry from her father, whereas a concubine does not. Given the emphasis on the dowry from Caleb to Achsah and the fruitful and generous nature of that dowry, this distinction seems apt. Achsah's father provides for her life; the concubine's father sends her empty-handed to her husband, which leads to her death. Achsah is won as a wife by the courage of her husband, Othniel. The concubine is lost as a wife by the cowardice of her husband, the Levite. Achsah is not only named but also vocal. Although we never hear Othniel's voice, we do hear Achsah's voice as she confidently requests good gifts from her father. The concubine never speaks and is spoken to only once, after she is dead. In the Achsah story, Caleb and Othniel cooperate for Achsah's flourishing. The concubine's story ends not with flourishing but with death.

When the two stories are set next to each other in this way, we begin to see that the fate of the concubine is a symptom of Israel's degeneration. Achsah's story set the benchmark for a thriving, God-honoring society: men and women cooperate for their mutual flourishing, and the evidence of this cooperation is seen in the lifting up of women from their place of subjection that follows the fall. Few in Israel are more subjected than this nameless concubine, and at this point in Israel's cycle of decay there is no one to care about her flourishing.

Dorsey suggests that the epilogue's structure is divided into two episodes. The first episode, the rape and death of the concubine found in chapter 19, has the classic chiastic structure.

a   concubine leaves her home in Ephraim (19:1–2)
   b   happy negotiations for the woman (19:3–4)
      c   hospitality in Bethlehem (19:5–9)

     d   TURNING POINT: Levite begins journey home (19:10–13)

    c′ inhospitality in Gibeah (19:14–21)

   b′ terrible negotiations for the woman (19:22–26)

a′ concubine is brought back to her home in Ephraim—dead (19:27–30)[1]

This structure suggests that the key moment is the Levite's decision to leave the father's house in Bethlehem in order to return to Ephraim.

The second episode is the subsequent war against the tribe of Benjamin, found in chapters 20 and 21.

a **first all-Israel assembly** (20:1–11)
- tribes hear about atrocity in which concubine was forcibly taken and raped by Benjaminites
- they vow, "none of us will <u>return to his home</u>" until justice is achieved

b **second all-Israel assembly** immediately preceding the war (20:12–17)
- Israel, enraged at the atrocity, <u>sent men through all the tribe of Benjamin</u> demanding that the culprits be turned over
- <u>Benjaminites refuse to turn over to the Israelites the men who violently took and raped the concubine</u>

  c **Israel defeated by Benjaminites** (20:18–25)
- two battles, each concluded with tally of casualties

    d **TURNING POINT: Yahweh promises victory** (20:26–28)

  c′ **Israel defeats Benjaminites** (20:29–48)
- two phases of the battle, each concluded with tally of casualties

b′ **next-to-last all-Israel assembly**, immediately following the war (21:1–15)
- Israelites pity surviving Benjaminites; they <u>sent word to the Benjaminites</u> and proclaim peace; Israelites attack Jabesh-gilead and slaughter all the inhabitants, saving alive four hundred virgins, whom they give to Benjaminites
- <u>Israelites violently capture and turn over to Benjaminites four hundred innocent young women</u>

a′ **last all-Israel assembly** (21:16–25)
- tribes condone Benjaminites' forcibly taking for themselves two hundred women at Shiloh
- then they <u>return</u> "each to his own tribe and family" (Dorsey 1999: 118)

---

1. Dorsey 1999: 117, slightly simplified and abbreviated.

This structure demonstrates that in fighting Benjamin, just as in fighting non-Israelite oppressors, Israel depends for victory on YHWH's support, which is withheld during the initial battles but given during the subsequent battles. However, the structure also highlights the terrible parallels between what the army of Israel does to the people of Jabesh-gilead and what the Benjaminites did to the concubine. As Dorsey notes, "The original crime of Gibeah is dwarfed by this greater act of villainy" (1999: 118). This structure also highlights a parallel between the Benjaminites' refusal to turn over the guilty men of Gibeah and the Israelites' eagerness to turn over the innocent virgin daughters of Jabesh-gilead and Shiloh.

Just as in the first prologue, the people of Israel lack the courage and persistence to cleanse the land and make it holy. Because of their lack of resolve and their lack of faith in YHWH (in the prologue, faith that He will give the victory against those who seem strong; in the epilogue, faith that He will preserve the tribes of Israel), the people of Israel end up assimilated to the ones they are supposed to oppose. They identify more strongly with the Canaanites (in the prologue) and with the Canaanized Benjaminites (here in the epilogue) than with YHWH's plans for their future.

The Levite and His Concubine

There is debate about why the concubine leaves her husband, with some manuscript traditions saying that she was "unfaithful" and others saying simply that she "was angry with him." If her infidelity was adultery, we must conclude that the Levite was being heroically merciful and gracious in seeking her out. Such a reading violates the trajectory of the text; the entire design of the book, so carefully crafted to demonstrate the degeneration of Israel, would be undermined if we suddenly had an example of a leader manifesting heroic virtue here at book's end. There is certainly no sign of heroic virtue during their time in Gibeah. Furthermore, most commentators agree that an adulterous daughter would not be warmly welcomed back to her father's house. Therefore, many commentators opt for the reading that she was angry. Susan Niditch points out that adultery is not the only sort of unfaithfulness and that in this cultural context the act of leaving could itself be seen as unfaithful.[2]

As noted earlier, the editor of Judges coordinates the two stories about a Levite so that the reader naturally sees them as stories about the same person. In both

2. Susan Niditch, *Judges*, Old Testament Library (Louisville: Westminster John Knox, 2008), 191.

stories the Levite now lives in Ephraim but has past connections with Bethlehem, suggesting that the editor wants us to understand the Levite of chapter 19 as being Jonathan, son of Gershom, son of Moses. He is not named again here, because anonymity serves such a strong function in chapter 19, but he is identified as being from the hill country of Ephraim, which is where Micah lived and where the Danites had settled, and having a concubine from Bethlehem, which is where Jonathan had been living before coming to work for Micah. These connections are strong enough to make identification natural for the reader.

We therefore come to the story with a suspicion about this Levite, already knowing that he has not been faithful to YHWH. The likelihood that this unfaithful Levite has suddenly become a Hosea-like model of compassion seems slim. When we then read that his concubine left him, it is reasonable to hear this marital rift as echoing the other marital rift in the book of Judges, that between YHWH and his people. The word used for the concubine's unfaithfulness is the same word used in 2:17, 8:27, and 8:33 to speak about the people of Israel being unfaithful to YHWH. There has been a progressive alienation between YHWH and His people throughout the book, framed in terms of adultery and prostitution. The people of Israel are prostituting themselves to the Baals and Asherahs, being unfaithful to their true husband, YHWH. Here in this story the Levite, whose office requires him to represent Israel before YHWH, stands in for the people of Israel in much the same way that most of the major characters thus far have stood in for the people of Israel. This suggests that the angry concubine is meant not only to stand as a character in her own right but also to stand in for YHWH. Her "unfaithfulness" is a breaking of the covenant with the Levite, which is something YHWH has been threatening for several chapters now. As we have seen throughout the book, the effects of sin match the sin. The Levite's abandonment of YHWH naturally bears fruit in his life when his concubine abandons him. The concubine's treatment both by the Levite and at the hands of the men of Gibeah is a graphic depiction of how Israel has been treating YHWH during this period in her history.

On this reading, the most probable reason for the concubine's anger with her husband is precisely his infidelity to YHWH. The woman had married a Levite, expecting to be joined with a representative of the covenant with YHWH, but now finds that her husband has made himself the priest of an idol, serving a renegade tribe. The prologue to Jephthah has YHWH responding to the cry of Israel only reluctantly, indicating that He is on the edge of abandoning them. The prologue to Samson omits any reference to the Israelites' cry for help, suggesting that they are no longer wishing for their bridegroom. A rupture is the next step in the progression, but we are shown it only indirectly, in this story about two nameless people whose marriage is disintegrating.

This typology makes yet more sense when we look at it from a New Testament perspective, in which YHWH is known to be triune. It is Christ who is sent out from the Father to be the Bridegroom for the bride, God's own people. In this sending He empties Himself and comes into the world "dowerless," not relying on His own divine power. His mission is to lead us back to the Father's house. But He is despised and rejected. Ultimately, His body is broken and distributed to His people as a sacrament producing repentance and communion.

The concubine returns to her father's house in Bethlehem, marking her as from the tribe of Judah, as was Achsah in chapter 1. When the Levite follows his concubine to Bethlehem, he finds that there is a place prepared for him there. The lengthy description of the father's hospitality is hard to understand unless the number of days that the Levite stays in his father-in-law's house has some significance. I would suggest that here near the end of Judges we have a picture of Israel planted in the promised land and given the opportunity to start again in the new Eden, coming into Bethlehem, the "house of bread," the house of the Father who is their help (Abi-ezer), and beginning the process of new creation. But the Levite leaves on the fifth day. The creation and naming of human beings happened on the sixth day. He leaves unnamed and unregenerate. His concubine follows him into this state of almost nonbeing, and she becomes a sacrifice for him, betrayed by him, laying down her life for him. Her body is then broken and distributed to YHWH's people, though the repentance and reconciliation produced by this act are distorted and imperfect. Nonetheless, the concubine is the most complete christological type in the book of Judges.

The shocking, though unsurprising, lesson of the text is that the threat to life and flourishing facing the Levite (and by extension Israel) is no longer external but internal. The Levite tells his servant that he does not want to stop at the city of the Jebusites, because it will be unsafe; he prefers to press on to reach an Israelite city. But the Canaanization of Israel is now so complete that this is no guarantee of safety. The story of the men of Gibeah's demands for the rape of the Levite deliberately echoes the story of Sodom and Gomorrah from Gen. 19, leading to the horrifying conclusion that those worthy of YHWH's destruction and judgment are no longer only outside the covenant community but within it as well. Indeed, Gibeah turns out to be a more dangerous place even than Sodom. As we discover in 1 Sam. 10:26, Gibeah is also King Saul's home, and this portrayal of the men of Gibeah as worse than the men of Sodom contributes to the lifting up of Judah as the tribe from which the hoped for, legitimate king should come.

Although the Levite is protected by being inside his host's home, he is unwilling to risk his own well-being in the face of the possibility that the mob will break into the house, and so he gives his concubine into their power in his place. The substitutionary nature of her suffering is striking. The text is perfectly clear about what happens: "They wantonly raped her, and abused her all through the night until the morning" (19:25). When the Levite emerges in the morning, he finds her lying by the door of the house, with her hands on the threshold. It is unclear if she is already dead. He seems to think she is still living, since he tells her to get up, but she is unresponsive. Throughout the book we have looked at the treatment of women as what Schneider calls "a barometer of how the Israelites are faring" (2000: 246). The abandonment of the concubine by her husband, her gang rape by men of Benjamin, her death as a result of that abuse, and the cowardly way her husband responds to her death are all indicators that Israel is not faring well at all.

In 1898 Josephine Butler, a British Christian working in a mission for prostitutes, heard this story as hauntingly familiar. "'Her hands were upon the threshold.' *They are there still.* That corpse lies at our doors, prone. Its cold dead hands are upon our threshold, stretched out in dumb, dread appeal to all the families and homes of the earth. We are none of us guiltless, men or women. Our silent acquiescence in the crime of this murder has contributed, is contributing, to the woe which follows and is following."[3] Butler goes on to meditate on how many women are the victims of such violence every day, all around the world, saying that the presence of the concubine on the threshold should remind us of Christ at the threshold, standing at the door and knocking. He has told us that he comes in "the least of these." Butler gives support to the idea that, if there is indeed a type of Christ in the book of Judges, the most likely contender is the concubine from Bethlehem whose husband betrays her to her death, who faces that death in silence, and whose body is then broken for the uniting of Israel.

Phinehas

Phinehas, son of Eleazar, son of Aaron, appears in connection with four different stories in the Deuteronomistic History. He first appears in Num. 25, when

---

3. Josephine Butler, "A Typical Tragedy: Dead Hands on the Threshold," *The Storm-Bell*, no. 10 (December 1898): 112–13.

the people of Israel have begun to worship the Baal of Peor because the men of Israel are being seduced by the women of Moab, who then introduce them to this form of Baal worship. While the people are weeping in repentance at the tent of meeting, an Israelite man arrives bringing a Midianite woman "into his family" (Num. 25:6). Phinehas responds to this by killing both the man and the woman, which turns back a plague that God has sent against the people of Israel to punish them for their unfaithfulness. Because of this action, God says of Phinehas, "I hereby grant him my covenant of peace. It shall be for him and for his descendants after him a covenant of perpetual priesthood, because he was zealous for his God, and made atonement for the Israelites" (Num. 25:12–13). A few chapters later, Phinehas goes into battle against the Midianites as a priestly representative, "with the vessels of the sanctuary and the trumpets for sounding the alarm in his hand" (Num. 31:6). In Josh. 22, Phinehas is the emissary sent from the Israelites at Shiloh to reprimand the Reubenites, Gadites, and the half tribe of Manasseh, who have built an altar to the Lord at the boundary between the land of Canaan and their possession in Gilead. In this instance Phinehas is able to broker peace, since the Gileadites assure him that their altar is a memorial replica only, not meant to replace the worship center at Shiloh.

So the character of Phinehas is concerned with fidelity to the great commandments of not worshiping any god but YHWH and not marrying with the people of the land. Now he reappears in the final epilogue of the book of Judges. He made an implicit appearance in the Gideon story, as noted in that chapter, in that Gideon is replicating Phinehas's battle strategy and may be attempting to imitate him in the establishment of a religious center at Ophrah. Now, in Judg. 20, he is presented as the same Phinehas who was a young man during the journey in the wilderness and who was serving as a priest during the occupation under Joshua.

Assuming that this identification is historically accurate and not merely symbolic, this suggests that the stories in Judges are arranged not chronologically but thematically. This impression is reinforced by the presence of Jonathan, the grandson of Moses, in the previous epilogue. Jonathan has—shockingly enough—fallen into idolatry. There is no suggestion that Phinehas has fallen away. He is still faithfully serving before the ark. At the end of the first prologue, the people of Israel gathered to weep before the Messenger of the LORD, and here they are weeping again, in the presence of the ark, with Phinehas as their intermediary. It is unclear whether Phinehas is consulted before the first two failed attempts to conquer Benjamin, but he is certainly consulted before the third, successful attempt (20:27–28). Barbara Organ summarizes Phinehas's significance:

Phinehas may not have an active role in the narrative, but he certainly has a symbolic function, that of legitimizing the Israelites' ritual activity, especially at such a critical juncture in their life. Once again the survival of the people is at stake. Phinehas also links the period of the Benjaminite war to the generation following the conquest. The contemporaries Joshua and Eleazar die at the end of the Book of Joshua. The Book of Judges opens with the explicit statement that the generation after Joshua "did not know Yhwh" (Judg. 2:10) and began to "do what was evil in the sight of Yhwh." The generation of the exodus did not live to enter the land, but the next generation, that of Joshua and Eleazar, remained faithful (Judg. 2:7). Phinehas is the faithful priest who continues to serve Yhwh in the sanctuary, just as one would expect of the priest with whom Yhwh made a perpetual covenant (Num. 25:12–13).[4]

War with Benjamin

The Levite's decision to cut up his concubine into twelve pieces is not explained. It is a shocking act, violating all biblical teaching about the respect to be shown to the dead. The fate of being unburied is wished on enemies, not on loved ones, and is a sign of YHWH's disfavor.[5] One might think that the Levite is driven to this dishonoring act by grief and guilt, but when the people of Israel gather, he does not confess his fault and does not express grief; rather, he tells a distorted and dishonest version of what happened, concealing his own cowardly betrayal of his concubine.

The decision to punish Gibeah is made by the Israelites as a spontaneous response to the Levite's story, without taking time to consult the ephod or the priest to discover YHWH's will. Only after they have taken a vow to stay in the field until they have punished Gibeah, and only after the Benjaminites have taken the side of their murderous compatriots, refusing to hand them over, do the Israelites "inquire" of God. The question is the same as it was at the very beginning of the book: "Who shall go up?" And the answer is also the same: "Judah shall go up first." But this time the war is not against Canaanites. It remains a war that is intended to cleanse the land, but the pollution of the land is now within Israel.

At first it seems that the Israelites will finally fight for the cleansing of Canaan the way they were always commanded to fight, the way they have failed to fight throughout this book. They appear, at long last, to have committed fully to the

4. Barbara E. Organ, "Pursuing Phinehas: A Synchronic Reading," *Catholic Biblical Quarterly* 63 (2001): 216.
5. See, for instance, Deut. 28:26; Ps. 79:2; Eccl. 6:3; Isa. 14:19; Jer. 16:4.

command for holiness. And yet, despite the clear direction from YHWH, the first two attempts to conquer Benjamin fail. After the first defeat, they "wept before the LORD until the evening" (20:23) when they inquired whether they should continue their battle. YHWH told them to go up again. Again, they were defeated. This time they not only wept before the Lord; they also fasted and offered sacrifices. And they were told to go up again.

This experience of failure after obedience is not explained explicitly. However, there is a clue in the way in which the Israelites conquer Gibeah on their next attempt. They use the same strategy that was used in Josh. 8 in the battle against Ai. In that story as well, there had been failure followed by weeping and inquiring of the Lord. There the cause of Israel's failure was disclosed. Israel had sinned by taking "some of the devoted things" (Josh. 7:11). They had been commanded to offer the belongings of the conquered Canaanites to the Lord, since the war in Canaan was meant to be a holy war, not a war of aggrandizement for the people of Israel. Achan, one of the men of Judah, had kept some of the booty, a crime for which he was put to death. Only after this sin was dealt with could the Israelites conquer Ai.

The strong similarities between the two successful battles would suggest that the reasons for their initial failure should also be parallel. The events of Judges leading up to this culminating story offer ample evidence of the Israelites' infidelity and disobedience, but here so many Israelites have been implicated that to execute them all would be to leave almost no one. YHWH's grace is seen in that He does not demand the death of all His people who have been idolaters, who have married with the Canaanites, or who have been doing whatever is right in their own eyes. Instead, He accepts Israel's identification of the men of Gibeah as primary offenders and sends His people into battle against the tribe of Benjamin, who have given such a vivid demonstration of their Canaanization. They have not simply taken belongings plundered from the Canaanites; they have taken the disobedience and immorality of the Canaanites. The corruption is not external, as with Achan, but internal.

However, after the victory has been won, we discover that such corruption is not confined to Benjamin. The cleansing of the land cannot be completed because those assigned to do the cleansing are themselves contaminated. The army of Israel, like Achan, is hoarding something they are unwilling to sacrifice to God. They are unwilling to sacrifice the tribe of Benjamin. When Benjamin is reduced to only six hundred men, the Israelites find they cannot bear to risk the disappearance of one of the twelve tribes. This is a stunning lack of faith. Remember that all the

Israelites were descended from one man, Abraham, and all through only one of his sons, Isaac. YHWH was able to build a great nation from a small beginning, even in the face of apparent infertility. Surely YHWH could have preserved Benjamin given the survival of six hundred men, but this possibility is not even discussed. Instead, the Israelites decide that they must solve this problem. They must find wives for Benjamin.

After the battle of Ai, the people of Israel celebrated a ceremony of covenant renewal with YHWH (Josh. 8:30–35). But here, after the battle of Gibeah, there is no such renewal. The concern is not with keeping covenant with YHWH; the concern is only with the rebellious tribe of Benjamin. The men of Israel cannot give their own daughters to the Benjaminites since they have made a vow not to do so. Here again, as with Jephthah, we have an instance of a rash vow, made by men, and here again the harsh consequences of the vow fall on young virgin girls. If the army of Israel wished to show compassion to the Benjaminites, it should have been at their own expense. When the sons of Jacob traveled together to Egypt, Judah offered to become a slave to Joseph in order to keep Benjamin free since he had made a vow to his father that he would protect Benjamin (Gen. 44:17). That proof of genuine brotherly love and responsibility led to the reconciliation of all the brothers with Joseph. Here at the end of Judges, however, the men of Judah along with the rest of the tribes claim to be loving and compassionate toward Benjamin, but all the cost of that putative love is paid by others.

What follows is painful and ironic and horrible. The people of Israel recapitulate the sin of Gibeah that they set out to punish, but on a much larger scale. They themselves become a violent mob, taking young girls by force first from the city of Jabesh-gilead and then from the city of Shiloh. In Jabesh-gilead they first kill all the other inhabitants, destroying a town full of fellow Israelites. In Shiloh they pollute a festival to YHWH that involved the young girls going out dancing in the fields. The war against Benjamin started as an attempt to purify the land, but by the end of the attack of Jabesh-gilead the land is far more polluted than ever before. The war started with the appearance of outrage over a violent rape and the appearance of concern for justice to be done for a murdered woman, but by the end of the abduction of the girls of Shiloh relations between men and women are far more violent and destructive than ever before.

I've been amused by the scene in *The Pirates of Penzance* when the major general's daughters are being threatened with being married against their wills to the pirate band. The major general's mild reproof—Oh no, you mustn't do that!—produces laughter. But this story in Judges isn't funny. It's the ultimate slide away from chapter 1, where we saw a family united for a woman's flourishing. Now not only parents and husbands are failing, but the entire nation is complicit in the abduction and rape of the daughters of Israel. And the abduction of the girls of Shiloh adds blasphemy to the mix. The same Israelites who wept and sacrificed before YHWH in chapter 20 are desecrating His worship by the end of chapter 21.

In 2 Sam. 13, David's son Amnon rapes his half-sister Tamar, but David does not punish him: "When King David heard of these things, he became very angry, but he would not punish his son Amnon, because he loved him, for he was his firstborn" (13:21). This statement invites questions. We know that "the Lord disciplines those whom he loves" (Heb. 12:6; cf. Prov. 3:12), so surely the claim that David's nonpunishment of his son Amnon was the result of his love cannot be taken at face value. A loving father would not allow his son to do such a heinous thing without punishment; a loving father would also protect and give justice to his daughter. A just and righteous king would protect the weak against the strong and would side with the victim against her oppressor. David's refusal either to discipline his son or to protect his daughter is a failure of his responsibility both as a father and as a king. It is not loving; it is cowardly. It is also disastrous for Israel, since it leads to civil war when Tamar's brother Absalom does what David would not do.

The Israelites' treatment of the surviving Benjaminites is similar to David's treatment of Amnon. The softness and compassion of the men of Israel toward Benjamin is a cowardly love, not a righteous love. Instead of righteous love, we see an abnegation of responsibility leading to an inappropriate accommodation to unrighteousness, disobedience, violence, and disorder. This epilogue ends as it began with the statement that everyone in Israel was doing whatever seemed right in his or her own eyes. Even though YHWH was consulted in this war against Benjamin, even though the war was undertaken in an effort to restore justice and avenge unrighteousness, it has not led to any change in the situation of pervasive, systemic disobedience. Instead, Israel has become worse than Benjamin in their desire to redeem Benjamin, which is a picture of what has been happening all through the book. The Israelites have taken on the characteristics of the Canaanites because they have not wanted to drive them out.

Many readers of this sad story at the end of Judges are most struck by the tragic lack of unity within Israel, and so they see the Israelites' desire to preserve Benjamin as laudable. However, unity is not the only good that YHWH desires for His people. He also desires holiness. The Israelites purchase unity at the expense of holiness, a common temptation in the church of our own day. When a community is willing to sacrifice holiness for unity, the whole community becomes corrupted, as is vividly portrayed in this story. Unity at the price of holiness is not loving and will not be lasting.

All of us, including the Benjaminites, need a redeemer who can become one with us and take our sin to himself without himself becoming sinful. We need a redeemer who transforms us into his likeness rather than being transformed into ours. We need a redeemer who will not be distracted by sentimentality or cowardice from the surgery that we need if we are to be free from sin. The men of Israel were not able to offer such redemption to Benjamin. They were unable to be compassionate without being weakened by sentiment, unable to do the hard thing that courageous love required. In *A Grief Observed*, C. S. Lewis says, "The more we believe that God hurts only to heal, the less we can believe that there is any use in begging for tenderness. . . . Suppose that what you are up against is a surgeon whose intentions are wholly good. The kinder and more conscientious he is, the more inexorably he will go on cutting."[6] Here representatives of all Israel gather and are betrayed by their own tenderness into doing evil rather than what is right.

YHWH also has compassion on Benjamin, but His compassion is fully loving, never weakened by a distaste for unpleasantness or pain. His compassion leads to restitution and the restoring of balance among the tribes. Before the taking of the land, Moses blessed Benjamin, saying, "The beloved of the LORD rests in safety—the High God surrounds him all day long—the beloved rests between his shoulders" (Deut. 33:12). The tragedy of Benjamin's fall is thus great, for Benjamin was to have been beloved and safe, resting in Jerusalem. But after a time of punishment, YHWH restores Benjamin. The first king of Israel is from Benjamin—indeed, he is from Gibeah. The first act of Saul's kingship is to go from Gibeah to Jabesh-gilead on a rescue mission. The people of Jabesh-gilead are being besieged by the Ammonites, and they send messengers to all the towns near them, asking for help. One messenger comes to Gibeah. Saul has been anointed as king by Samuel, but he has not yet been recognized as king by the people, and he hears the news as he is coming in from the fields where he has been plowing with his oxen. "And the spirit of God came upon Saul in power when he heard these words, and his anger was greatly kindled. He took a yoke of oxen, and cut them in pieces and sent them throughout all the territory of Israel by messengers, saying, 'Whoever does not come out after Saul and Samuel, so shall it be done to his oxen!' Then the dread of the LORD fell upon the people, and they came out

6. C. S. Lewis, *A Grief Observed* (New York: HarperCollins, 2009), 32–33.

as one" (1 Sam. 11:6–7). If there was any doubt that this story linking Jabesh-gilead and Gibeah was meant to be heard as echoing the story of the war with Benjamin, the cutting up of the oxen places the matter beyond question. Saul, a Benjaminite, comes from Gibeah, the scene of Benjamin's shame, and rescues the town of Jabesh-gilead, where Benjamin was saved by slaughter of the townspeople. Just as punishments fit crimes in the Bible, so does restitution. It is only after Saul undoes the damage that was done to Jabesh-gilead on behalf of his tribe that he is recognized as king.

By the end of Judges, the question of the extermination of the Canaanites has come to look very different from what it appeared to be at the book's beginning. At that point we considered some parallels between God's command to Abraham to sacrifice Isaac and God's command to the Israelites to sacrifice the Canaanites in holy war. In both cases YHWH has every right to demand the sacrifice, since life and death belong to Him, especially human life, since human beings owe Him fealty in a way that animals and other creatures cannot. In both cases He allows human beings to serve as His assistants in offering such sacrifices, only so that they may learn a new role. Abraham learned that YHWH Himself will be the provider of such sacrifices, even as YHWH Himself took both sides of the covenant on Himself, agreeing to pay if either side was broken.

Here at the end of Judges, the people of Israel have been shown that they are not fit to offer the *herem* sacrifice, for they are not fit to be a priestly people. The final statement of the refrain ends the book: "In those days there was no king in Israel; all the people did what was right in their own eyes." Doing what is right in our own eyes rather than in YHWH's eyes is the root of all our sin. This was the sin of Eve and of Adam. By ending the book with this refrain, the author of Judges is making clear that sin remains dominant, and indeed has grown in domination during this period. Rather than taking the land, the people of Israel have been overtaken. Rather than driving out the Canaanites, the people of Israel have been Canaanized. Like Abraham, the people of Israel learn a new role: they are not the priests; they are the guilty who are in need of a perfect sacrifice. As we read the book of Judges, we are to identify with Israel's sin. We too are incapable of serving as our own priest, for we need a high priest who is "holy, blameless, undefiled, separated from sinners, and exalted above the heavens" (Heb. 7:26).

BIBLIOGRAPHY FOR JUDGES

Frequently cited works are listed here. Other works are documented in the footnotes.

Alter, Robert. 2014. *Ancient Israel: The Former Prophets: Joshua, Judges, Samuel and Kings; A Translation with Commentary*. New York: Norton.

Block, Daniel I. 1999. *Judges, Ruth*. New American Commentary 6. Nashville: Broadman & Holman.

Bluedorn, Wolfgang. 2001. *Yahweh versus Baalism: A Theological Reading of the Gideon-Abimelech Narrative*. JSOTSup 329. Sheffield, UK: Sheffield Academic Press.

Dorsey, David A. 1999. *The Literary Structure of the Old Testament: A Commentary on Genesis–Malachi*. Grand Rapids: Baker Academic.

Frolov, Serge. 2013. *Judges*. The Forms of Old Testament Literature 6b. Grand Rapids: Eerdmans.

Gunn, David M. 2005. *Judges through the Centuries*. Blackwell Bible Commentaries. Malden, MA: Blackwell.

Jordan, James B. 1999. *Judges: A Practical and Theological Commentary*. Eugene, OR: Wipf and Stock.

Kim, Jichan. 1993. *The Structure of the Samson Cycle*. Kampen: Kok Pharos.

Kline, Meredith G. 1999. *Images of the Spirit*. Eugene, OR: Wipf and Stock.

Matthews, Victor H. 2004. *Judges and Ruth*. New Cambridge Bible Commentary. Cambridge: Cambridge University Press.

Mobley, Gregory. 2005. *The Empty Men: The Heroic Tradition of Ancient Israel*. Anchor Bible Reference Library. New York: Doubleday.

Schneider, Tammi J. 2000. *Judges*. Berit Olam: Studies in Hebrew Narrative and Poetry. Collegeville, MN: Liturgical Press.

Stek, John H. 1986. "The Bee and the Mountain Goat: A Literary Reading of Judges 4." In *A Tribute to Gleason Archer*, edited by Walter C. Kaiser and Ronald F. Youngblood, 53–86. Chicago: Moody.

Sternberg, Meier. 1985. *The Poetics of Biblical Narrative: Ideological Literature and the Drama of Reading*. Bloomington: Indiana University Press.

Trible, Phyllis. 1984. *Texts of Terror: Literary-Feminist Readings of Biblical Narrative*. Overtures to Biblical Theology. Philadelphia: Fortress.

Waltke, Bruce K. 2004. *Light from the Dark Ages: An Exposition on Judges and Ruth: BIBL 615*. Audio course with printed notes. Vancouver: Regent College Audio. Citations from this source are from the accompanying written notes.

Webb, Barry G. 2012. *The Book of Judges*. New International Commentary on the Old Testament. Grand Rapids: Eerdmans.

✚ RUTH ✚

by Stephen E. Fowl

ACKNOWLEDGMENTS

There is always a particular satisfaction in writing the acknowledgments for a book. Although it appears at the beginning of a text, it is one of the last things an author writes. In this case it is a testimony to this volume's very odd path to publication that I first wrote these acknowledgments in 2012. Despite the long periods of waiting, I am very pleased that this work is now appearing in print.

Writing a commentary on a text outside one's field of professional expertise is a good way to be reminded of one's deep dependence on the work of others. In the course of writing I have accumulated numerous intellectual and personal debts. Many of these I can never repay in full. I hope to acknowledge some of these debts here as a form of down payment.

I am now well into my twenty-ninth year teaching at Loyola. With each passing year I realize what a significant role the Department of Theology has played in my formation as a scholar and a theologian. All of my colleagues, both old and new, contribute to the extraordinary collegiality we enjoy and the depth of our intellectual community. I am very grateful for their support. In addition, I received two faculty development summer research grants to support this work. I am happy to acknowledge those with much gratitude too.

My dear friends at the Church of the Servant King in Eugene listened to my ideas about Ruth and numerous other things over many years. As always, they pushed me to think harder and live more faithfully than I could ever have done on my own.

My wife, Melinda, has been my companion through countless writing projects. I am grateful for her steadfast love. She, our sons, Brendan and Liam, and our daughter-in-law, Madeline, provided welcome reminders that the rigors of writing need the regular distractions of home life if they are not to become too severe. I know that I do not appreciate that as much or as often as I should.

Jim Kinney, Rusty Reno, and Ephraim Radner all offered specific comments on this manuscript. They have improved it significantly. All subsequent errors, however, are my responsibility.

Although this is not all one might say about Ruth, it is true that this is the story of someone who out of love bound themselves to a people, to a place, and to God over the long haul. I am sure that when the Episcopal Cathedral of the Incarnation first got involved with Sandtown Habitat for Humanity, Sarah and Don Stevens-Rayburn never imagined that they too were binding themselves to a people, to a place, and to God out of love. Nevertheless, they have done so for over twenty years. In honor of that love I dedicate this book to them.

INTRODUCTION TO RUTH

Theological Commentary Writing: Anxiety from Two Sides

Before commenting directly on Ruth, I would like to offer some brief reflections on how I see the task of writing a theological commentary. Because I have written on this subject elsewhere at greater length, I will be brief here and indicate where readers seeking a fuller account of my views can find them.[1]

Many years ago I participated in a panel discussion at the Society of Biblical Literature (SBL) on the topic of theological commentary. My recollection may fail me, but I believe everyone on the panel was engaged in producing a theological commentary. We were divided more or less equally between those whose primary academic specialty is theology and those who are primarily biblical scholars. The room was filled and the presentations and discussion were lively.

I was reminded of this session recently as I read a review of the volumes published in this series so far.[2] The reviewer, Luke Johnson, is to my mind one of the most acute and theologically sensitive biblical scholars around. For the most part, he did not think very highly of the volumes in this series. I note this because his criticisms replayed the worries voiced by many of the biblical scholars at that SBL session many years ago: When listening to theologians speak about and offer examples of theological commentary, the biblical scholars wanted to know how the theological comments were dependent on, or at least connected to, interpretation

1. A good place to start might be the introduction to my commentary on Philippians in the Two Horizons Commentary Series (Grand Rapids: Eerdmans, 2005) and my *Cascade Companion to Theological Interpretation of Scripture* (Eugene, OR: Cascade, 2009).
2. Luke T. Johnson, "Interpretive Dance," *Commonweal*, February 24, 2012, 17–20.

of the texts in question. The biblical scholars were anxious because it appeared to them that what was passing as theological interpretation was simply a set of theological assertions and convictions arrived at independently of close engagement with the biblical text. Was the biblical text simply a stage on which theological ideas paraded? Were the theologians sufficiently aware and attentive to the rich and sometimes rough texture of biblical texts?

The theologians in the room had their own anxieties. They tended to worry that biblical scholars, left to their own devices, were so deeply formed by the methods and concerns of historical criticism[3] that they would have nothing of theological import or interest to say. Instead of theological commentary, readers would be bombarded with discussions of technical linguistic matters, speculation about textual precursors, and a steady replacement of textual interpretation with comments about historical, social, and cultural backgrounds and contexts. In these cases, whatever theology was present in the commentary would seem ill matched with the textual interpretation, mirroring what the biblical scholars feared with regard to the theologians.

The anxieties of biblical scholars and theologians have their roots in the modern fragmentation of theology into a set of discrete and often isolated subdisciplines. At any point in the history of Christianity, except the modern period, it would not have been possible to be considered a theologian if one did not have a facility with scripture and its interpretation. At its best, theology was a mode of exegesis. No one presumed the theologian offered the last word on the biblical text; no one expected theologians to speak with one voice, because the biblical texts were multivocal. Although premodern interpreters were quite diverse in their interpretive results, they did share the view that scriptural interpretation should primarily be directed toward and regulated by theological concerns. Theological concerns can be many and varied. Doctrinal, moral, political, ecclesiological, liturgical, and ascetical interests all represent types of theological concerns, and there are, no doubt, more beside these. Interpreting biblical texts in the light of ancient Near Eastern religious practice, Greco-Roman social and political life, or ancient literary genres, or using biblical texts as repositories of data about the historical Jesus, is not generally a way of keeping theological concerns primary. I should say that these are completely legitimate interests, and theological interpreters will want to pay attention to the work of those scholars operating with such interests. Aside from their intrinsic merit, these interests may inspire and inform one's own theological

---

3. For ease of expression I will use "historical criticism" as if it were a single thing rather than a discrete set of often competing practices and interests.

interests. Moreover, although there may be reasons to lament the fragmentation of the theological enterprise within the modern academy, this situation is neither surprising nor likely to change any time soon. Recognition of this fragmentation is one of the things that fuels the anxieties of theologians and biblical scholars when it comes to matters of theological commentary writing. In many respects a series such as this is an attempt to counter the fragmentation of the theological enterprise within the academy and the churches.

Although one can find manifestations of contemporary theological commentary that will feed the anxieties of both biblical scholars and theologians, one should recognize two further points. First and foremost, the interpretive landscape has changed, and for the better. Within the guild of biblical scholars, discussions about theological interpretation of scripture have now developed enough self-confidence that the case for interpreting scripture theologically does not depend on overheated claims about the bankruptcy of historical-critical approaches to scripture. The various methodological and hermeneutical challenges presented to historical criticism have enabled more self-reflective biblical critics to reformulate and revise their presumptions, interests, practices, and conclusions in ways that allow for the continuation of such forms of interpretation while also allowing for other self-reflective interests, practices, and conclusions to flourish.

Second, for nearly twenty years now, there has been an ongoing discussion about the nature, aims, and practice of theological interpretation of scripture. There are now monographs and textbooks discussing theological interpretation, other commentary series devoted to theological interpretation in addition to this one, and also a journal dedicated to the theological interpretation of scripture. Thus, against the background of the anxieties of both theologians and biblical scholars, theological interpretation has taken root as a contemporary scholarly practice. Hence, rather than offer a further apology for producing a theological commentary in the present, I will offer a few words about what I take to be some of the central presumptions and tasks of theological commentary.

Starting Points: Scripture as the Word of God and Human Words

It might appear that theological commentary should begin by addressing questions about the nature of scripture as the word of God. If the nature of scripture can be properly established, a theological interpreter can then demarcate methodologically what will count as a good interpretation of a scriptural text. Such good interpretation could then form the basis for sound theological reflection.

If one begins this way, one must initially reckon with the fact that although Christians confess that scripture is the word of God, they also recognize that modern historical studies have decisively shown that scripture is also a human work. The original texts that comprise the Bible were written by a variety of human authors (known and unknown) in diverse historical, linguistic, and cultural settings. Both the human authors of these texts and those who preserved, edited, and ordered these texts participated in and were subject to a host of social, material, and institutional forces that undoubtedly affected the composition of the Bible, even if scholars are not altogether sure how and to what extent this happened. Of course, one can simply interpret the Bible in this light and leave things at that. Much professional biblical scholarship does precisely this.

Upon deciding to treat the Bible as a human historical text to be read like any other, the remaining issue for theologians and Christians more generally is how to treat the Bible as the word of God. Once interpreting the Bible as a human book becomes its own end, the question is how to move from the results of that work either to theological claims, or to the moral and ascetical formation of Christians, or to any other edifying practice that Christians have traditionally based on scripture. There are no clear and distinct ways to do this. In the modern period, scholars have attempted to answer these questions by extracting timeless truths from the messy contingent human texts of the Bible or, more recently, through the biblical theology movement.

Neither of these options has been particularly successful from a theological standpoint. Successive attempts to distill timeless truths tend to end up either with anodyne abstractions that are too vague to do much theological work or with truths that are deeply enmeshed in contingent realities. The story of biblical theology in the modern period is marked by successive attempts to organize the rich diversity of scripture solely on the basis of criteria or themes derived only from that very same scripture. Theological criteria or themes are ruled out from the start. Indeed any proposal is doomed if one can show that its method of organizing the diversity of scripture is derived from theological concerns or convictions. If scripture's diversity is indeed a problem to be solved with resources derived only from scripture, the chances for success seem slim.

Despite this fact, works of biblical theology can sometimes result in rich interpretive results and deep theological reflection. Nevertheless, I think questions about the nature of scripture are not the best place to begin thinking about theological commentary. Instead, I am convinced that questions about the nature of scripture are subsidiary to and should be dependent on a doctrine of revelation, which is, in turn, dependent on a doctrine of the Trinity. The Christian God is the Trinity, whose inner life is reflected in the gracious and peaceful self-giving and self-communication of Father, Son, and Spirit. In creating all things, not only does the triune God freely will the existence of humans created in the image of God, but God also desires fellowship with humans, offering them a share in the divine life (cf. 2 Pet. 1:4). This is both a central intention with which God created and the end for which God created. Given this, God's self-presentation or self-communication is an essential element in establishing and maintaining the fellowship God freely desires to have with humans. Thus, God's self-revelation to humans is both the source and the content of a Christian doctrine of revelation. Revelation is directly dependent on God's triune being, and it is inseparable from God's freely willed desire for loving communion with humans.[4] In this light, the written text of scripture is subsidiary to and dependent on a notion of revelation that is itself directly dependent on God's triune being.[5]

A Better Place to Begin

Beginning with this recognition rather than debates about the nature of scripture allows for a recalibration of the relationships between God, scripture, and Christians in several ways. All of these will have an impact on how one proceeds with the task of theological commentary.

For Christians, the ends of reading, interpreting, and embodying scripture are determined decisively by the ends of God's self-revelation, which are directed toward drawing humans into ever deeper communion with the triune God and each other. In this way, scriptural interpretation is not an end in itself for Christians. One might even say that scripture itself indicates that the mediation of revelation through written scripture is not God's best desire for believers but a contingent response to human sinfulness. Recall that God speaks with Adam and Eve with an unbroken immediacy in the garden. This is also reflected in the description of God's interactions with Moses as speaking with a friend face-to-face (Exod. 33:11). Further, Jer. 31:31–34 indicates that the written covenant will ultimately be replaced by a covenant written on the heart, so that teaching, remembering, and interpreting scripture will be a thing of the past. In addition, when confronted with Moses's permission of divorce in Deut. 24:1–4, Jesus makes it quite clear that

4. See John Webster, *Holy Scripture: A Dogmatic Sketch* (Cambridge: Cambridge University Press, 2003), 13–15.
5. See *Dei Verbum* §2.

there is a gap between God's best intentions for humans and the scriptural words of Moses that are offered as a concession to human sinfulness (Matt. 19:1–9). These texts indicate that scripture is the result of God's condescension to human sinfulness.

At the same time, scripture is absolutely normative and authoritative for believers now since it reveals the mystery of God's reconciling of all things in Christ. Thus, although the interpretation and embodiment of scripture is not an end in itself, as Christians engage scripture "for teaching, for reproof, for correction, and for training in righteousness," they can confidently advance toward their proper ends in God, "proficient [and] equipped for every good work" (2 Tim. 3:16–17). Until God's law is written on our hearts after the manner of Jer. 31, scripture is God's providentially ordered and sufficient means for revealing the triune God to sinful humans.

Another avenue that opens up when Christians think of scripture in the light of their convictions about the triune God is in relation to the history and processes of the formation of scripture. Reckoning with these matters will be crucial for any theological commentary in the present. As noted above, any emphasis on scripture's dual nature as both human words and the word of God will obviously recognize that the text of scripture as we know it today is tied to a variety of historical, political, and social processes. Scholars may disagree about the nature of these processes, but it is hard to deny that a variety of forces, known and unknown, shaped and were shaped by the text of scripture.

Nevertheless, if revelation is seen as the triune God's self-communication, an activity that flows from the very nature of the Trinity, an activity that is graciously directed to drawing humanity into ever deeper friendship or communion with God and each other, then one can be more relaxed in approaching and analyzing the human processes that led to the formation of Christian scripture. This is because the triune God is not simply the content of revelation but the one who directs and sustains God's self-revelation with the aim of drawing humanity into ever deeper communion. Thus, the conviction that God's revelation is ultimately directed toward bringing about our salvation also entails a view of God's providential ordering of history so that God's ends ultimately will be achieved. In this way, Christians can fully recognize the human processes (whatever they may have been) that led to the formation of scripture. At the same time, such convictions about God's providence enable Christians to understand that, however scripture came to look the way it does, scripture reveals all that believers need to sustain a life of growing communion with God and each other.

In this respect, Christians would do well to take on the disposition displayed by Paul in Phil. 1:12–18. In this passage the imprisoned Paul begins by noting that, contrary to what one might expect, the gospel has advanced even in the midst of his imprisonment (1:12). Indeed, Paul's adoption of the passive voice here makes it clear that God, and not Paul, is the agent advancing the gospel. Paul goes on to note that many believers in Rome (most likely) have become bold in proclaiming the gospel. He observes that among these newly emboldened preachers, some preach from good motives and others preach from selfish motives (1:15). After commenting on each of these groups (1:16–17), Paul surprisingly announces that, no matter what the motives of these preachers, Christ is being proclaimed, and Paul rejoices in this (1:18).

The motives of the preachers, while important, seem secondary to the act of proclamation. It may appear that Paul pragmatically prefers to see the gospel preached than to wait until everybody's motives are pure. I do not think Paul sees the choice in quite this way. Ultimately, Paul is convinced that God is directing both his personal circumstances and the more general spread of the gospel. Thus, he need not be overly concerned about the motives of any particular set of preachers. Paul is able to see in the midst of his own circumstances that, despite appearances and contrary to expectations, God is advancing the gospel. Rather than expressing a preference for preaching from selfish motives over no preaching at all, this passage is an expression of faith in God's providential oversight of the gospel's progress.

From a theological perspective it is important to note that a very particular doctrine of providence underwrites Paul's account here. Paul is confident that God will bring the good work started in his and the Philippians' lives to its proper completion (Phil. 1:6). His view of God's providence leads him to fit himself and his various circumstances into a larger ongoing story of God's unfolding economy of salvation. Within this larger context, and only within this context, Paul's circumstances can be seen as advancing the gospel. This view of providence enables Paul to rejoice even in the face of a gospel proclaimed from selfish motives. If this disposition is extended to scripture, Christians can recognize the vicissitudes in the historical formation of scripture and still treat scripture as God's providentially ordered self-revelation.

One cannot sustain any notion of God's providence apart from a fairly robust notion of the Spirit's role in the various aspects of scripture's formation. John's Gospel offers a starting point for thinking about this. There Jesus speaks about the role the Spirit will play in the lives of those who will come to produce the

New Testament. The Spirit is the one who calls to mind all that Jesus taught (John 14:26). Jesus also promises that the Spirit will lead his followers into all truth, truth that they simply could not bear on that side of the crucifixion and resurrection (John 16:12–15). In addition, the Spirit will guide and direct the disciples concerning what is to come so that they can continue to abide in Christ (John 15:1–11). In calling to mind the words of Christ, in leading and confirming the disciples in all truth, and in speaking about the things yet to come, the Spirit's role in the lives of believers, and thus in the production of scripture, is comprehensive.

The Spirit's work in the operation of God's providential ordering of things sanctifies the means and processes that lead to the production of scripture, turning them to God's holy purposes without diminishing their human, historical character. Thus, in calling scripture "holy" Christians are not making a comprehensive claim about the purity of the motives of the writers and editors of scripture. These may well have been decidedly unholy. Even in the face of such unholy motives and actions, Christians are committed to the belief that the triune God has revealed a passionate desire to have fellowship with them, even in the light of their manifest sin. Scripture is chief among God's providentially ordered gifts directed to bringing about this reconciliation and fellowship. Thus, scripture is holy because of its divinely willed role in making believers holy.

In this light, the theological commentator need not reject out of hand any work of historical biblical scholarship. At the same time, theological commentators need not cede their own interests to the interests of historical biblical scholars. Even if one can imagine the interests of biblical scholars as a coherent whole, they need not determine the interests of theological commentators. This will lead theological commentators to make use of the work of historical biblical scholarship on an ad hoc basis when and to the extent that such work helps advance the ends of theological commentary. This, of course, raises the question of what the interests of theological commentary might be.

To answer this question, one may begin by noting, again, that scripture is God's providentially ordered vehicle for bringing us to our true home, that is, a life of ever deeper friendship with God and others. Believers' diverse engagements with scripture aim to bring them closer to their true end in God. Given this assumption about scripture, it would seem that, whatever else it might do, theological commentary seeks to enhance the prospects that believers' engagements with scripture will achieve their goals. These prospects would be enhanced as, for example, a commentary opens new vistas with regard to one's understanding of a text, thus edifying one's faith and practice. Other times, a commentary may enable a reader to better attend to aspects of the text that might otherwise have passed without notice, sharpening one's capacities to attend to God through better attention to scripture. Still other times, a commentary may help one avoid errors of various sorts. These examples seem typical, but by no means do they exhaust the possibilities.

Opening new vistas, refocusing attention, and helping believers avoid error are just some of the ways a theological commentary might enhance the prospects that believers' diverse engagements with scripture will bring them into deeper friendship with God and neighbor. To the extent that theological commentators seek to enhance the prospects that believers' engagements with scripture will direct them to their ends in God, commentators will always need to keep such ends in view. In my recollections of that SBL session noted above, the theologians may have been worried that biblical scholars would not focus their attention in this way at all. Alternatively, my hunch is that biblical scholars tend to think that many contemporary theological commentators focus far too much on the ends of Christian faith and life and devote too little time to the text. Keeping the ends for which believers are called to engage scripture at the forefront, however, is not a task unique to theological commentary. Monographs, thematic works, and other types of theological writing might also do this.

In ways that are very different from a monograph, theological commentary has the obligation to attend to what has been written. This is both an intellectual and a theological discipline in that it requires a willed submission to another's writing with the aim of making that writing clearer to contemporary readers. The commentator's discussions, debates, arguments, and insights derive a large measure of their importance from their capacity to clarify another's work, a work that has its own givenness. Thus, all commentary writing, and theological commentary writing in particular, demands a particular type of attentiveness and humility.

To borrow a distinction arising from Aristotle and some of his ancient commentators, theological commentary is a *stochastic* rather than a creative form of *techne* (art/craft). In our contemporary world Matthew Crawford has helpfully elucidated this distinction with regard to repairing motorcycles. Unlike creative artists, such as an architect or builder whose ends are achieved when the building stands or falls, *stochastic* artists, such as those involved in medicine and motorcycle repair, never fully achieve their ends.[6] This is because the doctor and the mechanic and the theological commentator are working on things that are not

6. Matthew Crawford, *Shop Class as Soulcraft* (New York: Penguin, 2009), 81. As Aristotle says, "It is not the function of medicine simply to make a man quite healthy, but to put him as far as may be on the road to health; it is possible to give excellent treatment even to those who can never enjoy

of their own making. This both requires and cultivates humility in those who are accomplished in these crafts. "Because the stochastic arts diagnose and fix things that are variable, complex, and not of our own making and therefore not fully knowable, they require a certain disposition toward the thing you are trying to fix. This disposition is at once cognitive and moral. Getting it right demands that you be *attentive* in the way of a conversation rather than *assertive* in the way of a demonstration."[7] There are numerous ways in which such attentiveness and humility are formed in people over time. Developing one's capacity for textual attentiveness tends to require the acquisition of certain skills, background knowledge, and critical judgments. These are all honed and perfected in the course of actually attending to specific texts.

Moreover, I assume that textual attentiveness requires attention to what previous commentators have said. I value the work of those who have commented on Ruth before me, and I have tried to learn from it. Theological commentary, however, is not simply the repetition or translation of the comments of the past. There are times when I will follow a traditional line of interpretation and times when I will argue for a better alternative or simply continue an interpretive conversation in a slightly different direction. Indeed, theological interpretation has less to do with bringing a dispute to a resolution than it is does with continuing a productive discussion.

Developing such textual attentiveness and the appropriate humility requires, among other things, excellent teachers as well as institutions to help sustain this teaching. In the past, churches and monastic communities provided both the teachers and the institutional contexts for forming appropriately attentive commentators. Although that is still the case to some degree, today the academy is the context in which such formation takes place for almost all commentators. This present commentary is not the place to champion or to lament this state of affairs. Nevertheless, recognizing this may clarify why close textual attentiveness is often cultivated and practiced apart from concerns with the ends for which believers' are called to engage scripture. This situation also helps to explain one of the challenges facing all theological commentators. That is, at its best, theological commentary will deftly combine rich textual attentiveness with a vigorous interest in directing and inspiring believers' engagements with scripture so that they are led into ever deeper friendship with God and neighbor. This task is by

---

sound health" (Aristotle, *Art of Rhetoric*, trans. J. H. Freese, Loeb Classical Library 193 [Cambridge, MA: Harvard University Press, 1926], 1355b12).

7. Crawford, *Shop Class*, 82.

no means easy. There is no single recipe for combining these two components of theological commentary. As with all *stochastic* arts, however, the recipe itself is much less important than the result.

Matters Regarding Ruth

In preparing this commentary I have worked with both the Hebrew text of Ruth and the Septuagint translation. I must admit, however, that I would be quite happy if my Hebrew turns out to be as good as Augustine's Greek. In any case, this is not a commentary that will methodically work through the Hebrew text of Ruth on a verse-by-verse basis. There are several such commentaries on Ruth available in English, and I have made use of those works when appropriate. When I do make comments on the Hebrew or Greek texts of Ruth, I aim to make my comments intelligible and helpful to someone who is reading Ruth in a good English translation.

Although it is not the shortest book in the Old Testament, Ruth is quite short at only eighty-five verses. These eighty-five verses relate the story of Ruth, a Moabite widow, her widowed mother-in-law, Naomi, and Naomi's relative Boaz. The story is set "in the days when the judges ruled [or "judged"]" (1:1).[8] The scope of the entire text covers several generations, but the bulk of the action really takes place on two separate days and one night.

Five verses into the book, the Israelite Naomi and her two Moabite daughters-in-law, Ruth and Orpah, find themselves widowed and in Moab. Naomi decides to return to her home in Bethlehem. Ruth and Orpah seek to return with her. Naomi tries to dissuade them. She is successful in the case of Orpah, but Ruth binds herself to Naomi, Naomi's people, and Naomi's God. Upon returning to Bethlehem, Ruth seeks to provide for herself and Naomi by gleaning in the fields. She encounters Boaz, a kinsman of her late father-in-law and late husband who shows her great kindness. As the harvest is ending, Ruth presents herself to Boaz late at night on the threshing floor. She seeks a marriage with him, and Boaz is eager to oblige. Several legal obstacles need to be overcome, but this is accomplished to the satisfaction of all. Ruth conceives a son who becomes the grandfather of David.

---

8. Bush (1996: 18–30) covers a variety of scholarly opinions about the date of Ruth. Bush's view is that setting Ruth within the history of the development from Standard Biblical Hebrew to Late Biblical Hebrew provides the only gauge for dating Ruth. After reviewing the various characteristics of Ruth, Bush places its composition late in the transitional period from Standard to Late Biblical Hebrew, sometime in the late preexilic or early postexilic period.

As befits such a concentrated story, many things are presumed or left unsaid. For example, although we get a clear picture that Ruth and Naomi are destitute when they return to Bethlehem, it turns out that Naomi owns a field. We only learn this because in chapter 4 Boaz tells an otherwise unidentified close kinsman of Naomi's that she wishes to sell the field. We readers had no prior knowledge of this field or about Naomi's wishes regarding its sale. This is just one example of the gaps in the story. Where there are gaps, commentators will seek to fill them in. For the most part, modern commentators seek to fill in various gaps by focusing on the motives for the actions of the central characters. As Danna Fewell and David Gunn note in their study of Ruth, "Careful and imaginative 'gap filling' enriches the reading experience."[9] Fewell and Gunn offer a "loosely feminist" account of Ruth, recognizing that the book is set in an ancient patriarchal culture. This leads them to generate psychological profiles of the various characters in the book. These profiles provide a basis for their speculations about various characters' motives. In her commentary Kirsten Nielsen (1997) is also interested in the motives of the characters in Ruth, though she seeks to situate the characters' motives in an ancient culture in which honor is a highly valued commodity and which has well-defined, if only partially known, codes for dealing with such matters as marrying and distributing and redistributing property. In addition to reflecting on the motives of the characters in the story, she displays what she takes to be the motives of those who produced the story. She finds the story itself arises as a type of propaganda defending David's right to the throne despite his Moabite ancestor.

These are exemplary works from which I have learned much. As a rule, these commentaries do not address theological concerns. In one respect this is not a surprise. There are only two places in Ruth where God acts, or where it is claimed God has acted (1:6; 4:13). Thus, the book of Ruth does not offer much by way of its own theological reflection. When modern commentaries do offer theological reflection on Ruth, they tend to treat the story as a dramatic example of the sort of care and concern God wishes Israel to show to widows and aliens in their midst. Thus, such commentaries treat Ruth as one way of embodying the commands found in such texts as Exod. 22:21–23; 23:9; Lev. 19:33–34; Deut. 10:17–19; 24:19–22 (Sakenfeld 1999: 4). Christians reading Ruth would then be encouraged to make their communities similar places of welcome for widows and aliens. There is nothing wrong with this. The world needs such communities now more than ever.

9. Fewell and Gunn 1990: 16. Although in a more traditional commentary form, Tod Linafelt (1999) tends to follow Fewell and Gunn when it comes to speculating about the characters' motives and psychological states.

In addition, the characters in Ruth, especially Ruth and Boaz, display the virtue of *hesed*. This term is often translated as "loyalty" or "kindness" in the NRSV. "It refers to care and concern for another with whom one is in relationship, but care that specifically takes shape in action to rescue another from a situation of desperate need, and under circumstances in which the rescuer is uniquely quali-fied to do what is needed" (Sakenfeld 1999: 11–12). Given these concerns, one might understand Jesus's parable about neighbor love, also known as the parable of the good Samaritan (Luke 10:30–37), as a New Testament parallel to the story of Ruth. Although I agree that these are some of the theological lessons found in Ruth, it seems to me that there is more to thinking theologically with and about Ruth than this.

One traditionally Christian way of reading Old Testament texts is to read them figurally, especially to read them as prefiguring Christ. I think there are ways of reading such figures in Ruth. I am also eager to point out ways in which Ruth prefigures the inclusion of Gentiles into the people of God in Christ, a theme of particular importance in Matthew, Luke, Acts, and many of Paul's writings. This sort of figural reading certainly has a christological and pneumatological impetus; it is christologically shaped, but it is not always strictly about Christ.[10]

This practice of figural reading is not common anymore in either the academy or the church. It is, nevertheless, a crucial practice for reading theologically. Let me offer a truncated account of why it is crucial based on arguments I have made more extensively elsewhere. For the first part of this argument for figural reading, I will need to speak, all too briefly, about the "literal sense" of scripture. For now, let me propose a working definition:[11] the literal sense of a passage will include those meanings conventionally ascribed to a passage by faithful Christian communities and therefore presumed to be intended by God. Thus, the literal sense will be those meanings Christians conventionally ascribe to a passage in their ongoing struggles to live and worship faithfully before the triune God. In this way the literal sense is primary, the basis and norm for all subsequent ways of interpreting a text. Take, for example, the famous passage in Isa. 7:14, "Look, the young woman [or "virgin"] is with child and shall bear a son, and shall name him Immanuel." If this verse is read solely in the context of the book of Isaiah,

10. Both Isadore of Seville and the *Ordinary Gloss* treat Ruth as a figure of the Gentile church.
11. For fuller accounts that situate the literal sense of scripture in the history of theology, see Stephen Fowl, *Engaging Scripture* (Oxford: Blackwell, 1998), chap. 1; Fowl, "The Importance of a Multivoiced Literal Sense of Scripture: The Example of Thomas Aquinas," in A. K. A. Adam, Stephen E. Fowl, Kevin J. Vanhoozer, and Francis Watson, *Reading Scripture with the Church: Toward a Hermeneutic for Theological Interpretation* (Grand Rapids: Baker Academic, 2006), 35–50.

it appears that the child in question is the son born to Isaiah of Jerusalem as related in Isa. 8. It is equally clear that Matthew and the Christian tradition generally take this verse to be a prophetic announcement of the birth of Jesus almost 750 years later. Christians can grant that both of these are the literal sense of Isa. 7:14. This is because the God who inspires these words is perfectly able to make them refer to both of these characters. This is what Augustine and Aquinas both mean when they speak of the possibility of there being many literal senses of the same passage.[12]

If this stands as a working definition of the literal sense, then figural interpretations will use a variety of interpretive techniques to extend the literal sense of scripture in ways that enhance Christians' abilities to live and worship faithfully in the contexts in which they find themselves. Why is this important? A central and widely shared Christian conviction about scripture is that God has providentially ordered scripture so that, despite its manifest obscurities, it provides Christians with a set of lenses though which to view and comprehend the world as they seek to negotiate their paths faithfully through it. If Christians are to use scripture as the basis for ordering and comprehending the world, then they must also recognize that there will be times when the literal sense of scripture may not offer a sharp enough vision to account for the world in which they find themselves. In those cases Christians will need to read scripture figuratively using a variety of interpretive techniques to extend the literal sense. In this light, it is not surprising that Christians have located figures or foreshadowings or anticipations of Christ and aspects of the Christian life in the Old Testament even if such things are not immediately evident to readers. Of course, these interpretive matters are hardly ever straightforward or clear. This is in part why, if Christians are to engage scripture as part of their ongoing struggles to live and worship faithfully before the triune God, they will inevitably find themselves discussing, arguing, and debating matters of scriptural interpretation. In this respect, for Christians figural reading will be both necessary and necessarily contested.

I would suggest (but do not have the time, space, or resources to prove) that modern commentators' interest in the motives of the characters in Ruth despite the text's reticence in these matters is a non-theological analogue to the theologians' interest in reading Ruth figurally. Each of these interests provides a way of going above and beyond what is offered in the text of Ruth in order to edify particular types of readers; each provides ways of forging connections between what is said

12. See Augustine, *Confessions* 12.31; Thomas Aquinas, *Summa Theologiae* Ia, Q. 1, Art. 10.

and further things that readers might want to know. At their best, both of these practices incite further thinking, reflection, and consideration.

The arguments for figural reading offered here and elsewhere can do little more than clear some conceptual space within which it makes sense for theological interpreters to offer figural accounts of biblical texts. The real test comes in offering such readings in the course of a sustained engagement with specific texts. It is in such engagements, rather than through ever more sophisticated accounts of figural reading, that figural readings will edify and enlighten or not. Hence, it is time to turn to Ruth. The English text included in the commentary is a lightly modified version of the NRSV with modifications indicated in the notes. Readers might also benefit from studying the Jewish Publication Society translation as well as the striking translation of Ellen Davis in *Who Are You, My Daughter?*

RUTH 1

¹·¹In the days when the judges judged, there was a famine in the land, and a certain man of Bethlehem in Judah sojourned[a] in the fields of Moab,[b] he and his wife and two sons. ²The name of the man was Elimelech ("My-God-is-king") and the name of his wife Naomi ("My-pleasantness"), and the names of his two sons were Mahlon ("Sickness") and Chilion ("End-of-the-line");[c] they were Ephrathites from Bethlehem in Judah. They went into the fields of Moab and remained there. ³But Elimelech, the husband of Naomi, died, and she was left with her two sons. ⁴These took Moabite wives; the name of one was Orpah ("Back-of-the-neck"[d]) and the name of the other Ruth. When they had lived there for about ten years, ⁵both Mahlon and Chilion also died, so that the woman was left without her two sons or her husband.

⁶Then she started to return with her daughters-in-law from the fields of Moab, for she had heard in the fields of Moab that the Lord had had remembered his people and given them food. ⁷So she set out from the place where she had been living, she and her two daughters-in-law, and they went on their way to go back to the land of Judah. ⁸But Naomi said to her two daughters-in-law, "Go back each of you to your mother's house. May the Lord do good-faith with you, as you have done with the dead and with me.[e] ⁹The Lord grant that you may find security, each of you in the house of your husband." Then she kissed them, and they wept aloud. ¹⁰They said to her, "No, we will return with you to your people." ¹¹But Naomi said, "Turn back, my daughters, why would you go with me? Do I still have sons in my womb that they may become your husbands? ¹²Turn back, my daughters, go your way, for I am too old to have a husband. Even if I thought there was hope for me, even if I should have a husband tonight and bear sons,

¹³would you then wait until they were grown? Would you then refrain from marrying? No, my daughters, it has been far more bitter for me than for you, because the hand of the Lord has turned against me." ¹⁴And they lifted up their voice and wept still more. And Orpah kissed her mother-in-law. But Ruth stuck by her.ᶠ ¹⁵So she said, "See, your sister-in-law has gone back to her people and to her gods; return after your sister-in-law." ¹⁶But Ruth said, "Do not press me to leave you or to turn back from following you! Where you go, I will go; where you lodge, I will lodge; your people are my people, and your God my God.ᵍ ¹⁷Where you die, I will die—there will I be buried. May the Lord strike me down,ʰ and more as well, if even death parts me from you!" ¹⁸When Naomi saw that she was determined to go with her, she said no more to her.

¹⁹So the two of them went on until they came to Bethlehem. When they came to Bethlehem, the whole town was stirred because of them; and the women said, "Is this Naomi?" ²⁰She said to them, "Call me no longer Naomi ("My-pleasantness"), call me Mara ("Bitterness"ⁱ), for the Almighty has dealt bitterly with me. ²¹I went away full, but the Lord has brought me back empty; why call me Naomi when the Lord has dealt harshly with me, and the Almighty has brought calamity upon me?"

²²So Naomi returned together with Ruth the Moabite, her daughter-in-law, who came back with her from the country of Moab. They came to Bethlehem at the beginning of the barley harvest.

Notes

This translation of the book of Ruth is a combination of the author's translation, the NSRV, and other indicated sources.

ᵃ I have followed the Jewish Publication Society translation of *lagur* as "sojourn." This rightly conveys the sense that Elimelech and his family are more like refugees than immigrants; they do not intend to stay.

ᵇ The phrase "fields of Moab" (*sedeh moab*) is different from "land of Moab" (*eretz moab*), which also appears in the Old Testament. Davis (2003: 4) suggests that the field is emphasized in Ruth because this is where women's character is revealed.

ᶜ The translations of the names comes from Davis 2003: 4.

ᵈ This translation is also from Davis 2003: 5.

ᵉ This is the first time *hesed* appears in Ruth. I have followed Davis's translation "do good-faith" (2003: 16). She also notes that since the Lord demonstrates *hesed* to Israel, "every person who enters into covenant with YHWH is expected to demonstrate that same quality" (17).

ᶠ The Hebrew word translated by Davis as "stuck" is the same word used in Gen. 2:24 to describe a man leaving his father and mother and sticking to his wife. She adds, "Although there is no indication of a sexual bond between the two women, Ruth is quietly making a bold statement of love in sticking by a woman whom others would see as God-forsaken" (2003: 23).

ᵍ Neither the Greek nor the Hebrew has a future-tense verb or any verb at all in this clause. The NRSV translation of "Your people shall be my people, and your God my God" seems to rely on the fact that 1:17 uses future-tense verbs. Of course, this may be because 1:17 refers to events that can only be in the future. Nielsen (1997: 45) and Davis (2003: 27) each opt to supply a present-tense verb. I have followed them here since this establishes the bond between Ruth and Naomi at the moment Ruth says it.

ʰ The Hebrew here is a typically formulaic oath. The NRSV properly translates it "May the Lord do thus and so to me." Although accurate to the Hebrew, we do not use such a formula in English to make oaths. I have followed Nielsen (1997: 45) in the translation above.

ⁱ The translations of these names follow Davis 2003: 34.

Commentary

Five brief verses at the beginning of the book introduce the temporal setting for this story and the geographical location of the central characters when the story begins, as well as offering an explanation for why they relocated to Moab rather than remaining in Bethlehem. The story begins "in the days when the judges judged." This helps to explain the location of Ruth in the Christian canon. The book is located in the time of the judges and follows the conclusion of the book of Judges. Ruth concludes with the birth of Jesse the father of David, thus nicely introducing the books of Samuel.

Ruth is not situated during the time of any particular judge but during the time "when the judges judged," as a literal translation of the MT or LXX might read.[1] In this light it is useful to remember that the book of Judges ends with the brief recognition that there was no king in Israel at that time and "each man did what was right in his own eyes" (Judg. 21:25).[2] Although the NRSV opts for a gender-neutral translation, "all the people did what was right in their own eyes," this translation misses something important about both Judges and Ruth. Judges is full of stories about men doing what is right in their own eyes in ways that often result in disaster for women. Think of Jephthah and his daughter in Judg. 11:29–40. In addition, there is the very troubling story of the Levite, his concubine, and the men of Gibeah in Judg. 19—men doing right in their own eyes, resulting in rape, murder, and ultimately civil war. This leads to punishment for the men of Jabesh-gilead and the distribution of women from Jabesh-gilead to the men of Benjamin and the subsequent kidnapping of young women from Shiloh during the "festival of the Lord" (Judg. 21:8–24). By the end of Judges one would be quite justified in reckoning any woman who willingly associated herself with Israel and Israel's God as rash or even suicidal. Yet Ruth does this. Her

1. The targum to Ruth identifies Boaz with Ibzan, the Bethlehemite who served as judge after Jephthah and before Elon (Judg. 12:8–10). The midrash, *Ruth Rabbah* 1.1, describes Boaz as a contemporary of Deborah (Rabinowitz 1983: 16).

2. In *Ruth Rabbah*, Rabbi Aha indicates that this was a time when most Israelites had turned from God and that the famine related in Ruth 1 is God's judgment on that time (*Ruth Rabbah* proem 2).

story narrates a bridge between Judges and the books of Samuel, which present the story of King David, Ruth's great-grandson.

It is also interesting to recall that in the ordering of books in the Hebrew Bible, at least from the medieval period, Ruth is one of the five *megilloth* or "rolls" (along with Song of Songs, Ecclesiastes, Esther, and Lamentations). Each of these is to be read during a particular festival. Ruth, the one who gleans in Boaz's field, is understandably tied to Shabuoth (the Feast of Weeks, or Pentecost), a harvest festival. This is also the time when Jews commemorate Moses coming down from Mount Sinai with the law. There is much one might make out of Ruth's connection with the Feast of Weeks. First, in Lev. 23 the Feast of Weeks is established with a provision that reminds the Israelites that in harvesting their fields they must not harvest all the way to the corners of the fields. In addition, they are to leave the gleanings of their fields for the poor and the alien (Lev. 23:22). Second, it is at the Feast of Weeks, Pentecost, that the Spirit of God falls on the first followers of Jesus, drawing in Jews from all over the Roman Empire to hear the mighty deeds of God in their own tongue (Acts 2:8–13). In this way Luke reflects the reconstitution of Israel in the light of the death and resurrection of the Messiah. Moreover, Pentecost offers us a foretaste of the movement of the church from Jerusalem, to Judea and Samaria, to the ends of the earth (Acts 1:8). Perhaps this movement is anticipated in the person of Ruth, the Moabite who joins herself to the people of Israel and Israel's God, returning with Naomi from outside Israel back to Bethlehem.

If one follows the liturgical ordering of festivals, then Ruth comes after Proverbs and Song of Songs. Although this liturgical ordering of the scrolls is traditional, there does appear to be some flexibility in it. In some manuscripts the texts are arranged in their presumed chronological ordering.[3] Thus, Ruth follows right after Prov. 31:10–31. In Prov. 31 we find an acrostic encomium to a "capable wife." The Hebrew term here is similar to the one Boaz uses to describe Ruth in 3:11. Moreover, much of the description of this woman in Proverbs either fits Ruth particularly or is easily imagined of her and her life beyond the end of the story. As the encomium closes, we are reminded that "a woman who fears the LORD is to be praised" (Prov. 31:30). Thus, one can see a connection between the end of Proverbs and Ruth.

---

3. See the discussion on L. B. Wolfson, "Implications of the Place of the Book of Ruth in Editions, Manuscripts, and Canon of the Old Testament," *HUCA* 1 (1924), 151–78. In the Talmud (B. Bat. 14b) Ruth is listed as first in the Writings, followed by Psalms. This is perhaps following a chronological order as Ruth's setting in the time of the Judges antedates the other Writings. In addition, by ending with the genealogy of David, Ruth nicely sets the stage for Psalms.

The beginning of Ruth also sets the story in a time of famine in the land, driving Elimelech, Naomi, and their two sons, Mahlon and Chilion, from Bethlehem (literally, "house of bread") into the fields of Moab in search of a sustainable life. Such a journey may remind readers of Abraham and Jacob, who both travel to Egypt in times of famine (Gen. 12:10; 42:1). The text of Ruth never reveals what sort of characters Elimelech, Mahlon, and Chilion are. In *Ruth Rabbah* 1.4, the midrashic tradition indicates that Elimelech left Bethlehem not because he lacked food but because he did not want to share the surplus food he had with more needy kinsmen. The targum of Ruth seems to counter this by claiming that Elimelech was a great man and a leader in Bethlehem.[4] By 1:3 Elimelech is dead, and in the next verse his two sons have each married Moabite women and then died.[5]

Thus, we are left with three widows, Naomi, Ruth, and Orpah. Quickly after that, Naomi decides it is time for her to return home (1:6).[6] She has heard that the Lord has attended to the situation of his people and has given them bread.[7] Bethlehem is again a house of bread. Although Moab had been a place of food for Naomi and her family, it was also a place of death and bitterness. Now that the Lord has renewed attention to the plight of the Bethlehemites, it makes sense for Naomi to return. It is less clear what Ruth and Orpah are to do. Both women appear to be under Naomi's authority.[8] Hence, they begin the journey with her. Fairly quickly, however, Naomi seeks to resolve any uncertainty about their future in Judah by sending them back to their mothers' houses (1:8).

Naomi gives them a blessing, asking that God would show the same *hesed* to Ruth and Orpah that they had shown to her and to the dead. The term *hesed* will play a central role in understanding the text of Ruth. In a general sense the term denotes a faithful goodness. In the LXX the Greek word *eleos* (often rendered into English as "mercy") usually translates the Hebrew *hesed*. The NRSV, the King James Version, and the New American Standard Bible (among others) all use the

---

4. See *Targum of Ruth*, trans. D. R. G. Beattie (Collegeville, MN: Liturgical Press, 1994), and the commentary by Etan Levine, *The Aramaic Version of Ruth* (Rome: Biblical Institute Press, 1973), 44.

5. The targum attributes all these deaths to the fact that Elimelech allowed his sons to take Moabite wives, violating Deut. 23:3. The targum also identifies Ruth as the daughter of Eglon (Judg. 3:12–14).

6. Davis (2003: 13) notes that the verb translated "return" or "turn back" occurs twelve times in Ruth 1. Elsewhere this verb is used to speak of a radical spiritual reorientation.

7. The same verb translated as "attended to" or "looked out for" is also used in Exod. 3:16 in reference to the Lord's renewed attention to the plight of the Israelites in Egypt.

8. J. Schipper, "Translating the Preposition *'m* in the Book of Ruth," *VT* 63 (2013): 663–69, argues that the use of the Hebrew preposition *'m* in 1:7 serves to communicate that Orpah and Ruth not only accompany Naomi but are under her authority. If this is correct, it resolves any uncertainty about Ruth's and Orpah's motivation in following Naomi.

phrase "deal kindly." The translation above follows Ellen Davis (2003) and uses the phrase "do good-faith." Because of its strangeness, this phrase causes us to pause and reflect on what might be involved in *hesed*.

In Mic. 6:8 the Israelites are told that all God requires of them is "to do justice, and to love kindness [*hesed*], and to walk humbly with your God." This text from Micah raises the prospect that justice, *hesed*, and humility before God are connected. This would lead one to think that success in cultivating one of these virtues leads to and may presume some measure of success in cultivating the other two. If justice requires one to give to others what they are due in God, and if humility is based on rightly knowing one's own state relative to God and others, then *hesed* would be that grace which recognizes but is not constrained or limited merely by what is due to others and by where one stands relative to others and God. This would seem to fit Ruth quite well. She goes well beyond justice in her dealings with Naomi and acts with both grace and boldness toward Boaz without ever seeking to aggrandize herself.

Moreover, although to show *hesed* clearly requires an inner capacity for mercy and kindness, *hesed* is primarily displayed in a pattern of action (hence, "do good-faith"). As the story of Ruth unfolds, we will see a fuller picture of what *hesed* looks like in Ruth's actions. Here in chapter 1 we already learn from Naomi that both her daughters-in-law have already shown *hesed* in the ways they have cared for her and in their care of the three dead men. It is not immediately clear what it means to show *hesed* to the dead. In *Ruth Rabbah*, Rabbi Zeir's comments indicate that the issue of showing *hesed* to the dead has to do with physically caring for the bodies and preparing them for the grave.[9] This gives some insight into the later work of Joseph of Arimathea and Nicodemus in John's Gospel and the various women in the Synoptics who prepare Jesus's body for burial. They are showing *hesed* to the dead. Indeed, in the case of Joseph of Arimathea and Nicodemus, these actions are the primary ways they display their discipleship. Moreover, in the early years of the church, pagan opponents of Christianity noted the ways in which believers cared for their dead.[10] In our contemporary world where we are

---

9. In *Ruth Rabbah* 2.14, Rabbi Zeir notes that the scroll of Ruth does not give specific direction about what is clean or unclean, what is permitted or forbidden relative to corpses. Its point, then, must be "to teach how great is the reward of those who do deeds of kindness" (in Rabinowitz 1983: 35).

10. See the letter of the emperor Julian to Arsacius, "Why do we not observe that it is their [the Christians'] benevolence to strangers, their care for the graves of the dead and the pretended holiness of their lives that have done the most to increase atheism [i.e., Christianity]? . . . When the impious Galileans support not only their own poor but ours as well, all men see that our own people lack aid from us." *Letter to Arsacius, High Priest of Galatia* (Loeb Classical Library).

systematically isolated from death and large corporations control much about the burial process, it is important to recall that for much of the church's history showing *hesed* to the dead was a central Christian practice.[11]

Although she will claim that the hand of the Lord has been stretched out against her during her sojourn in Moab, Naomi asks that this same Lord "deal kindly" with Ruth and Orpah as they remain in Moab.[12] In the face of Ruth's and Orpah's resistance (1:10), Naomi commands them to return to their own families just as she is returning to hers. Why would Naomi separate herself from those who have shown her *hesed*? Her motives here are unclear. It is clear that she will not be able to provide sons for them to marry (1:11), and from Naomi's perspective "rest" or "security"[13] is best found in the "house of [a] husband" (1:9). Perhaps, like Judah, who saw nothing but death in retaining any connection to Tamar (Gen. 38), Naomi sees that both Ruth and Orpah are childless widows and tied in some way to the deaths of her husband and sons. Perhaps God's hand is against them in the same way that God's hand has been stretched out against Naomi.[14] Perhaps she simply wants what is best for them and thinks that is more likely to happen in Moab than in Judah. We never learn of her motives. It is clear, however, that despite the fact that both women have shown her *hesed*, she thinks that she and they do not have a future together.

In the midst of much weeping Orpah heeds Naomi's directive. Unlike the LXX, the MT does not explicitly say Orpah returned to her family. Rather, she simply kisses Naomi and is never mentioned again in the text. Neither the LXX nor the MT offers any sort of evaluation of Orpah. She has done what Naomi commanded; this could hardly be blameworthy. Indeed, as Nielsen indicates, Orpah's very conventional response makes Ruth's response look even more meritorious (1997: 48). Both Judaism and Christianity, however, have filled in the silence of the text here. The midrash *Ruth Rabbah* relates a horrifying story of Orpah being

11. See Michael L. Budde's essay "The Church and the Death Business," in Michael L. Budde and Robert Brimlow, *Christianity Incorporated: How Big Business Is Buying the Church* (Grand Rapids: Brazos, 2002), 83–108.

12. The syntax of the Hebrew in 1:9a is quite difficult. J. Schipper, following a suggestion by R. Holmstedt, comments, "A new train of thought independent of the blessing, Naomi's speech shifts towards matters of practical advice that, unlike the blessing formula, do not involve Yhwh." "The Syntax and Rhetoric of Ruth 1:9a," *VT* 62, fasc. 4 (2012): 644. It seems to me that the most this claim can sustain is that Naomi's speech does not necessarily require the work of YHWH. She is not ruling that out. Moreover, the issue of divine and human agency in Ruth is often hazy, even when the syntax is less than hazy. Finally, in the LXX there is no ambiguity. God's help is invoked throughout 1:8–9.

13. The Hebrew, *minuha*, suggests rest and security (cf., e.g., Gen. 49:15; Mic. 2:1).

14. This is the supposition of Fewell and Gunn (1990: 73–74).

gang raped on her way back to her family.[15] The Talmud (b. Sotah 42b) offers a more generous, though mixed, account. Because of her tears over Naomi, Orpah is granted four gigantic sons, one of whom is Goliath. This then allows for the observation that the heirs of the one who stays end up defeating the heirs of the one who leaves. From the Christian side, Rabanus Maurus in his commentary on Ruth treats Orpah as an example of those who after being baptized return to pagan ways.[16] They are like the grain that is sown among the rocky soil. It springs up but is unable to withstand the heat of the sun because its roots are shallow, and it withers and dies (cf. Matt. 13:1–9; Mark 4:1–9; Luke 8:4–8).

Ruth, however, clings to or "sticks by" Naomi. The Hebrew verb translated here as "cling" is the same verb used in Gen. 2:24 to speak about a man leaving his father and mother and clinging to his wife and becoming one flesh with her. In this light Ruth is forging a bond with Naomi, her people, and her God that only death can break. The LXX says that Ruth "followed" Naomi, using the same verb used of disciples of Jesus.

Naomi makes one last attempt to get Ruth to turn back, citing the example of Orpah, who has returned to her people and her gods (1:15). Ruth then gives voice to her clinging. She will go where Naomi goes. Indeed, she has no more gods of her own or people of her own. In 1:17 she even invokes the name of the Lord to underwrite her commitment, binding her to Naomi for life.

Modern readers long to know why. What leads Ruth to make this extraordinary declaration of love and commitment? The text gives us no answer. Perhaps her family had died; perhaps she saw some reason to hope that things would be better with Naomi; perhaps God spoke to her. We never learn about motive. Instead, we see faith embodied but not explained. This is not all that different from Abraham. Abraham is called from his people, his home, and his gods. Without much insight into his motives, we read that he does what God asks. He believes God, and it is reckoned to him as righteousness. We must reckon Ruth, too, as righteous on the basis of her faithfulness. In fact, she may exhibit even greater faith than Abraham. In Gen. 12, 15, and 17, Abraham is given some rather extravagant promises from God to believe in. Ruth receives nothing like this. She is much more like Matthew the tax collector who simply responds to Jesus's request to follow him by dropping everything and following (again without revealing any motive). Moreover, it is Ruth who makes extravagant promises to Naomi. These promises are in some ways

15. *Ruth Rabbah* 2.20 (in Rabinowitz 1983: 38).
16. PL 108:1204A-B (in Smith 1996: 13). Maurus is significant because the *Ordinary Gloss* on Ruth is basically comprised of his commentary with some small additions.

quite close to the promises that the Lord makes to Abraham in Gen. 17:7 and to Jacob as he is leaving the promised land in Gen. 28:15. Just as God promises to be with Abraham and his heirs wherever they may go, Ruth binds herself to Naomi, her people, and her God. Ruth's promise stands in sharp contrast to the scribe who offers to follow Jesus wherever he goes (Matt. 8:19). Like Naomi, Jesus promises the scribe little, not even a place to sleep at night. The Gospels seem to imply that this scribe does not live up to his rash promise. Ruth, however, clings to Naomi and brings fullness to Naomi.

One might further question whether Ruth loves Naomi or Naomi's God. In answer to this Ellen Davis notes that it is common for people to come to God by loving people who love God: "Many, and perhaps most, people come to God because they know and love someone who knows and loves God" (Davis 2003: 28).

The Christian tradition treats this passage in particular and Ruth more generally as a type of all Gentiles who turn to God. Ambrose typifies this when he writes, "Ruth entered the Church and was made an Israelite, and deserved to be counted amongst God's greatest servants; chosen on account of the kinship of her soul, not of her body. . . . Continuing in our Father's house, we might, through her example, say to him who, like Paul or any other bishop, calls us to worship God, *Your people are my people, and your God is my God.*"[17] Such kinship of soul rather than kinship based on common DNA matches that new family that Jesus forms, a family that is constituted not by blood ties but rather by those who hear the word of God and do it (Luke 8:19–21; 11:27–28).

In the face of this astonishing profession of fidelity, love, and steadfast commitment, Naomi is silent. She has no hope to offer Ruth. She does not appear to be in any position either to reciprocate or to affirm Ruth's actions. She simply relents and allows Ruth to go with her.

We may get further insight into how to understand Ruth's actions here by looking at the way the text constantly refers to her as "Ruth the Moabite" (cf. 1:22; 2:2, 21; 4:5, 10). In Num. 25:1–5 Israelite men begin to have sexual relations with the women of Moab. These women encourage the Israelite men to sacrifice to their gods. "Thus Israel yoked itself to the Baal of Peor" (Num. 25:3). This provokes God's anger, and Moses commands the judges of Israel to kill any who have yoked themselves to the Baal of Peor (Num. 25:5). Against this backdrop Ruth the Moabite provides the antitype to this passage. She is a Moabite woman who joins herself to Israel's God and through whom God brings further blessing to Israel.

17. Ambrose, *Commentary on Luke* 3.30, PL 15:1685A. This comment was included in the additions to the *Ordinary Gloss* (in Smith 1996: 32).

Ruth and Naomi arrive in Bethlehem in 1:19. We learn nothing about the journey. Their arrival, however, excites the women of the city. Bush (1996: 91), among others, argues that the Hebrew here should not be read as a question but as an exclamation of positive surprise. Thus, Naomi is remembered and welcomed back, indicating that she and Elimelech left on good terms. In the midrash on Ruth, the surprise has to do with the change in Naomi's appearance due to her reversal of fortune.[18] In either case, no mention is made of Ruth. She neither speaks nor is spoken of in this paragraph.

For her part, Naomi takes on a persona like Job. The Lord has embittered her life and witnessed against her. Naomi recognizes no charge against her. Like Job, she is an innocent sufferer (Nielsen 1997: 52). Thus, she should be called Mara or "bitter one" rather than Naomi, which means "my pleasantness" or "sweetness."

Naomi clearly identifies the Lord as the cause of her afflictions. There is nothing more in the text to sustain this judgment. Indeed, the Lord neither speaks nor acts directly in the book of Ruth. If we are to make judgments about God's purposes and actions in this story, we will, like Naomi, have to exercise our own powers of discernment. There are, however, some reasons for us to doubt that Naomi is the best judge of her own circumstances. She claims that she left Bethlehem full and now the Lord has brought her back empty (1:21). If the term "full" refers to a general level of blessing and prosperity (e.g., Deut. 33:23), then it is clearly not the case that Naomi and Elimelech left Bethlehem "full." They were refugees from a famine. Naomi returned, as she says in 1:6, because the Lord had remembered his people and given them food. If this is what Naomi means by leaving full and coming back empty, then she has misjudged the situation under which she left.

Alternatively, if *Ruth Rabbah* is correct in taking Naomi's claims of fullness seriously, then it seems that she and Elimelech were wealthy and left Bethlehem to avoid sharing with their poorer neighbors. If this were the case, then Naomi hardly has a complaint against the Lord. One would expect something more like penance or contrition than lament. One might also expect a more hostile reception from those Naomi and Elimelech left behind.

Of course, it is also possible to take "full" to mean that Naomi went out with a husband and two sons and is returning a childless widow. It is likely that this is what she means. Nevertheless, it completely neglects the fact that she is returning with Ruth, the one who has shown *hesed* to her and her dead husband and sons, the one who has pledged to become one of her people, worship her God,

---

18. *Ruth Rabbah* 3.6 (in Rabinowitz 1983: 48).

and remain with Naomi until they are parted by death. Naomi may have suffered affliction in Moab, but she is not empty. Indeed, by the end of Ruth, the women of Bethlehem tell Naomi that the Lord has truly blessed her with a daughter-in-law who is worth more than seven sons (4:15). Although we might assume that Naomi agrees with this judgment, she does not offer it herself.

Thus, in the light of any of these scenarios, we have some reason to think that Naomi's initial judgment about the Lord will require revision. This might also lead one to avoid pronouncing too quickly on the movements of God's providence. As both Job's friends and Job himself learn, it is easy to make overhasty assertions about what God is and is not doing in the world.

Chapter 1 concludes by reinforcing Ruth's Moabite origins. As noted above, Ruth's commitments to Naomi do not erase the fact that she is a Moabite and that she and Naomi have both come from Moab. We also learn that things in Bethlehem are going well enough that there is barley to harvest.

RUTH 2

²:¹Now Naomi had a kinsman on her husband's side, a man of considerable substance,ᵃ of the family of Elimelech, whose name was Boaz. ²And Ruth the Moabite said to Naomi, "So, I'm going to go to the field and glean among the ears of grain, behind someone in whose eyes I find favor."ᵇ She said to her, "Go, my daughter." ³So she went. She came and gleaned in the field behind the reapers. As it happened, she came to the part of the field belonging to Boaz, who was of the family of Elimelech. ⁴Just then Boaz came from Bethlehem. He said to the reapers, "The LORD be with you." They answered, "The LORD bless you." ⁵Then Boaz said to his worker-lad who was in charge of the reapers, "To whom does this worker-girlᶜ belong?" ⁶The worker-lad who was in charge of the reapers answered, "She is the Moabite worker-girl who came back with Naomi from the fields of Moab. ⁷She said, 'Please let me glean and gather among the sheaves behind the reapers.' So she came, and she has been on her feet from early this morning until now, without resting even for a moment."

⁸Then Boaz said to Ruth, "Now listen,ᵈ my daughter, do not go to glean in another field or leave this one, but keep close to my worker-girls. ⁹Keep your eyes on the field that is being reaped, and follow behind them. I have ordered the worker-lads not to bother you.ᵉ If you get thirsty, go to the vessels and drink from what the worker-lads have drawn." ¹⁰Then she fell prostrate, with her face to the ground, and said to him, "Why have I found favor in your sight, that you should take notice of me, when I am a foreigner?" ¹¹But Boaz answered her, "All that you have done for your mother-in-law since the death of your husband has been fully told me, and how you left your father and mother and your native land and came to a people that you did not know before. ¹²May the LORD reward you for your

R U T H

deeds, and may you have a full reward from the LORD, the God of Israel, under whose wings you have come for refuge!" [13]Then she said, "May I continue to find favor in your sight, my lord, for you have comforted me and spoken kindly to your servant, even though I am not one of your servants."

[14]At mealtime Boaz said to her, "Come here, and eat some of this bread, and dip your morsel in the sour wine." So she sat beside the reapers, and he heaped up for her some parched grain. She ate until she was satisfied, and she had some left over. [15]When she got up to glean, Boaz instructed his worker-lads, "Let her glean even among the standing sheaves, and do not reproach her. [16]You must also pull out some handfuls for her from the bundles, and leave them for her to glean, and do not rebuke her."

[17]So she gleaned in the field until evening. Then she beat out what she had gleaned, and it was about an ephah of barley. [18]She picked it up and came into the town, and her mother-in-law saw how much she had gleaned. Then she took out and gave her what was left over after she herself had been satisfied. [19]Her mother-in-law said to her, "Where did you glean today? And where have you worked? Blessed be the man who took notice of you." So she told her mother-in-law with whom she had worked, and said, "The name of the man with whom I worked today is Boaz." [20]Then Naomi said to her daughter-in-law, "Blessed be he by the LORD, whose kindness [*hesed*] has not forsaken the living or the dead!" Naomi also said to her, "The man is a relative of ours, one of our nearest kin." [21]Then Ruth the Moabite said, "He even said to me, 'You should stick with the workers who work for me until they finish all the harvesting for me.'" [22]Naomi said to Ruth, her daughter-in-law, "It is better, my daughter, that you go out with his worker-girls, and they won't press themselves on you in another field."[f] [23]So she stayed close to the worker-girls of Boaz, gleaning until the end of the barley and wheat harvests; and she lived with her mother-in-law.

Notes

[a] Translation from Davis 2003: 38–39. Although the Hebrew can sustain the NRSV's "a prominent rich man," the phrase translated as "considerable substance" also connotes moral character. Boaz, of course, displays this over the course of the story.

[b] This verse follows Davis (2003: 42–43), who argues that the Hebrew suggests Ruth's resolve. The NRSV translation conveys the sense that Ruth is asking for Naomi's permission to glean.

[c] Davis (2003: 44–45) translates the Hebrew *na'ar* and *na'arah* as "worker-lad" and "worker-girl."

[d] The Hebrew is cast as a question, "Haven't you heard, my daughter?" The English, "Now listen," accurately conveys that this question is really more of an assertion.

[e] Again, this is another assertion cast as a question in Hebrew.

f I have followed Davis's (2003: 64) translation here as she continues the interplay of "workers" and "worker-girls."

Commentary

Boaz is introduced in 2:1 as a man of great substance, might, and wealth; he is also a relative of Elimelech.[1] If Boaz had neglected any prior obligations to take care of Ruth and Naomi, neither the text nor his subsequent behavior indicate that he was blameworthy. Nevertheless, upon their return to Bethlehem it is not clear how Naomi and Ruth will eat, where they will stay, and who will care for them.

After many verses of silence, Ruth and Naomi have a brief conversation in 2:2–3. Ruth tells Naomi that she is going to glean in the fields in order to find some food for them. Naomi agrees with this plan. Deuteronomy 24:19 (cf. Lev. 19:9; 23:22) explicitly states that after harvesting, any leftover grain should be available to the widows, the aliens, and the poor for gleaning. Ruth matches all three of these descriptions. On one level it would appear that Ruth has a God-given right to glean. Alternatively, Ruth herself indicates that she will need the "favor" of the owner(s) of the field if she is to be successful. Whatever obligations the Torah imposes on landowners and whatever rights it grants to gleaners, it is also clear that in practice the poor are dependent on the goodwill of those who have more. This may be one more way in which the practice of justice and *hesed* are intertwined. In the practice of gleaning, it is easy to imagine that one can observe the strictures of the laws on gleaning and the poor may still not have enough to eat. Moreover, the proper combination of justice and *hesed* can mitigate the stigma that might fall on those who have to rely on gleaning to survive. As it turns out, Ruth ends up gleaning in the field belonging to Boaz.

At this point in chapter 2, Boaz arrives on the scene. He greets the reapers and then asks the servant in charge about Ruth. We do not learn why Ruth has caught Boaz's eye. She is not one of his hired workers, and she is evidently very attractive.[2] The worker-lad identifies Ruth as the young woman from Moab who returned with Naomi. The worker-lad then relates that Ruth asked permission to

1. The targum takes the Hebrew phrase generally translated as "a man of great might and wealth" to mean that Boaz is "strong in the Law," i.e., a Torah scholar.

2. The midrash *Ruth Rabbah* 4.4 (in Rabinowitz 1983: 52) clears up this question. Noting the linguistic connections between the Hebrew phrase translated "as it happened" or "by chance" in 2:3 and the Hebrew phrase for nocturnal emissions in Deut. 23:10, Rabbi Johanan claims that whoever saw Ruth was sexually excited. See also the discussion in Amy Richter, *Enoch and the Gospel of Matthew*, Princeton Theological Monograph Series (Eugene, OR: Pickwick, 2012), 117.

glean, has worked unceasingly since then, and is now taking a rest. The last clause of 2:7 is a bit obscure. A wooden translation of the Hebrew would be "This is her sitting the house a little." The LXX is clearer—"She has not rested in the field even a little"—but does not seem closely tied to the Hebrew text. The rest of the text makes it clear that Ruth is not off in the distance. Rather, whether gleaning without ceasing or in the house, she is quite near to Boaz. Despite the textual obscurities at the end of 2:7, we can say two things with confidence about Ruth at this point. She has displayed both modesty and diligence in her actions, and she is now close enough to Boaz for him to speak to her directly.

Boaz wants Ruth to remain working in his field, and he offers to make her work easier. She is to stay close to his worker-girls; the Hebrew verb is the same one used in 1:14 to describe Ruth clinging to Naomi. Boaz has ordered the male workers not to "touch" her, thus protecting her from sexual harassment or assault.[3] Finally, he makes sure that she will have water, a necessity if one is to work in the Judean sun.

In 2:3 Ruth set out with the hope of finding favor with someone. Boaz's offer both exceeds her expectation and raises the question why. In answer, Boaz refers to Ruth's own actions with Naomi. She has left father, mother, and homeland to venture to an unknown place out of loyalty to Naomi. Moreover, she has sought refuge under the wings of the Lord, and Boaz asks the Lord to reward her for this.

Boaz invokes the Lord's blessing on Ruth's display of *hesed*. When Ruth speaks, she returns to speaking of Boaz as the primary agent of blessing here. She has found favor in *his* eyes; *he* has comforted her;[4] *he* has "spoken to her heart" (2:13); *he* has treated her like one of his Israelite workers, though she is not an Israelite.[5]

Although Ruth herself may not have described her actions in the way Boaz does, Boaz's description would have been recognizable to attentive Israelites. Psalms 17:8; 36:7; 63:7; and 91:4 all use the image of shelter under God's wings as a way of describing both a place of safety and God's care and compassion. The word used to designate God's wing, *kanap*, is the same word that Ruth will use in 3:9 when she asks Boaz to cover her with the corner of his garment. "For what Ruth asks Boaz to do is the very same fulfillment of what Boaz asked the Lord to do" (Nielsen 1997: 60). In this section Ruth persistently links her good

3. The Hebrew *nagah* is also used in Gen. 20:6 where God tells Abimelech that God has kept Abimelech from "touching" Sarah.
4. The verb *niham* (comfort) describes God comforting people in Isa. 12:1; 51:12; 52:9; 66:13; Pss. 71:21; 119:82. It is important to note, however, that "comfort" in this sense means a change in material conditions and not simply a change of emotional states.
5. This exchange recalls the dialogue between God and Moses in Exod. 32:7–13, where God identifies idolatrous Israel as Moses's people, only to be reminded by Moses that Israel is God's people.

fortune to finding favor in the eyes of Boaz. For his part, Boaz seeks to establish the Lord as the primary actor here. As the story moves to its completion, these two perspectives will move closer together as Boaz begins to embody the blessing that he has asked the Lord to give to Ruth.[6] Given that the book of Ruth rarely ascribes agency to the Lord, this way of looking at things is not that surprising.

In the next episode (2:14–17) Boaz continues to shower favor down on Ruth, inviting her to dip her bread in the vinegar and to partake of the roasted grain. Ruth is able to eat her fill (something that she may not have been able to do for some time) and to bring home leftovers for Naomi. Then, after the meal, Boaz commands his workers not to harass Ruth and to arrange things so that she finishes the day with an extraordinary abundance of grain. The ephah of threshed grain that Ruth brings home would have been far more than any gleaner might have expected. This would have been enough for several weeks' food.[7] Although she does not speak in this passage, Ruth is the focus of everyone's attention. Having left Naomi that morning empty, she returns full, even overfull, at the end of the day. This does not fully resolve the precarious position of Ruth and Naomi, but things are looking up.

Chapter 2 closes with Ruth and Naomi discussing the day's events and how to proceed. This paragraph (2:18–23) is filled with surprises and textual puzzles. Ruth returns to town with so much grain that Naomi is naturally curious about where she gleaned. After Ruth also takes out the leftovers from her lunch, it would have been clear to Naomi that this was more than just an average day spent gleaning. Her questions "Where did you glean? Where did you work?" followed by "Blessed is the man who took notice of you" indicate that Naomi understands that someone has been extravagantly generous with Ruth.

Ruth explains that Boaz is the one who has "taken notice" of her. Naomi's response in 2:20 bears looking at more closely. "Blessed be he by the LORD who has not forsaken his kindness [*hesed*] to the living or the dead." The English and the Hebrew both reflect an ambiguity regarding whose kindness has been displayed here, the Lord's or Boaz's. The LXX clearly understands it as the Lord's kindness. Given that Ruth has attributed this kindness to Boaz alone and that Boaz consistently identifies the Lord as the ultimate source of the favor he has shown Ruth, Naomi's ambiguous blessing covers both of these possibilities.

---

6. Linafelt (1999: 36–37) suggests that Boaz is deflecting attention away from his interest in Ruth. This may be the case, though motive here is hard to determine. In fact, Linafelt can adduce no real evidence for his speculations.

7. Davis (2003: 59) and Bush (1996: 133) both indicate that an *ephah* was somewhere between 22 and 39 liters. That much grain would have weighed between 30 and 50 pounds.

Although both Boaz and Ruth may have specific, though undisclosed, reasons for speaking as they do about the source of the blessings bestowed on Ruth,
Naomi's comments remind readers that from a theological perspective *hesed* has
its origin and derives its character from God and God's dealings with the world.
At the same time, *hesed* often requires human agency in order to be manifested in
the world. As a theoretical matter, it may at times be important to be clear about
these two distinct agents, God and humans. With regard to any particular set of
actions, however, the relationships between the activities of these two agents might
be difficult to disentangle. In certain cases one might want to disentangle them.
If, for example, there appeared to be some gap or difference between what God
would count as *hesed* and what humans would call *hesed*, it would be important
to note this. In addition, for a variety of contingent reasons, people may want to
focus their attention on one agent rather than another. Hence, clarity would be
important. Nevertheless, the ambiguity of Naomi's remarks suggests that readers
should generally avoid trying to disentangle what has been so fruitfully tangled
together.

On the basis of the combined remarks of Boaz, Ruth, and Naomi, it would
seem that the book of Ruth is not particularly interested either in constructing or
in disentangling chains of divine and human agency. Instead, readers are invited
to cultivate both the perceptual virtues that will enable them to discern God's
workings and the virtue of hope in God's providence when the workings of God
are obscured. Indeed, God's providence, rather than the capacity to identify direct
examples of God's agency, seems to be a central element in the story. Further, as
one grows in holiness, becoming ever more closely conformed to the image of
Christ, it should be both more difficult and less important to distinguish between
one's own desires and actions and those of God.

Naomi goes on to identify Boaz as "our" relative and "one of our nearest kin"
(2:20). This is the first time that Naomi has spoken as if she and Ruth shared a
common situation and might share a common destiny. In addition, Naomi names
Boaz as their *goel*, a term often translated as "redeemer," though here it is better
translated as "close kin." When applied to God, the term refers to God's capacity to
rescue one from danger or distress. When applied to humans, the redeemer is one
who can buy back land that has been sold to outsiders out of economic necessity,
or buy back people sold into slavery (Lev. 25:24–25, 47–55). Further, a redeemer
may be one who is authorized to receive money in restitution for wrongs done to
a dead family member. In Num. 35:9–28 a *goel* is one authorized to avenge the
murder of a family member (Linafelt 1999: 42; Bush 1996: 137). Naomi does

not appear to be relying on these technical roles a "redeemer" might play. Rather, she seems to use the term more broadly of someone who acts to deliver a member of their family, tribe, or clan. Naming Boaz this way sets the stage for the role he will seek to play in chapters 3 and 4.

In response to Naomi's identification of Boaz as a close relative, Ruth says that Boaz had invited her to continue to glean, sticking close to his male servants (2:21). In fact, Boaz had said that Ruth should stay close to his female servants (2:8), though his instructions regarding Ruth in 2:15–16 are given to his male workers. It is unclear why Ruth states things this way.[8] Whatever Ruth's reasons, Naomi suggests that it would be more appropriate for Ruth to stick close to the female workers. She does this, gleaning with them throughout the barley and wheat harvests.

---

8. One obvious possibility is that by sticking close to the male servants, Ruth may find a husband. Rabbi Hanan b. Levi (*Ruth Rabbah* 5.2, in Rabinowitz 1983: 69) interprets this discrepancy to indicate that Ruth still retains a measure of the sexual wantonness characteristic of Moabite women (cf. Gen. 19:33–35; Num. 25).

RUTH 3

^{3:1}Naomi her mother-in-law said to her, "My daughter, I need to seek some security for you, so that it may be well with you. ²Now here is our kinsman Boaz, with whose worker-girls you have been working.^a See, he is winnowing barley tonight at the threshing-floor. ³Now wash and anoint yourself, and put on your best clothes and go down to the threshing-floor; but do not make yourself known to the man until he has finished eating and drinking. ⁴When he lies down, observe the place where he lies; then, go and uncover his feet and lie down; and he will tell you what to do." ⁵She said to her, "All that you tell me I will do."

⁶So she went down to the threshing-floor and did just as her mother-in-law had instructed her. ⁷Boaz ate and drank, and his heart was good.^b Then he went to lie down at the end of the heap of grain. Then she came quietly and uncovered herself at his feet,^c and lay down. ⁸In the middle of the night the man was startled and turned over, and there, lying at his feet, was a woman! ⁹He said, "Who are you?" And she answered, "I am Ruth, your servant; spread your cloak over your servant,^d for you are next-of-kin." ¹⁰He said, "May you be blessed by the LORD, my daughter; this last instance of your loyalty [*hesed*] is better than the first; you have not gone after young men, whether poor or rich. ¹¹And now, my daughter, do not be afraid; I will do for you all that you ask, for all the assembly of my people know that you are a worthy woman. ¹²But now, though it is true that I am a near kinsman, there is another kinsman more closely related than I. ¹³Remain this night, and in the morning, if he will act as next-of-kin for you, good; let him do so. If he is not willing to act as next-of-kin for you, then, as the LORD lives, I will act as next-of-kin for you. Lie down until the morning."

[14]"So she lay at his feet until morning, but got up before one person could recognize another; for he said, "It must not be known that the woman came to the threshing-floor." [15]Then he said, "Bring the cloak you are wearing and hold it out." So she held it, and he measured out six measures of barley, and put it on her back; then he went into the city. [16]She came to her mother-in-law, who said, "How did things go with you, my daughter?"[e] Then she told her all that the man had done for her, [17]saying, "He gave me these six measures of barley, for he said, 'Do not go back to your mother-in-law empty-handed.'" [18]She replied, "Wait, my daughter, until you learn how the matter turns out, for the man will not rest, but will settle the matter today."

Notes

[a] The Hebrew in 3:1 and the beginning of 3:2 is again cast as a question that functions as an assertion.
[b] Following Davis (2003: 76).
[c] This is Nielsen's translation (1997: 71), for which she offers a persuasive case on 68–69.
[d] The Hebrew term here, unlike the term translated "worker-girl" above, refers to a member of a household, which is a more marriageable status.
[e] The Hebrew here is more literally translated "Who are you, my daughter?" Clearly, the issue is not one of recognition, hence the NRSV's "How did things go with you, my daughter?" See the discussion of this verse below.

Commentary

In 1:9 Naomi asked that the Lord would provide security for each of her daughters-in-law in the form of new husbands. As chapter 3 begins, Naomi takes the initiative to find security for Ruth in the form of a husband. Naomi's plan seems similar to the plan that Tamar executes in Gen. 38, securing a future for herself through Judah. This fits with the explicit connection between Ruth and Tamar that appears in 4:12. In addition, attentive readers will recall that Ruth descends from Moab, who was conceived when, in the wake of the destruction of Sodom and Gomorrah, Lot's oldest daughter conceived a child after "lying"[1] with her drunken father (Gen. 19:33–35).

Naomi reveals that Boaz, whom she has already identified as a kinsman-redeemer, will be winnowing barley that evening. This in itself is not unusual. The breeze that typically picks up around sundown would blow the chaff away.

---

1. In Gen. 19 the Hebrew verb *shkb*, "to lie," is used to speak of the sexual encounter between Lot and his daughter. The verb is also used simply to indicate sleep. The same verb appears eight times in Ruth 3.

The threshing floor is where the winnowing would take place. Hosea 9:1 indicates that the threshing floor is a place where prostitution was common. This activity might be tied to religious fertility rights or the fact that workers away from home might use that situation as a chance to have sex with other women.[2] Hosea uses the image to describe Israel's idolatry.

Naomi then describes the subterfuge she wants Ruth to carry out. The first part of this plan is clear. Ruth is to make herself as attractive as possible and hide herself until Boaz finishes eating and drinking and lies down for the night. Naomi's instructions regarding Ruth's preparations are similar to Ezek. 16:9–10. At the beginning of Ezek. 16 the Lord recounts how the people that became Israel were desolate and unloved, orphaned among the nations. God's compassion and grace lead God to choose Israel, dressing and anointing her as a bride in preparation for her wedding. Although Ezekiel does not use the term *hesed*, the Lord's love for Israel and the Lord's actions regarding Israel certainly display a form of *hesed*. In this light, Naomi appears to plan a situation where Boaz will have the opportunity to extend *hesed* to Ruth in the same way that the Lord showed *hesed* to Israel.

After that, there is a great deal of obscurity in 3:4 and the subsequent descriptions of Ruth's actions in 3:7 and 3:8. There is a range of ways of interpreting the Hebrew here. At one end of the spectrum, Ruth is simply told to uncover Boaz's feet and lie down at his feet. Some argue that "feet" is a euphemism for genitalia. Thus, Ruth is instructed to expose Boaz's genitals.

Alternatively, Nielsen argues that because in 3:8, 14 the term translated as "feet" clearly refers to a place (i.e., at Boaz's feet), the term should be understood this way in 3:4–7. This would mean that Ruth, rather than Boaz's feet, is the object of the verb "uncover" (Nielsen 1997: 68–69). That is, Naomi is urging Ruth to expose herself at Boaz's feet. This also makes the best sense of Ruth's request in 3:9 that Boaz cover her with the corner of his garment. Whichever of these possibilities one prefers, it is clear that Ruth is being instructed to offer Boaz a sexual encounter. Since Naomi's stated motive here is to provide security for Ruth, and since she understands that such security comes from having a husband, one should also infer that Ruth's offer is connected to marriage.

Naomi is convinced that Boaz will give Ruth further instructions. As it turns out, Ruth is the one who gives further instructions. Naomi does not entertain the prospect that Boaz would refuse Ruth's offer. Nevertheless, for many weeks Ruth has gleaned in Boaz's fields, enjoying his favor, yet he had not made his hopes

2. Of course, it is when he is away from home on business that Judah visits Tamar, whom he takes to be a prostitute.

and intentions known. As Ellen Davis notes, there is a great deal of uncertainty surrounding this plan: "With the element of uncertainty looming large, what is most striking in the scene that now unfolds is the profound mutual trust expressed by Naomi, Ruth and Boaz. Each of them ultimately stakes everything on the good judgment and good-faith (*hesed*) of the others. Only through the genuine caring of each of the three can urgent need—and now, the possibility of deep humiliation—turn into something completely different, namely, fulfillment and rest" (Davis 2003: 72). The only motive given for Naomi's instructions in 3:1–4 is to find security for Ruth so that things may go well for her. We are not told of any other motives. It would appear, however, that although long-term security is the goal, Naomi's plan exposes Ruth to some danger. Ruth could be seen and recognized, or Boaz might not react favorably when faced with a potentially scandalous situation.

We learn little about Ruth's reaction to this plot. Rashi, at least, understands that Ruth has some reservations about the specifics of the plan. In his reading of the story, Ruth does not want to be mistaken for a prostitute, so she brings her clothes to the threshing floor and adorns herself there.[3] Nevertheless, as this scene ends, Ruth commits herself to following Naomi's instructions.

Ruth follows Naomi's instructions and then some. Boaz eats and drinks until "his heart was good." The Hebrew idiom here may reflect some level of intoxication (1 Sam. 25:36; 2 Sam. 13:28; Esth. 1:10). It can also reflect a happy or joyful disposition independent of any alcohol (1 Kgs. 8:66; Prov. 15:15). Whether alcohol induced or not, Boaz is in a good mood as he goes to sleep, establishing the preconditions for the success of Naomi's plan. For her part, Ruth stealthily approaches Boaz and either uncovers his feet or, more likely, uncovers herself and lies down at his feet.

We are not told when Boaz goes to sleep. Instead, 3:8 begins "in the middle of the night." This is the time when everything is dark and momentous things happen (e.g., Exod. 12:29; Judg. 16:3; Job 34:20). Almost as if the narrator were in the dark too, the characters are simply identified as "the man" and "a woman." In the middle of the night Boaz wakes up shaking or shuddering and rolls over. The Hebrew here indicates that he is startled or frightened, though some think that, having been "uncovered," Boaz is shivering from cold.[4] If it is Ruth who is uncovered, then Boaz is probably not cold. We do not learn why Boaz wakes up

---

3. Rashi, note to Ruth 3:6, available at https://www.sefaria.org/Rashi_on_Ruth.3.6?lang=bi.
4. Edward F. Campbell, *Ruth*, Anchor Bible 7 (New York: Doubleday, 1975), 122; Nielsen (1997: 72); and Linafelt (1999: 53) all emphasize fright. Fewell and Gunn (1990: 86–87) speculate that Boaz wakes

in a fright. The why is less important than the fact that he reaches out his hand and finds a woman at his feet.

Boaz quite naturally asks the woman who she is. Ruth identifies herself as "your servant" (1:9). This identification is telling in several respects. First, Ruth notes that she is Boaz's servant. In 2:8–13 when she and Boaz first speak, Ruth calls herself a "foreigner" (2:10). In addition, she notes that although Boaz has treated her as his servant, she is not his servant. Further, the Hebrew term used in 2:13, *shiphha*, is different from the term used here in 3:9, *amah*. Some argue that this is a significant distinction, with *shiphha* indicating someone on the lowest rung of the social ladder and *amah* signifying someone of marriageable status. Given that in 1 Sam. 25:23–35 Abigail uses both terms as synonyms to refer to herself, there may be less in this distinction than some think.[5]

At this point in Naomi's plan, Boaz should take matters in hand and give Ruth instruction. Instead, Ruth is the one who instructs Boaz. There is a textual ambiguity in the wording of Ruth's request. Ruth asks Boaz to spread his "wing" over her. The Masoretic vowel tradition reads the plural "wings."[6] The consonantal text reads the singular "wing."[7] The plural harkens back to Boaz's wish in 2:12 that the Lord would bless Ruth for seeking refuge under the "wings" of the Lord, the God of Israel. In this case Ruth is inviting Boaz to fulfill his own wish by acting as the Lord's agent, providing her with protection.

In the case of the singular, the term would here be a reference to the corner of Boaz's garment. In both Deut. 22:30 and 27:20, to uncover another man's "wing" (*kanaph*) is to perpetrate adultery. Most significantly, in Ezek. 16:8 the Lord speaks of finding Israel desolate and despised. We then read, "I spread the edge of my cloak [*kanaph*] over you, and covered your nakedness: I pledged myself to you and entered into a covenant with you." Seen in this light, Ruth's request that Boaz spread his *kanaph* over her is a request for marriage. Taking into account Ezek. 16:1–14, it does not directly matter whether the relevant term is singular or plural. In each case Ruth is in effect inviting Boaz to play the role of Lord to her Israel, to offer her marriage, security, and a covenantal relationship. As Ruth

---

up, finds himself naked with a woman at his feet, and is terrified by what might have happened while he was in a drunken state. This speculative option goes well beyond what the text indicates.

5. Campbell (*Ruth*, 101) notes that the terms appear to be synonyms.

6. This version is known as the *qere* (what is to be read). This reflects the fact that the Hebrew text used for public reading is consonantal. The Masoretes later added vowel points. When they preferred a particular reading, they would indicate that although the consonantal text contained one reading, the preferred reading is the one that should be read.

7. This version is called the *ketib* (what is written). It reflects the consonantal version of the Hebrew text, the written form of the text inherited from scribal tradition.

describes things, this is perfectly appropriate because Boaz is a *goel*, a near kinsman, a redeemer.

In response to Ruth's request or invitation, Boaz invokes the Lord's blessing on her. He identifies her current act of kindness (*hesed*) as greater than her prior one. It is clear that Boaz sees her action in terms of seeking marriage with him rather than with younger men.[8] The question is in what sense Ruth's decision is an act of kindness. Is it a kindness to Boaz, seeking him rather than a more vigorous younger man? Is it a kindness to Naomi for Ruth to seek a marriage that will provide them both with security independent of Ruth's own desires? The contrast Boaz draws between the younger men and himself in 3:10 indicates it was a kindness to him. Alternatively, when Boaz first praised Ruth and sought God's blessing for her, it was because of all she had done for Naomi (2:11–12). Moreover, Naomi's plan at the beginning of chapter 3 was to gain security for Ruth (and by implication Naomi herself?) through a husband (cf. also Naomi's wish for Ruth and Orpah in 1:8 that the Lord would bestow *hesed* through providing them with husbands).[9] There does not seem to be any reason to opt for one of these options over another. They can all be correct, and they do not mutually exclude each other.

Boaz characterizes Ruth as a "worthy woman" (3:11). Indeed, this is not simply his view; he claims that everyone in town knows this. This designation seems to point in two directions. The Hebrew phrase *esheth hayil* is not common. It serves as the linguistic counterpart to the designation of Boaz in 2:1 as an *ish gibbor hayil*. This connection is lost in the typical English renderings of this phrase in 2:1 as "a wealthy man" or "a prominent man." Boaz's designation of Ruth also points to the same phrase in Prov. 31:10, which is used to launch a description of the virtuous/worthy/capable wife. Thus, despite Ruth's relatively low status according to most of the social markers of her day, Boaz describes her in a manner that makes her a most fitting wife.[10] Moreover, it is clear that, in the mind of Boaz at least, there is nothing in Ruth's actions that is morally questionable. Indeed, according to the midrashic interpreters, the major moral struggle in this

8. The Hebrew that is generally translated as "going after" in 3:10 is sometimes used for the aggressive pursuit of a sexual relationship (Prov. 7:22) and thus serves as a fitting metaphor of Israel's idolatry (Hos. 2:7). It is also used to describe Rebekah and Abigail following after messengers to meet their respective husbands, Isaac and David (Gen. 24:5–8; 1 Sam. 25:42).

9. See Fewell and Gunn 1990: 84–85. They may be relying too much on speculations about Boaz's emotions and motives.

10. Making a similar claim, Davis (2003: 84) notes, "In partial contrast to Boaz, Ruth's 'substance' [worth] is entirely one of character."

episode focuses on Boaz's nightlong battle with his "Evil Inclination" to avoid having intercourse with Ruth.[11]

By reading this episode through Ezek. 16:1–14, one can see that Ruth's actions come to stand for the Gentiles' longing to be joined to Israel under the corner of the Lord's cloak. Although the outlines of this plan come from Naomi, it is Ruth who takes the initiative. Instead of waiting for instructions from Boaz, Ruth urges him to bring her under his cloak, just as she took the initiative to join herself to Naomi, Naomi's people, and Naomi's God. In these ways Ruth also exhibits the great lengths to which Gentiles may go to be joined to Israel. This connection invites one to investigate this matter further from the perspectives of Matthew and Paul, as they both share an interest in the relationships between Jews and Gentiles in Christ, particularly as Matthew includes Ruth in his genealogy of Jesus.

The Lord's redemption of and fellowship with Israel as reflected in Ezek. 16:1–14 and elsewhere is so appealing, fascinating, and compelling that Gentiles are drawn to the Lord. On an individual scale, the Moabite, Ruth, displays this Gentile longing to be joined to Israel and its God. Thus it is not surprising that Matthew would include her in his genealogy of the Messiah, the redeemer of Israel, whose life, death, and resurrection signal both the time and the manner of Israel's redemption and the radical opening of that covenantal relationship with God to all nations. In this respect, Ruth also foreshadows Jesus's encounter with the "Canaanite" woman in Matt. 15:21–28.[12] In that episode another Gentile woman, acting on her own initiative and outside the conventional norms, draws benefits from Israel's savior. This more piecemeal inclusion of the Gentiles is transformed into an open invitation after the resurrection in Matt. 28:19–20.

Although, unlike Matthew, Paul does not invoke Ruth in his writings, one can reflect on this encounter from a Pauline perspective. Boaz's welcoming of Ruth anticipates the reception of Gentiles into the body of redeemed Israel constituted by the followers of Jesus. As Paul sees it, this inclusion of the Gentiles fulfills God's promise to Abraham that through him and his seed the nations would be blessed (cf. Gen. 12:3; Gal. 3:15–18).[13] Ruth's subsequent union with Boaz anticipates the making into one new person of Jew and Gentile in Christ described in Eph. 2:11–22. As Ruth and Boaz become one flesh, we get an anticipatory

---

11. See *Ruth Rabbah* 6.4; 7.1 (in Rabinowitz 1983: 81, 82). The targum connects Boaz's struggle to that of Joseph when Potiphar's wife tries to seduce him (Gen. 39:6–8).

12. Of course, by Matthew's time there had not been any Canaanites on the scene for over one thousand years.

13. Thus, although Paul might characterize God's promise to Abraham in Gen. 12:3 as an act of divine *hesed*, he clearly sees the fulfillment of this promise as a matter of justice.

glimpse of those who are "far off" being joined together with those who are "near" to form one new person in Christ (Eph. 2:13–14).

In addition to foreshadowing Eph. 2:11–22, the union of Ruth and Boaz is a sort of enactment of Isa. 2:1–4. In Isa. 2 we learn of the effects of God's redemption of Zion. Redeemed Zion enjoys a renewed intimacy with God. The common life of its inhabitants is marked by peaceableness. Weapons are turned into farming implements. When the nations see what God has done here in the city, they are fascinated by it, attracted to it, compelled to come near, and ultimately drawn into the intimacy that God enjoys with Israel. Listen to what they say: "Come, let us go up to the mountain of the LORD, to house of the God of Jacob; that he may teach us his ways and that we may walk in his paths" (Isa. 2:3). As all the peoples of the world see both God's redeeming, loving relationship with Israel and the sort of common life this forms and sustains within Israel, they are drawn to God. There is a beauty here that manifests itself in lives that are reconciled with God and with others and in a common life founded on justice, fidelity, and truthfulness.

This way of looking at things connects the salvation of the nations quite closely to Israel's manifestation of a particular common life. God forms and sustains a people whose life with God and each other exudes such radiance that the world is drawn to God. In this way God's desire that all the nations of the earth will be blessed through Abraham and his heirs is brought to fruition. The world is drawn to or courted by God rather than coerced into a relationship with God. All of this is displayed at a personal level in Ruth. From the outset of the story, she has been drawn to Israel and Israel's God for reasons that are never made explicit in the text. There was something about Naomi and Naomi's people and God that drew Ruth. The text of Ruth leaves this matter underdetermined. In doing so, it may allow for a great number of ways by which Gentiles may find Israel's life with God compelling enough to be drawn in.

Recognizing that in the first couple of centuries of the church it was relatively common for theologians as diverse as Origen and Tertullian to point to the church as the fulfillment of Isa. 2 helps to reinforce this connection between Isa. 2:1–4, Ruth's marriage to Boaz, and Eph. 2:11–22. Listen to Origen as he responds to that early critic of Christianity, Celsus. Celsus charges that Christians are nothing more than the rebellious offspring of a rebellious Jew. In response Origen notes:

> "In the last days," when our Jesus came, each one of us has come "to the visible mountain of the Lord," to the Word far above every word, and to the house of God which is "the church of the living God," "a pillar and ground of truth." . . . And all

the nations are coming to it and many nations go, and we exhort one another to the worship of God which has shone out in the last days through Jesus Christ, saying, "Come, and let us go up to the mountain of the Lord and to the house of the God of Jacob, and he will proclaim to us his way and we will walk in it." . . . No longer do we take the sword against any nation, nor do we learn war any more, since we have become children of peace.[14]

Other early Christian theologians such as Justin Martyr (*Apology* 1.39) and Irenaeus (*Against Heresies* 4.34.4) make similar connections between Isa. 2 and the one body of Jews and Gentiles in the church. I will try to summarize some of the characteristics of the early church that led them to make this connection.

First, in the earliest Christian communities, at least for a time, Gentiles were drawn to a predominantly Jewish body. Acts relates this most clearly. Indeed, much of the first seven chapters of Acts focuses on the reconstitution of Israel in the light of the death and resurrection of the Messiah. Most of these transformations and restorations take place in and around Jerusalem. In time, however, the first followers of the resurrected Christ, all of whom were Jews, spread out from Jerusalem. In halting, sometimes faltering ways that do not reflect well Boaz's welcome of Ruth, these Jews are led by the Spirit to preach to Gentiles. Much to their surprise, the Gentiles receive the gospel in large numbers. This may more closely match Boaz's surprise at Ruth's "following after" him rather than other, younger men.

Paul, the apostle to the Gentiles, always begins by preaching to Jews first when he enters a new town. Acts, Romans, and Galatians in particular make it clear that Christianity is a Jewish movement to which Gentiles are drawn and grafted in. Indeed, the first theological controversy these followers of Jesus have to address is whether the Gentiles who join themselves to these outposts of redeemed Israel need to become Jews. That is, do they need to be circumcised and observe such things as Jewish food laws? Despite the fact that Paul, among others, vociferously argues that Gentiles need not become circumcised to be part of the body of Christ, he also is unequivocal in his commitment to seeing the church as being continuous with God's redemption of Israel. It is the Gentiles who have been grafted in to a Jewish group and not the other way around.

Having said that, Paul in particular recognizes that it is equally important for these first Christians to form and comprise a single body of Jews and Gentiles

---

14. Origen, *Contra Celsum* 5.34, trans. Henry Chadwick (Cambridge: Cambridge University Press, 1965). I have made some small revisions to the translation of Henry Chadwick.

united in the body of Christ. Gentiles neither need to become Jews nor are they second-class citizens in God's redeemed Israel. To the extent that the first churches manifested these practices so often associated with Isa. 2, attracting and welcoming the nations, being places of peace and practicing forgiveness and reconciliation, they were able to offer concrete testimony to God's redemption of Israel through the life, death, and resurrection of Christ. Unless the body of Christ is able to offer such concrete testimony, as Paul so clearly saw, it becomes difficult to speak of Isa. 2 finding its fulfillment in these local manifestations of redeemed Israel, which we know as the first churches. Thus, Paul saves some of his sharpest criticisms for those whose doctrines and practices threaten the actual concrete manifestation of a unified body of Jews and Gentiles in Christ.

It becomes clear that Ruth's encounter with Boaz in 3:6–13 is the climactic moment in this brief story. The Moabite woman seeks security for herself (and Naomi) under the wing of Boaz (and, by implication, Israel and Israel's God). As with most of our actions, it is often difficult to discern with whom and where the impetus for things actually begins. This is true here in Ruth too. At the critical moment, in response to Boaz's question in 3:9, Ruth initiates the invitation for marriage, and Boaz responds with welcome and blessing from the Lord. He commits himself to do what Ruth has asked. As it turns out, however, there are several potential complications that need to be addressed.[15]

Most immediately, Boaz indicates that he is not the closest male relative. There is another. This matter will need to be addressed, but it cannot be dealt with in the middle of the night. Boaz invites Ruth to rest there with him until morning. Before morning, Ruth and Boaz make sure that Ruth leaves the threshing floor unnoticed and also that she brings back some grain to Naomi. The end of chapter 3 thus parallels the end of chapter 2. Ruth returns home to Naomi with grain and news. Naomi's question to Ruth is rendered in the NRSV as "How did things go with you?" (3:16). The Hebrew repeats the same question Boaz asks in 3:9, "Who are you?" Clearly, visual recognition is not the issue here. Ruth's response makes it plain that she and Naomi recognize each other. At the same time, as Ellen Davis notes, Ruth has taken on a new identity. "She took the risk of bitter humiliation and loss of reputation. But in so doing, she found the most profound regard" (Davis 2003: 91). This moment solidifies the new identity to which Ruth pledged herself in chapter 1, binding herself to Naomi, Naomi's people, and Naomi's God.

15. Nielsen (1997: 78) notes that this impediment is parallel to the sorts of impediments to the fulfillment of promises that arise in the patriarchal narratives.

Ruth relates "all that the man had done for her," and displays the grain that Boaz gave her so that she would not "return empty-handed." This reflects the same term that Naomi used in 1:21 to describe her situation: "I went away full, but the LORD brought me back empty." Both Ruth's news and the grain indicate that Naomi's fortunes are improving. The chapter concludes with Naomi urging patience to see how things will develop. Having initially charged the Lord with causing her emptiness, Naomi's counsel of patience here indicates that she is growing in her awareness that God's providence can often unfold in unpredictable ways and at a pace that we often cannot anticipate.

RUTH 4

⁴:¹No sooner had Boaz gone up to the gate and sat down there than the next-of-kin, of whom Boaz had spoken, came passing by. So Boaz said, "Come over, so-and-so;ᵃ sit down here." And he went over and sat down. ²Then Boaz took ten men of the elders of the city, and said, "Sit down here"; so they sat down. ³He then said to the next-of-kin, "Naomi, who has come back from the fields of Moab, is selling the parcel of land that belonged to our kinsman Elimelech. ⁴So I thought I would tell you of it, and say: Buy it in the presence of those sitting here, and in the presence of the elders of my people. If you are going to act as redeemer, then act as redeemer; but if you will not act as redeemer, tell me, so that I may know. For there is no one except you to act as redeemer, and I come after you." And he said, "I will act as redeemer."ᵇ ⁵Then Boaz said, "The day you acquire the field from the hand of Naomi, you are also acquiring Ruth the Moabite, the widow of the dead man, to maintain the dead man's name on his inheritance." ⁶At this, the next-of-kin said, "I cannot act as redeemer for myself without damaging my own inheritance. Take my right of redemption yourself, for I cannot act as redeemer."

⁷Now this was the custom in former times in Israel concerning redeeming and exchanging: to confirm a transaction, the one took off a sandal and gave it to the other; this was the manner of attesting in Israel. ⁸So when the next-of-kin said to Boaz, "Acquire it for yourself," he took off his sandal. ⁹Then Boaz said to the elders and all the people, "Today you are witnesses that I have acquired from the hand of Naomi all that belonged to Elimelech and all that belonged to Chilion and Mahlon. ¹⁰I have also acquired Ruth the Moabite, the wife of Mahlon, to be my wife, to maintain the dead man's name on his inheritance, in order that the name of the dead may not be cut off from his kindred and from the gate of his native

place; today you are witnesses." [11]Then all the people who were at the gate, along with the elders, said, "We are witnesses. May the LORD make the woman who is coming into your house like Rachel and Leah, who together built up the house of Israel. May you produce children in Ephrathah and bestow a name in Bethlehem; [12]and, through the children that the LORD will give you by this worker-girl,[c] may your house be like the house of Perez, whom Tamar bore to Judah."

[13]So Boaz took Ruth and she became his wife. When they came together, the LORD made her conceive, and she bore a son. [14]Then the women said to Naomi, "Blessed be the LORD, who has not left you this day without a redeemer;[d] and may his name be renowned in Israel! [15]He shall be to you a restorer of life and a nourisher of your old age; for your daughter-in-law who loves you, who is more to you than seven sons, has borne him." [16]Then Naomi took the child and laid him in her bosom, and became his nurse. [17]The women of the neighborhood gave him a name, saying, "A son has been born to Naomi." They named him Obed; he became the father of Jesse, the father of David.

[18]Now these are the descendants of Perez: Perez became the father of Hezron, [19]Hezron of Ram, Ram of Amminadab, [20]Amminadab of Nahshon, Nahshon of Salmon, [21]Salmon of Boaz, Boaz of Obed, [22]Obed of Jesse, and Jesse of David.

Notes

[a] The Hebrew here is *peloni almoni*, which is a nonsensical rhyme. Davis (2003: 97) suggests it is like "Joe Schmoe." I use "so-and-so" following Linafelt (1999: 65).

[b] In this verse I follow Davis (2003: 98). Davis's translation captures the fact that the Hebrew lacks a direct object for the verb "redeem." As she notes, the lack of an object puts the focus on the subject. Moreover, this ambiguity opens the door to Boaz's claim that buying the land also entails marrying Ruth.

[c] I continue to follow Davis's translation of this term, first begun in 2:5 (Davis 2003: 45).

[d] Although the NRSV is perfectly within its rights to translate the Hebrew as "next-of-kin," the term can also be translated as "redeemer," and in this case the various overtones and connotations of redeemer seem appropriate (Davis 2003: 113–14).

Commentary

What Ruth initiated in the darkness at the threshing floor reaches its conclusion in the daylight before witnesses at the town gates. Despite all of this happening in a very public way, there are still a number of strange and obscure elements in 4:1–6.

Just as Naomi predicted at the end of chapter 3, Boaz sets out to resolve the issues raised by the fact that he is not the closest relative to Naomi and Ruth. We never learn exactly who this closer relative is. Despite the fact that Boaz must surely

know who this person is, he never refers to him by name. Instead, he refers to him
with what Linafelt calls a "rhyming Hebrew nonsense phrase,"[1] which is probably
well translated as "so-and-so." Why refer to him this way? His namelessness could
reflect a literary device, contrasting with Boaz's commitment "to maintain the
name" of Ruth's dead husband (4:5). It could also reflect an implicit criticism of
this relative for failing to be as generous as Boaz.[2]

Boaz encounters so-and-so at the gate to the town. This is a place where one
can carry out legal and commercial transactions, including issues around levirate
marriage (Deut. 25:5–10), in the presence of witnesses. Contrary to our expectations, Ruth is not the immediate subject of discussion here. Indeed, the rules
around levirate marriage do not seem to apply here. Neither so-and-so nor Boaz
is identified as a brother of Mahlon and Chilion. Moreover, if there were others
who would offer prospects for levirate marriage back in Bethlehem, it is not clear
why Naomi would have been so adamant that Ruth and Orpah return to their
homes to seek husbands at the outset of the story (Nielsen 1997: 85). Nobody
seems to expect that issues around levirate marriage apply here. This fact can help
explain why Boaz speaks first about a field that Naomi wishes to sell. This is all new
information to readers. How does Boaz know this? When did Naomi say this?
What was happening with the field (which must have belonged to Elimelech) while
they were in Moab? Why wait until now to sell? None of the people involved in
this transaction raise any of these questions. We are left, perhaps invited, simply to
follow along, keeping these questions at bay. The presence of the field does allow
Boaz to engage so-and-so over the prospect of acting as a kinsman-redeemer (*goel*).

The process for close kin to redeem land and property is laid out in Lev. 25:24–
34. We also read of Jeremiah redeeming a cousin's field in Jer. 32:7–15 as a hopeful
sign that the people of Judah would again possess their land in peace. Because
so-and-so is the closest kin, it is his responsibility to redeem the land if he is able.
Of course, a straightforward interpretation of Lev. 25:35–38 might indicate that
so-and-so should already have extended aid to Naomi and Ruth along the lines
that Boaz had done and is clearly willing to continue to do. In his favor, the man
does not hesitate to accept his obligations when Boaz presents them in 4:4.

In the light of the prescriptions for the Jubilee Year in Lev. 25, so-and-so would
have to return the land to Naomi or Elimelech's heirs. Fortunately for him, Naomi
is old and will not have further children, and Elimelech is dead. There is currently

---

1. Linafelt 1999: 65. The Hebrew is *peloni almoni*.
2. The first suggestion is Linafelt's (1999: 65). The second is Nielsen's (1997: 83) and Sakenfeld's
(1999: 69).

no one to whom the one who redeems this land would have to return it. This is a safe and secure opportunity for so-and-so.

At this point the text becomes obscure on several levels. In terms of what the text actually says, there are two traditions. One tradition has Boaz say that on the day that so-and-so redeems the field, "I [Boaz] will buy Ruth the Moabite, the widow of the dead man, to maintain the dead man's name on his inheritance."[3] Another tradition has Boaz assert that on the day that so-and-so redeems the field, "you [so-and-so] will also buy Ruth . . ."[4] If one follows the reading that has Boaz claiming to "buy" Ruth as his wife, then Boaz is making it clear to so-and-so that buying Naomi's field is not such a stable investment. Although it is not strictly a levirate marriage, Boaz's commitment "to maintain the name" of Ruth's dead husband (4:5, 10) casts his action in terms straight from the description of levirate marriage in Deut. 25. Should Boaz and Ruth conceive a child as he intends, a male child could buy back the field or it would simply revert back to him in the Jubilee Year. When so-and-so recognizes this, he understands that he cannot redeem the field without risking his own inheritance and he withdraws his offer. This reading makes good sense of this particular episode involving Boaz and so-and-so.

However, it does not fit well with 3:12–13, where Boaz indicates that there is someone who has a prior claim on the role of redeemer and that this is an impediment to Boaz taking Ruth under his wing. How can this be the case if Boaz in 4:5 is claiming that he will take Ruth as his wife when so-and-so redeems Naomi's field? Moreover, from the perspective of the narrative as a whole, this reading separates Naomi's fate, which is tied to the field, from Ruth's fate, which is tied to Boaz's promise. From the very beginning of this story Ruth has tied her fate to Naomi's, and Naomi has gradually come to see her prospects as tied to Ruth's.

Thus, the reading that connects so-and-so's purchase of the field with taking Ruth as his wife coheres better with what Boaz claims in 3:12–13. In addition, in 4:5 Boaz connects redemption of Naomi's field with taking Ruth as a wife in order to maintain the name of Elimelech and his son Mahlon. Here Boaz explicitly does what the narrative has implicitly done from the outset; he ties Naomi's fate and Ruth's fate together. The problem with this reading is that there does not seem to be any legal basis for Boaz to tie redemption of Naomi's field to levirate marriage

3. This version is called the *ketib* (what is written). It reflects the consonantal version of the Hebrew text, the written form of the text inherited from scribal tradition.

4. This version is known as the *qere* (what is to be read). This reflects the fact that the Hebrew text used for public reading is consonantal. The Masoretes later added vowel points. When they preferred a particular reading, they would indicate that although the consonantal text contained one reading, the preferred reading is the one that should be read.

to Ruth. Indeed, if there had been some basis for a levirate marriage, one would have anticipated either Naomi or Ruth exerting such a claim much earlier in the story. Moreover, on this reading, it would appear that Boaz is running the risk that so-and-so will opt to redeem the field and take Ruth as his wife. Although 3:12–13 presents this as a possibility, we always get the sense that Boaz wants to marry Ruth.

Both readings of 4:5 pose problems for readers in the sense that each raises questions that it does not provide the resources to answer. We should note, however, that neither so-and-so nor the elders who witness this interchange raise any objections. Indeed, as 4:7–12 indicates, these witnesses substantiate Boaz's claim to acquire all of Elimelech's material goods and to take Ruth as a wife to maintain Mahlon's name. Their invocation of Tamar and Judah indicate that they, too, see this as a version of levirate marriage even though it goes beyond the demands of the law. Of course, there may have been laws and customs at work here that are not known to us but were so well known to the characters in the story that they go without saying. The narrator does not, however, hesitate to explain the significance of the sandal to confirm a transaction (4:7). So it is odd that the narrator does not fill in any gaps in our knowledge of the law and its application here. Instead, we are invited to set our questions aside and to view Boaz's offer as one of extraordinary generosity. Just as he did with Ruth's gleaning, he goes above and beyond what is required here. Justice is mingled with *hesed* as in Mic. 6:8.

It is worthwhile to read this passage against the story of Judah and Tamar in Gen. 38. There Judah withholds his youngest son from entering into a levirate marriage with Tamar. Tamar is forced to seduce Judah into fulfilling that role himself. As Judah recognizes, "She is more in the right than I, since I did not give her my son Shelah" (Gen. 38:26). Judah fails both to do justice and to love *hesed*.

Like Tamar, Ruth goes to extraordinary lengths to get Boaz to spread his wing over her. Boaz, however, is not obligated in the way that Judah was. He also goes well beyond his obligations in agreeing to take Ruth as his wife, to maintain the name of Mahlon, and to redeem Naomi's field, thus assuring her of an income. If Ruth has shown *hesed* to Naomi, then one must also recognize that Boaz extends *hesed* to these two women as well as showing a form of *hesed* to the dead by seeking to maintain Mahlon's name.

This is particularly fitting in the light of the genealogy at the end of Ruth. Boaz is the descendent of Perez, the child born to Judah and Tamar. Thus, in his own past is the story of one who failed to do justice, let alone love *hesed*. In the case of Gen. 38, a bold woman (possibly a Gentile, see below) intervenes to ensure that justice is done. Boaz's very existence is dependent on Tamar's just act. Now in a similar situation, Boaz goes beyond the bounds of justice, extending *hesed* to Naomi and Ruth and also to the name of Mahlon.

Furthermore, both Ruth and Tamar appear in Matthew's genealogy of Jesus. It is likely that Matthew sees them both as Gentile women who seek to join themselves to Israel and Israel's God. They foreshadow the variety of types of reception that the first Jewish followers of the resurrected Christ extended to Gentiles who wished to join them in the body of Christ such as we read in Acts 10–11. There Peter needs to be prodded (seduced?) by a vision before he will agree to go visit the Gentile Cornelius. His steps are grudging, Judah-like, at the outset. The fact that the Holy Spirit falls on Cornelius and his household, just as the Spirit fell on the Jewish disciples in Jerusalem on Pentecost, convinces him both to baptize Cornelius and to accept hospitality from him. In the course of Acts 10 Peter moves from the response of Judah to that of Boaz when faced with Gentiles wanting to join themselves to Israel. The initial response of "the apostles and the believers" in Judea in Acts 11:1–14 again reflects the hesitation of Judah to fulfill his obligations to his Gentile daughter-in-law.

The tension over whether to receive Gentiles into the body of Christ in the manner of Judah or Boaz continues on through Acts 15. Prompted by the workings of the Spirit, Peter, Paul, Barnabas, and, ultimately, James come to extend the sort of *hesed* that Boaz does here in Ruth. For each of these New Testament characters, their recognition that Gentiles have received the Holy Spirit independently of becoming Jews convinces them that God is drawing the Gentiles into the body of the Messiah. The Spirit plays the role of Ruth and Tamar, wooing and inviting these followers of Jesus to provide refuge for the Gentiles under God's wings. Moreover, as Galatians reminds us, even pillars of the church, faithful disciples such as Peter and James, find it difficult to mirror the role of Boaz, reminding us of the extraordinary nature of his actions in Ruth 4.

Boaz and Ruth marry; they have intercourse. Nevertheless, the text informs us that it is the Lord who causes Ruth to conceive and bear a son. This is only the second time in the entire book that the Lord acts directly. In 1:6 the Lord breaks the famine in Bethlehem; in 4:13 the Lord causes Ruth to conceive and bear a son. Naomi's wish for her daughters-in-law in 1:8–9 and Boaz's wish for Ruth in 2:12 have been fulfilled.

At this point, Naomi becomes the focus of attention. The women (presumably the women of Bethlehem who speak in 1:19) praise God for providing Naomi with two specific things, a redeemer (*goel*) and a daughter-in-law whose love is better than that of seven sons. The term *goel* is used by Ruth when she asks Boaz to cover her with his wing, and it is used to describe "so-and-so," the potential redeemer in 3:12–13 and 4:1–5. In this case the term is being used more widely than simply the redeemer of land: this son will restore life to Naomi and care for her in her old age. Further, the Lord has blessed Naomi with a daughter-in-law whose love is better than that of seven sons.[5] This is an extraordinary evaluation of Ruth that parallels that of Boaz earlier in chapter 2. Moreover, the women imply that the fact that Ruth is this child's mother bodes well for his future. These words of blessing serve to reverse Naomi's bitter lament upon returning to Bethlehem empty and afflicted by God (1:20–21).

This reminds readers that Ruth is both a story of God's providence and a story of humans learning how to perceive, interpret, and name God's providence. In this regard the story urges both patience in how one interprets, perceives, and speaks about one's situation before God and a certain humility that leads one to repent of and reverse one's initial judgments in the light of subsequent events.

In the final verses of the book we are reminded twice that the child of Ruth and Boaz is the grandfather of David. First, in 4:17 there is a brief mention of the fact that Obed fathers Jesse, who fathers David. Then the book closes with a ten-generation genealogy from Perez, the child of Judah and Tamar, to David. This nicely leads into 1 Samuel, as reflected in the placement of Ruth in the Christian canon. If one keeps in mind the place David holds in 1 and 2 Samuel, Ruth reminds us that David's lineage is inconceivable without Tamar and Ruth. Recall also that Matthew introduces Jesus the Messiah as "the son of David, the son of Abraham" (1:1). Abraham is the one to whom God first promises blessing to the Gentiles. David is the king who decisively establishes Israel's national identity in the midst of a host of hostile nations. Throughout Matthew's Gospel, Jesus, the son of David, persistently frustrates the expectations of those who seek a king like David. Although Israel is surrounded and even occupied by a hostile empire, Jesus does not pursue any of the nationalist agendas that were current in his day. As the resurrected Christ ultimately makes clear, his reform, restoration, and redemption of Israel is directed to drawing the nations back to God rather than destroying them as Israel's enemies. This is the way the promise to Abraham is to be fulfilled. Indeed, Matthew has already signaled to us that Jesus, the son of David, will not so much be the nationalistic monarch who defeats Israel's enemies as he will be the one who is the direct descendent of two strikingly bold Gentile women, Tamar and Ruth.

---

5. Recall Elkanah's question to Hannah in 1 Sam. 1:8, "Am I not more to you than ten sons?" In that case the answer seems to have been no.

CONCLUDING THOUGHTS

In the course of commenting on the book of Ruth, I have noted some themes that recur throughout the story. One theme that appears periodically is the connection between God's providence and human capacities to recognize and rightly name God's activity in the world. Naomi returns to Bethlehem claiming that the Lord is the cause of her affliction. She left Bethlehem full and returns empty, even though she has Ruth with her. By the time the story has run its course, Naomi's material situation has improved dramatically and the future looks secure. Moreover, she is a grandmother. Her daughter-in-law, Ruth, has shown herself to be more valuable than seven sons. Even if Naomi does not say so herself, the Lord has taken care of her. The point here is not to deny the real hardships Naomi confronted both in Moab and in the times immediately after her return to Bethlehem. In addition, the inhabitants of Bethlehem and we modern people all recognize that many who suffer never receive the social and material blessings Naomi receives by the end of the story. Instead, the book of Ruth reminds believers that the movements of God's providence are often difficult to discern. We risk the sin of presumption if we are too quick to attribute afflictions to the Lord's displeasure with us. Moreover, such a disposition tends to blind us, as it did Naomi, to the very particular blessings that God places in our lives in the person of those like Ruth.

On a smaller scale, Ruth and Boaz disagree about the true source of the favor Ruth finds in the course of the story. Initially, Boaz seeks the Lord's blessing for Ruth because of all that she had done for Naomi and her family. Ruth tends to seek the same blessing from Boaz himself. Indeed, by the end of the story Boaz provides for Ruth the very things he has asked the Lord to provide for her. In a story that attributes very little directly to the Lord's doing, we readers receive little direct insight into the ultimate motives and causes behind movements of the story. The Lord does not require believers to be able to discern the precise movements and nuances of God's providence. Perhaps the story even encourages a tendency toward patient, faithful silence in these matters. Instead of devoting many words to discerning the movements of God's providence, in their respective ways Ruth and Boaz embody the commands of Mic. 6:8: do justice, love *hesed*, and walk humbly with God.

In addition, throughout this commentary I have tried to indicate places in the story of Ruth that seem relevant for understanding both Israelite identity and the relationships between Jew and Gentile. Large portions of the New Testament focus on these matters. As a way of concluding this commentary, I would like to put Ruth into a more direct conversation with two biblical texts that bring these issues into sharper focus.

The first text is Deut. 23:3–6. The book of Ruth never stops referring to Ruth as "Ruth the Moabite." This sets up an interesting tension with Deut. 23:3, which notes, "No Ammonite or Moabite shall be admitted to the assembly of the LORD." Deuteronomy 23:4 indicates that this prohibition is related to two things: the first concerns the Moabites' lack of hospitality to the Israelites after the Israelites had left Egypt and were journeying to the promised land; the second is the plot of the Moabite king Balak to get the seer Balaam to curse Israel in Num. 21–24. Finally, Deut. 23:6 goes beyond the initial prohibition of Moabites and Ammonites being in the assembly of the Lord: "You shall never promote their welfare or their prosperity as long as you live."

Ruth the Moabite joins herself to Israel and Israel's God; Boaz directly promotes her welfare and prosperity. Ultimately, the women of Bethlehem bless Ruth, likening her to Rachel and Leah, "who together built up the house of Israel" (Ruth 4:11), and Ruth the Moabite becomes a crucial link in the lineage of David the king. To gloss Rom. 9:6–7, it is clear that not all who are descendants of Moab are Moabites.

One could argue that Ruth stops being a Moabite once she binds herself to Naomi, Naomi's people, and Naomi's God. If this is so, it is worthwhile noting that the text of Ruth does not stop calling her a Moabite. Moreover, the midrash on Ruth rejects this explanation, claiming that Ruth and Orpah were not made proselytes, nor did they undergo ritual washing. It argues instead that the commandment of Deut. 23:3 had not been written at the time. Moreover, the midrash notes that the commandment prohibits Ammonites and Moabites but not the Ammonitess or the Moabitess.[1]

---

1. *Ruth Rabbah* 2.9 (in Rabinowitz 1983: 30). This teaching is offered in the name of R. Meir.

Regardless of the merits of this position, a Christian may also make recourse to John the Baptist's warnings against presuming too much about one's biological connection to the people of God (cf. Matt. 3:9; Luke 3:8). If God can raise up children of Abraham from stones, then surely it is not too much to imagine that God can raise up children of Abraham from among the Moabites.

The second text I want to look at with regard to Ruth is Matthew's Gospel. At the beginning of this commentary, I noted a tendency among modern commentators on Ruth to speculate about the motives of the various characters in the story in the light of the fact that the story reveals almost nothing about the motives behind various actions. At this point I would like to speculate some about the motives of one of the earliest interpreters of Ruth, Matthew the evangelist.[2]

In the genealogy of Jesus the Messiah, Matthew inserts five women: Tamar, Rahab, Ruth, "the wife of Uriah" (aka Bathsheba), and Mary. With the exception of Mary, Bathsheba is the only one who appears to be Jewish. She is the daughter of Eliam (2 Sam. 11:3), who is the son of Ahithophel, a member (along with Uriah the Hittite) of David's core of elite fighters (2 Sam. 23:34, 39). In the light of the fact that Matthew appears to take Tamar, Rahab, and Ruth as Gentiles, it is interesting that Bathsheba is known as "the wife of Uriah [the Hittite]" (cf. 2 Sam. 11:3), by her connection to a Gentile husband, rather than as a Jew.[3]

I do not know of any scholar who thinks that Matthew sought to help clear up Jesus's rather ambiguous bloodline. Instead, the genealogy is a way of setting us up to understand better the story that Matthew is about to tell. Nevertheless, it is curious that these women are included. By including Ruth in this genealogy, Matthew invites one to ask, What sort of understanding of Ruth did Matthew have such that it seemed like a good idea to include her in his introduction to the gospel of Jesus the Messiah?

2. See Richard Hays, *Echoes of Scripture in the Gospels* (Waco: Baylor University Press, 2016), 112, who notes that Matthew's inclusion of these women in the genealogy of Jesus "encourages the reader to recall their stories and ponder their significance for understanding the shape of Israel's story. They prefigure the mission to 'all nations' that is announced in the Gospel's closing chapter."

3. Although Rahab and Ruth are clearly Gentiles, one might question whether this is true of Tamar. If she is not, it raises questions about why Matthew includes these four otherwise unconnected women in Jesus's genealogy. *Jubilees* 41:1 and *Testament of Judah* 10:1 both identify Tamar as an Aramean, rendering her no more or less Jewish than Sarah, Rebekah, or Leah, who do not appear in Matthew's genealogy. In a recent article, however, Richard Bauckham notes that Philo (*On the Virtues* 220–22) identifies Tamar as a "Palestinian Syrian," otherwise known as a Canaanite, who converted to the worship of the one true God. "Thus Philo provides clear evidence that a Jewish exegete of the time of Matthew could consider Tamar to be of unequivocally Gentile origin." Bauckham, "Tamar's Ancestry and Rahab's Marriage: Two Problems in the Matthean Genealogy," *Novum Testamentum* 37, no. 4 (October 1995): 320.

Others have asked a version of this question before. Chrysostom, Origen, and Jerome all answer this question by identifying Ruth as one of the sinful women Matthew places in Jesus's genealogy so that "someone who is worshipped on account of sinners [and is] born from sinners washes out the sins of all."[4] Or in Herbert McCabe's words, "He belonged to us and came to help us, no wonder he came to a bad end, and gave us some hope."[5]

I do not doubt that Matthew clearly situates Jesus in the midst of sinners. Nevertheless, even though these women are not the standard Jewish matriarchs, they are not obviously more sinful than most of the men in this genealogy. Indeed, Judah declares that Tamar is "more in the right than I" (Gen. 38:26); Rahab saves Jewish lives such that in his epistle to Jewish believers James identifies her as someone who reveals her righteousness by means of her works (Jas. 2:25); Boaz calls Ruth's evening encounter with him an act of *hesed*. He also calls Ruth a "worthy woman" (3:11) and claims that his behavior toward Ruth is simply God's reward for her prior actions. The "wife of Uriah the Hittite" is hardly the only one at fault in the affair that leads to Uriah's murder. Thus, although Chrysostom, Origen, and Jerome want to show that Jesus has a strong connection to everyday sinners, the fact that scripture elsewhere gives such positive evaluations of Tamar, Ruth, and Rahab indicates that there may be more to say about Ruth's inclusion in Matthew's Gospel.[6]

One way of exploring this is to recall that from Matt. 1:1 we are presented with what appears to be a very Jewish story. Matthew presents the genealogy of the Messiah of Israel. Jesus is the son of David, the son of Abraham. At the end of the genealogy, Matthew helpfully points out that it was fourteen generations from Abraham to David, fourteen from David to the exile, and fourteen from

---

4. Jerome, *Commentary on Matthew*, trans. Thomas P. Scheck, Fathers of the Church 117 (Washington: The Catholic University of America Press, 2010). See also Chrysostom, *Homily on Matthew* 1.

5. H. McCabe, "The Genealogy of Christ," in *God Matters* (London: G. Chapman, 1987), 249. Cf. Davis (2003: 11): "All of this, the evangelist implies, is part of the messy world that the Messiah comes to redeem."

6. Amy Richter's *Enoch and the Gospel of Matthew*, Princeton Theological Monograph Series (Eugene, OR: Pickwick, 2012) argues that the five women in Matthew's genealogy (including Mary) are inserted because of their participation in unconventional and/or illicit sexual encounters that nevertheless bring about some good. This reverses a pattern found in *Enoch* where various disasters are introduced into the world through the sons of God engaging in sex with the daughters of men (Gen. 6) and also teaching them a variety of illicit arts. Although there is much in Richter's work I agree with, I think the case with regard to Ruth is not particularly strong. It relies on seeing Ruth as a "typical" Moabite, sexually wanton and idolatrous. Although Num. 25 presents Moabites this way, the book of Ruth does not present Ruth this way. As Davis (2003: 9) comments, "In Ruth sexuality is linked with moral character of the highest kind." Hays (*Echoes of Scripture*, 112) claims that rather than their dubious reputation, these women are notable for their "tenacious fidelity."

the exile until the birth of the Messiah. All of this yields the impression that an appropriately attentive observer of Israelite life ought to have been expecting something significant to happen at the time when Jesus was born. Moreover, an observant reader noting that the Messiah is the son of David and the son of Abraham might be puzzled by the fact that Matthew does not identify Jesus as the son of Moses. Nevertheless, by the time Jesus gets up from giving the Sermon on the Mount, it is clear that he is the new and better Moses. No doubt this is a claim that many of Matthew's Jewish contemporaries will resist. Regardless of how one responds to Matthew's presentation of Jesus as the new and better Moses, all will recognize that it is a claim that, at least at its outset, is only of interest to Jews. In addition, in Matt. 10:5–6 Jesus tells his disciples not to go to the Gentiles, only to the "lost sheep of the house of Israel." Only at the very end of the Gospel does the resurrected Christ instruct his followers to go and make disciples among "all nations" (Matt. 28:19). Even here, however, Matthew's Gospel is still a profoundly Jewish story. It is a story of God's redemption of Israel and God's desire to draw all the nations to God through the Messiah's redemption of Israel. Without breaking continuity with God's dealings with Israel, the end of Matthew anticipates a mission to Gentiles.

It is not surprising that Christian commentators on Ruth saw in this text an anticipation of this movement that unfolds in Matthew. For example, Isidore of Seville (ca. 560–636) speaks of Ruth as a type of the church. She is a Gentile stranger who leaves her native land (idolatry) and joins herself to the people of God.[7] The *Ordinary Gloss* also sees Ruth's declaration that she will join herself to Naomi and Naomi's people and Naomi's God as a foreshadowing of the Gentile church.[8] In a rough and ready way, one can grant this point and rejoice in God's providence. As an account of Ruth, however, it still leaves us with several loose ends that might warrant further reflection.

The text of Ruth says nothing about why Ruth acts as she does. Her attachment to Naomi, to Naomi's people and homeland, and to her God is surprising and seems to be an act of Ruth's own will. Boaz's evaluation of "all that [Ruth has] done" (2:11) also seems to treat these actions as Ruth's own work. If this is taken to be a type of the church, it might lead one to think that the church joins itself to God through its own work and the force of its own will. One way to address this problem is to understand Ruth's attachment to the people of God through texts such as Isa. 2:1–4 where, after seeing God's redemption of Israel, after Zion

---

7. See the text in Smith 1996: 7–8.
8. See PL 108:1204B–C (in Smith 1996: 13).

is established as the highest of the mountains, the nations stream to Israel. Israel's redemption is so fascinating and compelling that the nations are thereby drawn to God. In this way Ruth can foreshadow the ingathering of the nations into the redeemed people of God.

Naomi does tell Ruth and Orpah that she is returning to Bethlehem because the Lord has "considered his people and given them food" (1:6). In the LXX the term rightly translated here as "considered" is the same term Zechariah uses in the beginning of the Benedictus when he blesses the Lord God of Israel who has "looked favorably on his people and redeemed them" (Luke 1:68). It is much more telling, however, that Naomi returns to Bethlehem a broken and barren woman. She may be returning to the people of God, but she has nothing to offer her daughters-in-law. She is now to be called Mara, or bitter. God has dealt harshly with her. She went out full and is returning empty (1:19–21). Little about Naomi's situation would have enticed or compelled Ruth to throw in her lot with the people of God.

Perhaps here one might make a more overtly christological move. If Ruth is a type of the Gentile church, then Naomi must become a type of the crucified Christ who, when he is lifted up on a cross, draws all people to him (cf. John 12:32). The crucified one attracts through and despite his wounds, drawing in the nations in hopes that by his wounds they may find healing and resurrection. At the same time, one should also see in Naomi aspects of that broken, confused, and discouraged band of followers of Jesus displayed at the end of Luke's Gospel and continuing into the first part of Acts. Although they have encountered the resurrected Christ, received the Holy Spirit at Pentecost, been commissioned to bring the gospel to all nations (Luke 24:47), these Jewish followers of the resurrected Messiah are remarkably ambivalent about proclaiming this message to Gentiles. Indeed, their ambivalence is much like Naomi's in the first two chapters of Ruth.

All of this goes well beyond Isidore of Seville's idea that Ruth is a type of the Gentile church, but it is a more potent way to make that claim. As similar as this is to themes in Matthew, I think Matthew finds something different in Ruth and the other Gentile women. The role of these women is more complex. It is in this complexity that Ruth becomes particularly important. In Matthew, John the Baptist warns those Jews who go out to hear him that they should not rely on their biological connection to Abraham in order to escape the coming wrath (3:9). Although he warns his disciples not to go to the Gentiles, Jesus praises the faith of a Roman soldier (8:5–13). Jesus claims that Gentile Ninevites and the queen of Sheba will ultimately judge the unbelief of his Jewish contemporaries

(12:38–42). After some hesitation, he even heals the daughter of a "Canaanite" woman (15:21–28).[9]

In this light, right at the outset of his Gospel, at the beginning of this story that seems to be by Jews, for Jews, and about Jews, Matthew inserts three Gentile women and "the wife of Uriah the Hittite" into the genealogy of the Messiah. Through cunning, pluck, courage, steadfast love, and even murder, adultery, and unconventional sexual encounters, Tamar, Rahab, Ruth, and Bathsheba insert themselves, or find themselves inserted, into the story of God's dealings with the people of Israel. By alluding to many of the unusual and unanticipated ways that God is able to graft wild branches into the olive tree of Israel, Matthew shows that as far as the Messiah is concerned, the boundary between Israelite and Gentile is clear, important, enduring, and—at surprising times—porous.

Paul picks up this theme in Rom. 9–11. In making his claim that the word of God has not failed (Rom. 9:6), Paul notes that not all Israelites truly belong to Israel. Not all of Abraham's descendants are children of the promise. This leads Paul to note the reversals foretold in Hosea where "not my people" become "children of the living God" (Hos. 1:10).

Including Ruth with the other women allows Matthew to assert the enduring importance of Judaism to Christianity, to anticipate the inclusion of the Gentiles in redeemed Israel, and to suggest that Jewish identity is theologically significant for Christians but that the boundaries of that identity are more porous than we might think, echoing Paul in Rom. 9–11. I take it that neither Paul nor Matthew seeks to erase or supersede Judaism. The covenants and the promises are eternal. Moreover, God's righteousness is revealed in God's eternal plan to save both Jews and Gentiles by faith. In addition, the body of Christ incorporates Jews and Gentiles together without requiring the homogenization of either. Nevertheless, the four women in Jesus's genealogy in Matthew remind us of the unusual and surprising paths God takes people down as they are drawn to their true home in God. We risk the sin of presumption if we fail to recognize that, although it is not the norm, God can raise up children of Abraham from the very rocks around us. Thus, in this respect, Ruth can stand as a guard against presumption, a reminder, like Romans, Galatians, and Ephesians, that in Christ Jews and Gentiles are united into a new body and that the different parts of the body cannot dispense with nor despise one another.

---

9. Of course, by Matthew's time there had not been any Canaanites on the scene for over one thousand years.

BIBLIOGRAPHY FOR RUTH

Frequently cited works are listed here. Other works are documented in the footnotes.

Bush, F. W. 1996. *Ruth and Esther*. Word Biblical Commentary 9. Waco: Word.

Davis, Ellen. 2003. *Who Are You, My Daughter? Reading Ruth through Image and Text*. Illustrated by Margaret Parker. Louisville: Westminster John Knox.

Fewell, Danna, and David Gunn. 1990. *Compromising Redemption: Relating Characters in the Book of Ruth*. Louisville: Westminster John Knox.

Linafelt, Tod. 1999. *Ruth*. In Tod Linafelt and Timothy K. Beal, *Ruth and Esther*, Berit Olam: Studies in Hebrew Narrative and Poetry. Collegeville, MN: Liturgical Press.

Nielsen, Kirsten. 1997. *Ruth: A Commentary*. Old Testament Library. Louisville: Westminster John Knox.

Rabinowitz, L., trans. 1983. *Ruth Rabbah*. London: Soncino Press.

Sakenfeld, Katherine D. 1999. *Ruth*. Interpretation: A Bible Commentary for Teaching and Preaching. Louisville: Westminster John Knox.

Smith, Lesley, trans. 1996. *Medieval Exegesis in Translation: Commentaries on the Book of Ruth*. Kalamazoo, MI: Medieval Institute Press.

SCRIPTURE INDEX

SUBJECT INDEX